WHISKEY IN THE KITCHEN

**The Lively Art of Cooking with Bourbon,
Scotch, Rum, Brandy, Gin, Liqueurs . . .
and Kindred Spirits**

BY EMANUEL AND MADELINE GREENBERG

with Illustrations by Tom Goddard

WEATHERVANE BOOKS
NEW YORK

TO DAVID PAUL

a blithe spirit

Whiskey in the kitchen
Spirits in the pot
Flavor in the vittles
Take home a lot

Copyright © MCMLXVIII by Emanuel & Madeline Greenberg
Illustrations © MCMLXVIII by the Bobbs-Merrill Company, Inc.
Library of Congress Catalog Card Number: 68-29297
All rights reserved.
This edition is published by Weathervane Books
a division of Barre Publishing, Distributed by Crown Publishers, Inc.
by arrangement with the Bobbs-Merrill Company, Inc.
a b c d e f g h
Manufactured in the United States of America

TABLE
OF
CONTENTS

WHISKEY
IN THE
KITCHEN
CHAPTER
1

Whiskey in the kitchen? Oh, you mean one of those informal cocktail parties where guests keep the hostess company while she's fixing more canapés?

No, we don't mean that at all.

Some kind of joke, then? Like the Texas recipe for everything: "Pour 3 ounces of sour mash into the chef . . ."

Definitely *not!* We mean *cooking* with whiskey and the other potables—rums, gins, liqueurs, brandies and specialties like tequila and aquavit. Actually pouring them into the pot, frying pan, chafing dish, sauce, baste, marinade or whatever. The vast field of cooking with spirits, still relatively untapped, offers the innovative cook enormous possibilities for broadening his or her culinary horizons. Spirits can, and do, enhance literally every course on the menu. And the results are impressive enough to win applause from the most jaded guest.

Given today's penchant for savory, uncommon fare, it's a curious contradiction that *Whiskey in the Kitchen* should be the *first* volume devoted solely to cooking with whiskey and the other distilled spirits. (Wine and beer, though alcoholic, are not distilled spirits.) And while this may be a pioneering effort, there will assuredly be more forthcoming—for reasons we hope will become obvious as you read along.

Cooking with spirits makes such obvious good sense, especially for Americans, the wonder is that we don't do much more of it! Whiskey—spirits—are a part of our everyday life. Whiskey is what we *prefer* to drink. And the same felicitous qualities which we enjoy in our cocktails and highballs can also brighten our victuals and add zest to ordinary fare. Shorn of mystique and pretension, spirits in the pot are nothing more than flavoring agents or seasonings—concocted for us by master blenders and distillers. As with other seasonings, spirits in food are most pleasing when used with restraint.

Essentially, cooking with spirits amounts to cooking *away* the alcohol. Liquor, like vanilla and lemon extracts, loses its alcoholic (and incidentally caloric) content in cooking, leaving only the tantalizing scents and amiable flavors that stimulate appetite.

2

Don't expect a dominating taste of whiskey or gin, if that's what you happen to use, in the completed dish. Primarily, spirits should accentuate the *natural* flavor of the food, a sort of counterpoint to the main theme. They also add sprightly flavor of their own, varying in intensity, depending on the way they're used. More about that later.

Astute cooks have always known that spirits can serve as a significant extension of the herb and spice shelf. More than one august reputation for setting a distinctive, sophisticated table stems from the judicious wielding of the liquor bottle in the kitchen. Just consider the array: smoky Scotches and burnished Irish whiskies, robust bourbons, delicate Canadians, the popular American blends (mistakenly called "rye" in the East), not so lusty as bourbon or so muted as Canadian, and tangy, straight rye whiskey, now out of fashion.

The piquant botanicals in gin which perk up a martini readily transfer their breezy bouquet to gin-laced dishes. It shouldn't take an enterprising cook very long to realize that a stew calling for juniper berries can be even better with gin.

Ah, perhaps *you're* beginning to get ideas—and there's still so much more to explore. The sun-drenched rums—pungent Jamaica rum, bright Puerto Rican rum, Virgin Islands rum, Barbados rum, Martinique rum, Hawaiian rum—are all uniquely engaging. The brandy family includes eloquent cognac, bluff Armagnac, genial California brandy. Then there are the austere fruit brandies—dry but with the smack of the fruit: kirsch, Calvados, poire, framboise, slivovitz. And the languorous fruit liqueurs, from apricot to wishniak, often confused with the fruit brandies. Of course, liqueurs go far beyond the fruit category. Let's not overlook crème de menthe, "at once sweet and tart, soft and shrill, kummel like the oboe with its sonorous nasal timbre," anisette, cacao, café, tasting very much as the names imply, and such celebrated proprietary potions as Benedictine, Chartreuse, Cherristock, Cherry Heering, Cointreau, Galliano, Grand Marnier, Southern Comfort, Drambuie, Irish Mist. You'll find this happy breed complementing familiar foods in the 400 or so recipes that make up the body of *Whiskey in the Kitchen*.

Leaves from the Past

Cooking with spirits is gaining devotees by the day among chefs and restaurateurs, as well as in the home. Recent disciples might well be surprised to learn that the liquor bottle is no stranger to the pantry. The practice of flavoring meats, poultry, game, preserves and desserts with spirits is as old as distillation.

Chinese cuisine is studded with recipes that call for liquor as a seasoning agent. You'll find Chinese kitchens in our country making liberal use of gin and bourbon, adequate replacements (along with sherry) for the *Mei Kewi Lui* and *Hwang Chui* of mainland China. An English cookbook presents old recipes for plum-pudding topping and for pancakes "as cooked at the Palace"—both with rum. The French, of course, are universally envied for their way with food. Much of the appeal rests on the deft application of brandy and wine, which, incidentally, are frequently used together.

Isn't it as reasonable for an American housewife to cook with bourbon, rum and other spirits as for her French counterpart to cook with brandy? Indeed, the profusion of spirit choices available here offers the kitchen artist a veritable palette of flavors and aromas, compared to the single tone of brandy. And though we may draw inspiration from the Gallic success, let's remember that liquor in the pot is part of our own gastronomic heritage. Our forebears, in settlements and on plantations, were well aware of the kinship between hearty New World provender and the ardent spirits, and they were versed in the art of mating them for blissful results. Family chronicles, cookbooks such as they were, and cherished, handwritten heirloom records of favorite "receipts" show that these pioneers had declared their culinary independence from Europe early in the game. They flavored frontier victuals with any handy spirit. Old recipes variously suggest "rum, brandy, white brandy, French brandy, spice brandy (in which rose petals or peach leaves had been steeped), proof spirit, ratafia, Hollands gin and whiskey." "French brandy" signified grape brandy; "brandy" alone was fruit brandy. Colonial records as early as the 1600s refer to brandy made from apples—applejack.

Rum and the brandies were used as accents, much as we use vanilla and lemon extracts. There were innumerable fruit cakes and pound cakes flavored with the popular regional spirit. One from the Virginia colony, dated 1723, allowed the cook a choice of apple or peach brandy. But other liquor-spiced cakes and pies achieved a measure of fame. Pork Cake, in which salt pork was the shortening, called for "raiſinſ ſoaked in brandy." Marlborough Pie, a custard-applesauce conceit favored in New England, also took brandy. Our version of Marlborough Pie, with Calvados, appears among the desserts. Bride Cake, served at Tucker House, Williamsburg, and Old Hartford Election Cake, both brandied, are of pre-Revolutionary War vintage.

The early Germans in Pennsylvania, gallant trenchermen, were partial to a mincemeat made with 22 pounds of assorted ingredients, plus a quart of brandy and two quarts of whiskey. *The Williamsburg Art of Cookery or Accompliſh'd Gentlewoman's Companion, Being a Collection of upwards of Five Hundred of the moſt Ancient & Approv'd Recipes in Virginia,* lists more than 50 recipes requiring spirits in the making.

Cakes, steamed puddings, mincemeat and sweet sauces were the popular choices for combining with spirits. But fish, meat and meat sauces, game, preserved fruits and vegetables were also sprinkled with "luscious liquor."[1]

Portable Soup, beef or veal stock boiled down to a "thick glutinous consistence . . . and seasoned with brandy," may have been our earliest convenience food. Solemn assurance was given that, cut into squares and dried in the sun, "it will keep good a long time." Another curiosity, rum-pickled cucumbers: "One gallon of rum to two of water, pick and wash the cucumbers and put them in. Nothing more is necessary to obtain good pickles," or so the lady said. Calf's-foot jelly, sweet potatoes, pumpkin chips, preserved quinces, apple fritters, with brandy in both the batter and the filling, are among the spirit-seasoned favorites in early America.

[1] John Milton.

Menus Take on a Lively Look

Evidence of the new "whiskey rebellion" can be seen on the menus of fine restaurants and hotel dining rooms—course after course generously infused with the benevolent elixirs. A casual gleaning of menus around town turns up the following:[2] Oysters Rockefeller (Pernod), Poulet Vallée d'Auge (Calvados), Zarzuela de Mariscos (brandy), Beef and Bourbon (bourbon), Whiskey Cream Pie (Irish whiskey), Bloody Mary Soup (vodka), Lobster Hermitage (cognac and anisette), Bourbon Squash (bourbon), Rognons Flambés a l'Armagnac (Armagnac), Filet de Sole au Whiskey (blended whiskey), Tripes aux Whisky (Scotch), Pullet Jamaica (rum). As you'd expect, one also finds such classics as Duckling Bigarade, Crêpes Suzettes, Steak au Poivre, Mousse de Truite, Sauce Américaine, Lobster aux Aromates, Tripes à la Mode de Caën, various pâtés, Baba au Rhum, Cherries Jubilee.

The names resound like an honor roll of gastronomy. Even such an incomplete listing indicates, unmistakably, the trend toward cooking with spirits—and the lively vistas they open for the imaginative cook in the home.

It would seem that cooking with liquor is an idea whose time has come. From a nation with a frontier we have developed into an "affluent society." Emotionally, we are shedding inhibitions imposed by the Puritan ethic and are moving to fulfill our manifest epicurean destiny. There's an abounding interest in the sensual satisfactions of superbly prepared and exquisitely presented fare. Dining with élan, kitchen talents, *foodmanship* if you will, have assumed the dimensions of a subculture, calling for the same conversational fluency on the part of people who keep up with things as art movies and the professional football scene.

Even more pertinent is today's emphasis on entertaining at home. The modern hostess strives for the nuance, the audacious touch that will distinguish *her* dinner party: a ravishing roast, a suave dressing or sauce, an utterly luscious dessert! She needn't look any

[2] Many have been adapted for home preparation, and detailed recipes are given in the appropriate section, later on.

farther than the family liquor cabinet for inspiration. The spirits world offers the knowing *cuisinière* a completely fresh range of tastes and bouquets with which to work culinary magic. Recently a prominent distiller gave a dinner for the Wine and Spirits Wholesalers at which every course, appetizer to dessert, was anointed with some liquor. The stunt, to label it accurately, was an unqualified success—making its point neatly. However, home cooks are not advised to duplicate this feat. Merely dousing food with liquor does not *guarantee* enchanting results. Handled adroitly, however, a spirit-seasoned dinner can transform a mundane meal into a captivating experience. Your guests may not fully comprehend what delicious alchemy is being performed—but there are great expectations.

THE INTELLIGENT COOK'S GUIDE TO SPIRITS

CHAPTER 2

"Spirits" is the label given to the category of distilled alcoholic beverages.

Whiskies are spirits obtained from grain—principally corn, rye and barley.

Brandies are spirits obtained from grapes and other fruit—plums, apples, cherries, berries, pears.

Rums are spirits obtained from molasses and other sugar-cane products.

Liqueurs are obtained by combining spirits with flavoring agents, and then sweetening.

Gin and **vodka** are customarily obtained by additional processing of neutral spirits. Gin is flavored with juniper berries and other botanicals, usually during a second distillation. Vodka is filtered through charcoal to remove taste and aroma characteristics.

There are several well-known spirits which do not fit easily into any category: tequila, obtained from the agave, or century plant (not cactus); aquavit, neutral spirits flavored with caraway seed; Metaxa, an aromatic brandy-like liqueur.

It's easy to make whiskey, as any West Virginia mountaineer will affirm. (For "whiskey," read any other spirit. The basic principle is the same.) First the grains are coarsely ground, cooked with water, then cooled. Germinated barley (malt) is mixed into this gruel. Enzymes in the malt convert the starches into sugar. Yeast is then added. The yeast feeds on the sugar, changing it to alcohol, a process known as "fermentation." The alcohol content of the liquid at this point is seven percent, roughly between beer and wine. Finally, the alcohol is extracted by distillation. The distilling process is based on an elementary principle—alcohol is volatile and boils at a lower temperature (172.4°F.) than water (212°F). Heating a fermented mixture at a point between the two will separate the alcohol out in the form of vapors. When the vapors are cooled, they condense, returning to liquid form, and we have new alcohol.

The *art* of distillation, as opposed to the simple *act,* is quite another matter, requiring experience and sensitivity. The object is to retain all the pleasant, flavorful characteristics of the spirit while eliminating the undesirable elements. Compare a well-made whiskey

10

from a responsible distiller with a cheap, unknown product—the gap is enormous!

The differences in flavor, aroma and body among whiskey types—the qualities which interest us as cooks—depend on a number of things. Distilling temperature is perhaps primary. The lower the temperature of distillation the lower the proof . . . and the greater the flavor and substance in the whiskey. Proof, incidentally, is always expressed as double the alcoholic content: 100 proof is the equivalent of 50 percent alcohol content. The product of a distillation at or above 190 proof is labeled "grain neutral spirits," because it presumably lacks "distinctive taste, color and odor." The kind of grains and proportions in which they are used also influence flavor. All things being equal, corn produces a lighter product. The time and nature of aging will affect the finished product, although not so categorically as assumed. More age does not always make a better whiskey, or wine, for that matter. Light-bodied whiskies, for instance, do not benefit so much from lengthy aging as do the full-bodied, richly flavored types. A point to remember: *Spirits do not continue to improve after bottling. The only aging that counts is in wood.*

Any special treatment—the drying of barley over open peat fires in making Scotch whisky, for example—will affect the nature of the finished product. We shall refer to these factors later when examining the spirits in greater detail.

Whiskey

There are well over two dozen whiskey types recognized by the United States government. The most popular are bourbons, American blends, Scotch, Irish and Canadian whiskies.

Bourbon: The principal grain in bourbon is corn. In making straight bourbon, the alcohol must be distilled out at 160 proof or less, and aged in new, charred white-oak barrels for a minimum of two years. As a practical matter, most bourbons are distilled at lower proofs, to retain more of the congeners—flavor-giving properties—and they are kept in wood four years or more.

Sour-mash bourbon isn't sour, nor is it noticeably different in taste from sweet-mash bourbon. The term "sour mash" merely describes a technical aspect of production, a method of yeasting and fermenting.

Bottled-in-Bond bourbon is 100 proof and aged a minimum of four years under government supervision. It is not in any way a quality designation.

Corn whiskey is even cornier than bourbon, being made from at least 80 percent corn grain. Unlike bourbon, it may be stored in either used or uncharred barrels. It is a light-bodied whiskey.

Tennessee whiskey is very much like bourbon, except that it goes through an extra step. Tennessee whiskey is trickled through charcoal immediately after distillation. There are only two distilleries in the state of Tennessee: George Dickel and Jack Daniel.

Characteristic flavor: Bourbon is unique among whiskies in the complexity of its flavor. Researchers say they have detected notes of caramel, vanilla, dry wood, cumin, cereal, fruity undertones, buttery, nutty scents, as well as the characteristic taste of alcohol. Most of the last evaporates in cooking. These components are not apparent separately, but combine to give a round, rich and lingering taste. The potential of bourbon as a condiment has barely been tapped.

American blends are one of the two major native whiskey types, the other being bourbon. Simply stated, blends are a mixture of whiskies and neutral spirits. By law the whiskies in blends must be at least 20 percent by volume. In fact, the national brands contain 35 percent straight whiskies, including bourbon, in the blend.

Flavor characteristics: somewhat thin compared to bourbon. The alcohol element is more noticeable. Faint rye-flour aroma. Fruitiness, cooked caramel and dry-wood notes are not so apparent as in bourbon. Not particularly good for cooking except in special situations.

Rye: This is rye whiskey, not the blends mistakenly called rye along the East Coast. No longer popular, which is too bad, it can be a fine whiskey. The principal grain in rye whiskey, not surprisingly, is rye. Otherwise, it is made like bourbon.

Flavor characteristics: definite redolence of the rye grain. Bold single flavor, unlike the complexity of bourbon. Full-bodied. People who are familiar with sour-rye bread will notice the same appetizing tang in rye whiskey.

Scotch whisky[1] is a blend of two whiskey types: malt whiskey, from malted (germinated) barley, distilled out at 140 proof to retain volatile flavor elements; and grain whiskey, from corn and a little rye, distilled out at 180 proof or higher, similar to American grain neutral spirits. The malted barley is dried over open peat fires, which imparts the smoky taste for which Scotch is known. Although the grain whiskies may comprise as much as 80 percent of a blend, Scotch whisky acquires its taste from the malt whiskies. A minimum of three years' aging (four in the U. S.) is required, in a variety of cooperage including old sherry casks.

Flavor characteristics: The pronounced smoky taste that some Scots call "peat reek," and others "a gentle fragrance of peat reminiscent of heather-clad moorland in spring," typifies Scotch whisky. Smokiness varies in intensity, brand to brand, depending on the percentage and type of malt in the blend. Grain whiskey contributes alcohol flavors. Scotch blends are light-bodied. There are also unblended malt whiskies called "singles," which are fuller in flavor and body and have a malty undertone.

Irish whiskey is made from 80 percent barley (half malted, half unsprouted), plus wheat, oats and a bit of rye. It is distilled out at low proof in pot stills, like Scotch. Unlike Scotch, the malted barley is not dried over open fires; therefore Irish doesn't have the smokiness of Scotch. Long maturation, seven years, is a hallmark of Irish whiskey. The Irish ship both straight whiskies and blends, about half and half, to the States. The blends containing 25 percent to 35 percent pot-still whiskies are naturally lighter.

[1] The Scots and Canadians spell it "whisky," without the "e."

Flavor characteristics: Low distillation temperature and long aging produce a well-grounded, full-bodied liquor in which the flavor of the malt prevails.

Canadian whisky: Most people consider Canadian whisky to be rye. In point of fact, the principal grain is corn (much of it imported from the United States), supplemented with home-grown rye, barley and small amounts of wheat. Canadian whiskies are blends, mostly distilled out at quite high proofs and filtered before bottling. They are aged a minimum of two years in new oak barrels or previously used whiskey barrels.

Flavor characteristics: Lightness is the outstanding quality of Canadian whiskies. They bear a resemblance to American blends, a bit sweeter perhaps and more even. Subtleties of taste and aroma are hard to isolate.

Gin and Vodka

Gin and vodka are similar in that both are basically grain neutral spirits, distilled out at such high proof as to have no distinctive taste or aroma. However, flavor is then *added* to gin and *removed* from vodka.

London Dry gin: Commonly, neutral spirits are redistilled and the vapors passed through a cylinder packed with aromatic substances, among which are juniper berries, cassia bark or cinnamon, coriander seed, angelica and orrisroot, bitter almonds, fennel, dried lemon and orange peels and cardamom. The hot vapors extract the oils from the botanicals. When cooled and condensed, the spirits remain forever impregnated with the flavor of the herbs, spices, peels and plants in the cylinder. Gin is not aged, and the government maintains that aging doesn't improve gin.

The term "London Dry" is generic and has no special significance. Although there are minor differences in production, imported and American gins are very similar.

Flavor characteristics: Every distiller has his own secret recipe for making gin, but the essential flavor is always of juniper. The 20 to 30 supplementary botanicals lend a sprightly garden-fresh bouquet which snaps up many dishes.

Hollands gin is also called "genever" or "schiedam." It's quite another product from London Dry gin. Distilled out at extremely low proof, Dutch gin is heavy, with a pronounced malt-grain flavor, akin to that of whiskey. The prevalent plant flavor is juniper.

Old Tom gin is London Dry gin that has been sweetened with sugar syrup. It is no longer popular.

Sloe gin: Actually a liqueur, not a gin. See "Liqueurs."

Vodka is distilled from the cheapest, most abundant material available in a country. It *may* be made from potatoes, but is almost always made from grain, even in the U.S.S.R.

Commonly, grain neutral spirits are reduced in proof by the addition of demineralized water, then filtered through activated charcoal to remove congeners, the flavor components. Claims are made that vodka has no flavor. In fact, it does have alcohol flavor, though little else. That which makes vodka superb for mixed drinks, its neutrality, makes it undesirable in cooking. It is not recommended for cooking except in such specialties as "Bloody Mary Soup."

Rum

Just about every sugar-growing island produces rum. Rum-watchers claim they can identify a dozen varieties. Rums do come in a considerable range, but for reasonable purposes they can be divided into two basic types—light-bodied, the prototype for which are the Puerto Rican rums, and full-bodied, Jamaica rums being the leading example. Note that this does not mean light and dark color. Rums, like whiskies, are practically colorless when distilled. Color is developed during aging or artificially added. Since rums start as a form of sugar, the step converting starches into sugars, necessary in whiskey, is eliminated. The malty flavor prevalent in whiskies is also eliminated, accounting for one of the basic differences in taste between whiskies and rums.

Puerto Rican rums are made from molasses, fermented with cultured yeasts and distilled out at high proofs, up to 189 proof. Aging takes place in uncharred barrels. The white- or silver-label rums require one-year minimum aging, and the gold- or amber-labels three years. "Añejo" indicates a rum of extra age and extra flavor. Puerto Rican rums are filtered and color replaced artificially. Light-bodied rums also come from the Virgin Islands, Haiti, Dominican Republic, Mexico, Brazil, Philippine Islands and Hawaii.

Flavor characteristics: Very delicate. The white labels are lighter than all distilled spirits but vodka, gin and neutral spirits—better for cocktails than cooking. The gold labels offer a pleasant caramel flavor, a touch of molasses in the fragrance and a hint of sweetness. A versatile cooking spirit because of its delicacy.

Jamaica rums are made from a combination of molasses and dunder, skimmings from the top of the sugar-refining tanks. These rums are fermented by "wild" yeasts from the air, or introduced in a culture from the previous fermentation, as in the sour-mash process. They are distilled out at low proofs, 160° or below, and given plenty of time to mature in uncharred barrels, often seven years. Jamaica rums have a deep golden hue, but those shipped to America are darkened, since that is the preference here. Full-bodied rums are also made in Martinique, Barbados, Trinidad and British Guiana.

Flavor characteristics: An assertive pungency and an unmistakable taste and aroma of molasses—the deep, bass notes in the flavor scale. Surprisingly for so forthright a flavor, it accommodates very well to many foods.

151 proof rum: Quite a few Jamaica and Puerto Rican rums are now available at 151 proof, largely attributable to the resurgent interest in cooking with spirits. These potent rums are ideal for flaming, practically failure-proof, and they leave a rich, concentrated residue of flavor when the alcohol has burned off.

Demarara rum is from British Guiana, a lusty, full-bodied yo-ho-ho rum, associated with pirates and whalers. It is probably the original source of 151 proof rum. It has a slightly burnt, some say smoky, taste not found in other rums.

New England rum is a domestic rum made from West Indian molasses. Once very popular, but no longer, it is distilled out at less than 160 proof, and belongs in the full-bodied grouping.

Brandy

There are two classes of brandy—grape brandy and fruit brandy. When the label merely reads "brandy," the contents are from grapes, or, more accurately, wine. Brandy from fruit will name the fruit from which it has been distilled. Brandy is called the soul of the grape. It takes five gallons of wine to make one gallon of brandy. All brandies are blended. The particular flavor, bouquet and body desired by the shipper are achieved by mixing brandies of various types and ages. They run the gamut from very round and full-bodied to relatively light-bodied brandies.

Cognac is the most famous and probably the finest grape brandy in the world. Those labeled "Grand Fine Champagne" and "Fine Champagne" are the best of the cognacs. Only brandy from the Charente region of France may be called cognac. It is distilled out at 140 proof and aged in Limousin oak casks anywhere from five to 40 years, then blended. For all the control which the French government exercises over cognac, there are few regulations on labeling. The stars and letters are the shipper's evaluation of his own merchandise. However, reputable cognac firms adhere roughly to these standards. Three stars on a label indicates that the cognac averages five to seven years age, although there will be older and possibly younger cognacs in the bottle. V.S.O.P. cognac will run between ten and 15 years. The "P," for "pale," means that no artificial color has been added—a useful guide since cognacs darken naturally as they get older. Connoisseurs say the optimum age for cognac is between 25 and 40 years.

Flavor characteristics: Cognac may be the most complex and multifaceted spirit, and the most versatile for cooking. The grape is the essence of cognac flavor. There is no dominating note, rather a subtle weaving of taste, aroma and bouquet. (Bouquet is that part of the fragrance which is developed while resting in the cask. Aroma is the original grape odor.) Bouquet is really what cognac is all about. To isolate its inherent nature, pour some into a thistle-shaped glass and cover lightly. When the liquid has evaporated, sniff the lingering fragrance. The longer it persists, the finer the cognac is apt to be. Professional tasters are after the same essence when they swirl wine or brandy around in a glass. By enlarging the evaporation surface, they increase the fragrant vapors and get a concentrated whiff of the bouquet.

Armagnac is another distinctive French brandy, second only to cognac, produced only in the Department of Gers, to the south of the Charente. Armagnac takes a lot of age. A 50-year-old Armagnac is not a rarity. It is usually drier than cognac, but not so velvety.

American brandy comes mostly from California and is distilled at fairly high proofs, up to 170°, and aged two to eight years in oak. A small quantity of brandy is distilled out at lower proofs in pot stills (the kind used for cognac) and blended with the lighter-bodied brandies for flavor and substance.

Flavor characteristics: Quite light compared to cognac and the French brandies. The flavor of the grape is present, but muted. Hint of sweetness. Very clean, no off flavors. Only fair for cooking, but excellent in mixed drinks—highballs, sours, Alexanders.

Fruit brandies: There is scarcely a fruit which cannot be made into brandy. They are distilled at low proofs to hold more of the perfume of the fruit in the alcohol after distillation. For the same reason, many fruit brandies are not aged. Contact with the cask would alter or diminish the exquisite but fragile fruit essences. Pits and stones are left in the mash, imparting a characteristic bitter almond undertone to brandies made from cherries, plums, etc.

Fruit brandies are dry. Do not confuse them with the sweetened *fruit-flavored* brandies, which are in reality liqueurs. Kirsch or kirschwasser, from cherries, is the fruit brandy most important in cooking. It is a standard ingredient in Swiss Fondue and is used freely with fresh or cooked fruit. Other favorites are mirabelle, quetsch and slivovitz (all from plums), framboise (raspberry), applejack and Calvados (apple), eau de vie de poire (pear). Fruit brandies are bottled at relatively high proofs, so easy does it!

You may come across the term "eau de vie." It usually refers to fruit brandies, especially the colorless group. Actually, "eau de vie" is a vague term which translates as "water of life" and can be applied to any distilled spirit.

Liqueurs

Technically, liqueurs are distilled spirits which have been flavored and sweetened. But anyone who has been held in thrall by their voluptuous charm and gemlike hues knows how inadequate a definition can be. The world's storehouse of flavors is plundered by distillers to obtain the choicest fruits, herbs, seeds, spices, flowers, peels and roots, which are then transferred to the spirit base by various methods. By far the simplest is steeping, a process much like brewing tea. Fruit is allowed to rest in a spirit until the flavor is fully extracted. The liquor is sweetened with sugar or dextrose. Honey and maple syrup are used, too, but only rarely. A minimum sugar content of 2½ percent by weight is required, but most liqueurs contain from 10 percent to 30 percent sugar.

The spirit base of the liqueur is generally grain neutral spirits or brandy, but some specialties call for bourbons, Scotch whisky, Irish whiskey, rum or gin. Have a go at making your own liqueur. Why not! Steep some fruit, say wild cherries, in 100 proof vodka. When the vodka has extracted sufficient cherry flavor, anywhere from six months to a year, sweeten with sugar syrup (not granulated sugar). You may want to reduce proof to the 50° or 60° customary for fruit liqueurs. Commercial houses accomplish this by adding distilled water.

Liqueurs or cordials,[2]—the words are synonymous—have intense flavor, are relatively low in proof and high in sugar content. These factors combine to minimize or mask the alcohol taste common to all spirits. That's why you can use liqueurs much more freely—straight from the bottle as a topping or seasoning—without heating first to release the alcohol. Take full advantage of the ready-to-use quality of liqueurs.

Fruit-*flavored* brandies are actually liqueurs made with a brandy base and bottled at a minimum 70 proof. Fruit liqueurs run 50 proof to 60 proof, in the main. Crèmes are the sweeter liqueurs and have a velvety consistency.

There are shelves and shelves of liqueurs in the stores, and new ones keep coming. For convenience, they are grouped here somewhat arbitrarily in four categories. Color, beguiling as it may be, is no indication of flavor. Crème de menthe, for instance, may be purchased in green, white, gold and ruby—all tasting alike.

Fruits

It should come as no surprise that these liqueurs reflect the characteristic flavor and aroma of the fresh fruit or peel. Most are obvious, but are listed here to show what's available.

Fruit:	*Commercial Name:*
apricot	apricot, Abricotene, Apry
banana	crème de bananes
blackberry	blackberry
black currant	crème de cassis, Bolsberry
cherry	cherry, Cherristock, Cherry Heering, maraschino, wishniak
grapefruit	Forbidden Fruit (taste is of citrus rather than grapefruit, but it is made from Shaddock grapefruit, grown in the West Indies)

[2] Folklorists attribute "cordial" to the Puritans, who, it is said, enjoyed their Cherry Bounce—rum flavored with cherries—but not the naughty implication of the French word "liqueur." So they adopted the term "cordial," thereby salving their consciences.

melon	Reishu
orange	curaçao, triple sec, Cointreau, Grand Marnier
peach	peach
pineapple	crème d'ananas
raspberry	crème de framboises, Framberry
sloeberry	sloe gin (the sloeberry is actually a small wild plum; some cherry taste)
	prunelle (made from sloeberry and/or Italian (prune) plum; plummy taste)
strawberry	crème de fraises
tangerine	mandarino, manderine, Van Der Hum
mixture	Cordial Medoc (contains orange, cacao, cherry)

Plants

These include herbs, spices, flowers, seeds, roots, barks.

Monastery types draw their flavor from a multiplicity of plants and generally are described as "herby, spicy and aromatic." Although they have a family resemblance, there is significant variation, too, depending on which ingredient or combination is dominant. These liqueurs are descendants of the legendary elixirs developed by medieval monks and alchemists. The revered names are Chartreuse—containing 130 (count 'em) ingredients, available in green at 110 proof, or yellow, 86 proof—and Benedictine and its modern companion B&B. The latter is somewhat drier because of the 50 percent cognac base. Other established names in the group: Benai, Elixir d'Anvers, Fior d'Alpi, Galliano, Izarra, Roiano, Strega, Vielle Curé.

Anisette, anesone, mastic, Ojen, ouzo, Pastis, Pernod, Ricard, Sambuca are all in the licorice-anise family—a very large family indeed. Big range in proofs, from 50 proof to 92 proof.

Crème de menthe (Frappemint, Freezomint): mint, primarily peppermint.

Crème de violette, crème yvette: violet flowers and a little vanilla.

Ginger: the taste and the prickle of ginger.

Kummel: caraway.

Nassau Royale: mellow banana, vanilla, some say a hint of cacao.

Parfait Amour: flower petals, citron, vanilla.

Rosolio: rose petals, orange, vanilla, spice.

Peppermint schnapps: clean mint tang; less sugar and a little higher proof than crème de menthe.

The Familiar Flavors

Crème d'almond, Noyaux: almond, from kernels of fruit; pleasant bitter undertone.

Crème de cacao: chocolate and vanilla.

Chocla Menthe, Vandermint: chocolate and mint.

Crème de café, Café Brizard, Coffee House, Galacafé, Kahlua, Pasha, Tía Maria: coffee bean.

Koffie Menthe: coffee and mint.

Tea Breeze, Ocha: green-tea flavor and fragrance.

Crème de vanille: vanilla.

Whiskey-Base Cordials

Tiddy's: Canadian whisky, maple syrup.

Drambuie: Scotch whisky, herbs, heather honey; spicy aroma.

Irish Mist: Irish whiskey, herbs and herbal extracts, heather honey; more flowery-honey bouquet than Drambuie.

Pimento Dram: Jamaica rum, pimento, cloves; peppery aftertaste.

Rock & Rye: whiskey, rock candy, fruit juice; sometimes bottled with chunks of fruit.

Southern Comfort: bourbon whiskey, peach liqueur.

Swedish Punsch: arrack (aromatic rum flavor), tea, lemon, spices.

HOW TO MATE
FOOD AND SPIRITS
FOR FUN
AND COMPLIMENTS
CHAPTER
3

For the purposes of cooking follow the French lead: think of spirits as condiments. It is said that when a French chef is at a loss for something new, he'll toss a little brandy and a few shallots into the kettle, give the old dish a ritzy name, and *voilà*—a creation! Brandy is a staple of French *haute cuisine,* and such bold, free-wheeling attitudes are natural there. Don't attempt to follow suit immediately. In time you'll develop a personal reference library of tastes and be able to handle spirits with similar aplomb. Meanwhile, here are enough specific applications, culled from many kitchens, to start you in the right direction.

Affinities

Brandy mates well with coffee. After sipping a *café noir,* the people of la Charente splash a little cognac into the drained cup. The lingering coffee aroma mingles pleasantly with the cognac. As you'd expect, brandy and fresh grapes complement each other. Crosscut the bottom of seedless green grapes and marinate in brandy for a half hour. Spear with picks and dip in confectioners' sugar for an ingratiating nibble. (When the grapes are gone, sip the nectarous liquor.) In Gascony, home of both musketeer d'Artagnan and Armagnac, prunes achieve nobility by steeping in the native brandy for a week or so. A Las Vegas restaurant spikes its pancake syrup with brandy. A treat for late Sunday breakfast! La Quetsch, a Parisian delicatessen, soaks Camembert in cognac, then sprinkles with walnut meats. Thrifty French housewives sweep crumbles of Roquefort cheese into small crocks and moisten with brandy, transforming *fromage perdu* into a delicious spread—for crackers, melba rounds, toasted bread. Add cognac to diced candied fruits and stir into puddings, cakes; sauce over ice cream.

Bourbon displays its fondness for chocolate in mousse au chocolat and in chocolate topping for ice cream. Grated bitter chocolate and a dollop of bourbon in chili con carne is really something else. Add zip to salted (unsweetened) whipped cream with bourbon, then adorn tomato soup with it. Stir a little bourbon into bean soup, barbecue sauce and ground beef for burgers. Bourbon and peaches

24

in any form is a marriage made in heaven. Sprinkle peach halves with brown sugar and bourbon. Dab with butter and broil. Scrumptious garnish! Split four or five vanilla beans and steep in a pint of bourbon or brandy. After several weeks you'll have homemade vanilla extract with an extra flavor dimension.

Fruit brandies are cosy matched with fruits from which they're made, but don't hesitate to mix with other fruits. Kirsch and pineapple—a byword, almost like ham and eggs. Kirsch and strawberries or apricots, or framboise and raspberries are equally good. Sprinkle with sugar. A little sweetening makes fruit brandies bloom. Gourmandaise, the dessert cheese, *comes* perfumed with kirsch. Take the obvious cue and cream Gruyère with kirsch or Calvados. Don't forget the kirsch in duckling Montmorency and Swiss Fondue. Americanize French onion soup with a soupçon of applejack. One of Manhattan's finer restaurants serves a vivacious apple sorbet made with Calvados. Similarly, a modest dashing of pear brandy vitalizes lemon sherbet. (Who was it who said, "A girl could get drunk in New York just from eating desserts"?)

A light splash of rum, no more, accents sautéed mushrooms and revives canned cream of mushroom soup. Rum befriends chocolate, coffee, pineapple, lemon and lime. Marinate pineapple in rum, then dip in batter and deep-fry. No rum? Applejack will do handsomely. When making chocolate pudding, separate the children from the adults by stirring a teaspoon or so of rum into each grown-up's portion. (Gild the lily by topping with whipped cream to which crème de cacao or coffee liqueur has been added.) Rum in icings and fillings for cake—*delicioso*.

Scotch is not nearly so gregarious as rum, but its smoky tones add vigor to fish sauces and fumés, and, unexpectedly, to English trifle. The Scots stir it into marmalade. And Scotch whisky basted over a roasting loin of pork comes highly recommended.

Liqueurs, the *dolce vita* branch of the spirit family, lend themselves more easily to improvisation. They can be sauced over sherbets and ice cream directly from the bottle, mixed into parfaits, spooned over fruit. Try crème de menthe with pineapple, cherry with orange ice, blackberry on grapefruit sections, Roiano or chartreuse over fruit cocktail. Pit the verve of ginger liqueur against smug canned pears, against oleaginous duck or pork. Make up your own minted pears by marinating in crème de menthe; serve with lamb— a cunning replacement for mint jelly. Orange liqueur is engagingly versatile. It goes with just about everything—dessert omelets and soufflés, carrots, sherbets, pork, duck, chicken. Tip: When using liqueurs with meat, poultry or fish, you may want to cut the sweetness with lemon juice, brandy or whiskey. Lashings of anesone in coffee are a Roman tradition. One coffee emporium in New York's Italian community takes the logical next step. They soak the beans in an anise liqueur prior to grinding. More conventionally, moisten the rim of a coffee cup with anisette, then swirl in sugar. Sip the coffee through a licorice bouquet. Double your pleasure—coffee liqueur in coffee. Drop sugar crystals remaining in a bottle of Fior d'Alpi into coffee.

Spirits combined with butter and other seasonings make inspired bastes. Open with gin, parsley and butter on sole; curaçao, lemon juice and butter on chicken; bourbon and butter on lamb.

In a prerefrigerator era, spirits did double duty as preservatives. Restaurant chefs today store fresh truffles in brandy—to preserve *and* to flavor. Plantation cooks swathed fruitcakes in bourbon-saturated cheesecloth to similar ends. Heavy paper soaked in whiskey, rum or gin was used as a cover to keep jelly free of mold. An old recipe for preserved muskmelons concludes with this admonition, "Keep covered tight, in a cool place, with a paper wet in brandy or proof spirit on them." Still a good trick. Try it instead of paraffin.

Rules of the Road

1. Essentially, cooking with spirits amounts to cooking *away* the alcohol. Liquor, like vanilla extract, loses its alcohol and most of its bite when boiled, leaving the good smells and tastes that stimulate only the appetite.

2. Allow enough cooking time for the alcohol to evaporate. A tablespoon of whiskey in a skillet, over a hot burner, needs only a moment or two. Ten minutes should be sufficient in most circumstances. Be especially careful to burn off all the alcohol when flaming

just before serving. *Allow the fire to burn out naturally.* When feasible, simmer a minute or two after flames have died.

3. There are times when the bitter undertone of alcohol *is* welcome to cut the sweetness, as when using fruit brandies with desserts. But be wary when alcohol isn't cooked or flamed away, especially with high-proof spirits like the fruit brandies. A little goes a long way.

4. As a general rule, robust, full-bodied spirits are best in hearty, well-seasoned fare, and lighter-bodied types in delicate dishes.

5. Classic recipes often call for both wine and brandy. Some chefs add brandy to wine dishes even when not classically correct. With wines maturing younger and food cooking faster, they feel the need for brandy's body and fullness to support today's lighter wines. Framboise in a white-wine sauce, incidentally, is one to remember.

6. Working chefs use spirits to deglaze a pan in which meat or fish has been sautéed. The liquor loosens the browned, flavorful bits adhering to the pan. As the alcohol evaporates, the flavor essence of the spirit combines with the flavors in the pan, enriching the juices. If you don't care to make a complicated sauce, just swirl the spirit— brandy, bourbon, gin—with the pan juices, and use as a natural gravy. Dandy.

7. To bring up the aroma of a particular spirit, brush it fleetingly over a roast, broil or cake as it leaves the oven. This is comparable to the baker's trick of brushing warm cake with the expensive spread to leave a buttery halo. When sprinkling cake layers with liquor, cut the spirit with water to get a more even distribution over the dry surface.

8. When blending spirits with whole eggs or yolks, trickle in very slowly. Too rapid addition of spirits to eggs tends to coagulate (scramble) the eggs.

9. In hot soufflés, liquor helps to achieve a lighter, higher, hardier result. Heated alcohol stimulates egg and cream sauce mixtures to puff and expand.

10. Too much liquor will delay or even prevent ice cream or other frozen desserts from freezing, since alcohol lowers the freezing point of a mixture.

11. Granulated sugar does not dissolve readily in liquor. When

you want to combine sugar with liquor, first make up a simple syrup by combining a cup of sugar with a cup of water and heating until the sugar dissolves. Measure as you would regular sugar.

12. As with any condiment, moderation is the key to successful spirit cookery. The flavor should highlight, rather than dominate. If the liquor flavor is quickly apparent, chances are you've poured too generously. Use a light hand until you know your way around the whiskey bottle. Better too little than too much.

13. There's no such thing as cooking liquor. Use a quality product with a reliable name, as you would in drinks. On the other hand, it is both unnecessary and inappropriate to lace a gravy with 20-year-old Scotch or Grande Fine Champagne cognac. The only possible exception would be when using a small quantity, uncooked. In such instances a rare, aged spirit is a splendid investment.

14. Liquor in the pot is neither inebriating nor fattening. When the alcohol is driven off, it takes with it the calories and intoxicants. Liqueurs, with their sugar dosage, are the exception. But even there the calories remaining are minimal. When *drinking* liquor, you can figure the calories as roughly equal to the proof, for every ounce; i.e., one ounce of 86 proof whiskey contains 86 calories, one ounce of 100 proof bourbon contains approximately 100 calories.

15. Claims have been made that spirits tenderize and improve the texture of meats and game. There is no scientific verification, but our subjective impressions would confirm this belief.

The Burning Issue

Everybody knows how dramatic a dish looks presented flambé. Indeed, it is often assumed that flaming is a theatrical stunt, performed by skilled maître d's or show-off hostesses *just* for effect. Flaming at table does create a festive atmosphere. Blue flames licking at a bird will impress the most blasé guest. But don't overlook the gustatory dividends resulting from such theatrics.

The fact is there's much more flaming by chefs in the privacy of restaurant kitchens than in the public rooms. Blazing is the quickest way of evaporating alcohol, leaving only the quintessential spirit flavor. It's particularly appropriate in quick-cooking dishes where there isn't time to simmer the alcohol away. Flaming speeds deglazing by loosening the flavorful encrusted morsels so vital to a sauce. Burning liquor in direct contact with the food at the beginning of preparation seems to fuse the separate flavor components in a delicious harmony in which no single flavor dominates. On the other hand, flaming just prior to serving imparts a captivating aroma that complements and highlights the basic taste.

Flaming food is neither difficult nor complicated. You can be as successful at home as any professional, if you observe the following principles and techniques.

1. *The spirit must have sufficient alcohol.* Almost any liquor can be made to flame, but try not to go below 70 proof. Of course, you'll get a brighter, more enduring flame with 100 proof bonded bourbons or the fruit brandies which run 90 proof or higher. Three-star cognac, usually 84 proof, flames more readily than the older cognacs, bottled at 80 proof. Most flammable of all is 151 proof rum. Stand back when you light that.

If you'd like to flame with a low-proof liqueur which happens to be compatible with your tour de force, add sufficient 100 proof vodka or brandy as chefs do, to ensure a good blaze. Another professional trick is to sprinkle lightly with sugar before igniting. It makes for a brighter blaze.

You can have trouble with the contents of a bottle that's been opened for a while. Alcohol will evaporate and ultimately the proof will be reduced.

Every now and then you'll see recipes for flaming with wine. It can't be done unless you fortify the wine with a high-proof spirit. Don't try it unless you know what you're about.

2. *The spirit should be warm.* Heat the liquor just to the point where the alcohol begins to vaporize. It is the vapor which ignites. Warm the liquor by setting at the back of the stove or holding over low heat, like a candle. Don't get the liquor too hot or it may go up before you're ready. The pan and/or the food to be flamed, if it is hot, can also serve to warm the liquor.

3. *Use reasonable caution.* When setting alcohol aflame, use a long fireplace match or taper. Don't lean over the pan or chafing

dish. Leave sufficient space between you and the flames to avoid singeing fingers or any other part of your anatomy. Remove combustibles such as paper towels and decorations. Don't add spirits to the pan directly from the bottle in the presence of flames.

4. *Equipment*. Flame the spirit in a *shallow* pan, if possible. A flat, wide surface allows oxygen to reach the flame easily, a necessity in keeping any kind of fire going. A handsome chafing dish is nice if you actually do the cooking at the table. Otherwise, transfer the prepared dish to an attractive serving piece and do the final flaming at the table. The flames burn off quickly and are not terribly hot, so it's unlikely they'll damage your china, silver or heavy crystal.

5. *Lighting the spirit*. Depending on the dish, the spirit can be ignited in a long-handled ladle and drizzled flaming over the food, or it can be added to the pan and then blazed. Chefs have a special technique of their own. They add the spirit to the pan and then shake it over the fire. The alcohol spray releases vapors, which catch fire and spark the liquor in the pan. It's an impressive performance, but it takes an experienced hand.

Use the method which you find most comfortable. Of course, the dish itself may dictate the method. For instance, steamed puddings are sometimes too moist to be ignited. To ensure that your Christmas plum pudding flames, light a bonded bourbon in your ladle and spoon the flames over the pudding. This is the safest practice any time there's enough sauce in a pan to dilute the alcohol, or, for that matter, any time you're in doubt.

With desserts that have a lot of syrup, such as cooked or canned fruit, drain before blazing and serve the syrup separately.

On occasion, restaurants do flambé just for the spectacle. Shish kabob on a flaming sword, presented in a darkened room, is a case in point. What the restaurants do is saturate cotton with a tasteless fuel and place the wad near the handle. When lit, and the sword or skewer is held vertically, flames shoot up, enveloping the lamb cubes.

But it's just as simple to combine spectacle with savor. To serve a flaming shish kabob at home, simply pour an ounce of warmed brandy on a heatproof platter. Lay the prepared shish kabob across the platter and ignite the brandy. When the flame dies, slide meat off skewer onto individual plates.

Triple sec ladled over baked spareribs, then flamed, is another example of flare combined with flair. You'll think of many more once the possibilities become apparent.

One precautionary suggestion: Before flambéing for guests, try the act on the family. Remember, even veteran entertainers go through lengthy rehearsals before opening on Broadway.

APPETIZERS

CHAPTER
4

Cheese Canapés

Parmesan Crowns

1 cup grated Parmesan cheese
1 cup mayonnaise

1 large onion, grated
⅓ cup blended whiskey

Preheat oven to 475°F. Combine ingredients and blend in blender or beat with rotary beater. Pile on water crackers or sesame crackers and heat in oven for 2 or 3 minutes.
YIELD: About 3 dozen.

Blue Cheese Devils

3 ounces cream cheese
3 tablespoons blue cheese

1 tablespoon Scotch whisky

Put cream cheese in a bowl and let it come to room temperature. Add other ingredients and mix thoroughly. Chill for several hours to ripen. Spread mixture on crackers. Toast under broiler about two minutes, watching carefully, until cheese browns and puffs slightly.

This mixture can also be used to stuff celery or mushroom caps or spread on crisp cucumber or apple slices.

Cheddartini Puffs

¼ pound sharp cheddar cheese, grated
¼ teaspoon salt
¼ teaspoon dry mustard

1 tablespoon grated onion
½ teaspoon sugar
1 teaspoon dry vermouth
1 tablespoon gin

Mix all ingredients thoroughly. Spread on crackers. Toast under broiler about 2 minutes, watching carefully, until cheese browns and puffs slightly.

Dips

Shrimp Dip

1 cup chopped cooked shrimp
½ pint sour cream
¼ cup bourbon
1 teaspoon chopped onion
1 teaspoon chopped parsley

½ teaspoon paprika
¼ teaspoon thyme
¾ teaspoon salt
¼ teaspoon pepper

Put all ingredients into blender and blend until smooth. Remove from blender and chill. Serve as a dip for raw vegetables or seafood or crackers.
YIELD: About 2 cups.

Clam Dip

1 8-ounce package cream cheese
2 tablespoons gin
2 tablespoons sour cream
7-ounce can minced clams, drained
1 teaspoon minced fresh dill-weed (or ¼ teaspoon dried)

1 tablespoon chopped pimento
¼ cup finely chopped celery
½ teaspoon horseradish
1 teaspoon grated onion
¼ teaspoon salt
Paprika for garnish

Soften cream cheese and beat with gin and sour cream until well mixed. Add other ingredients and blend well. Turn into a serving bowl and sprinkle with paprika. Serve with potato or corn chips.
YIELD: About 2 cups.

Crisp Vegetable Dip

1 cup mayonnaise
1 large clove garlic, pressed
½ teaspoon salt

½ teaspoon freshly ground black pepper
2 teaspoons Puerto Rican rum
1 teaspoon chili sauce

Blend all ingredients together until well mixed. Serve with raw celery sticks, carrot strips, cucumber fringes, cauliflower flowerets, cherry tomatoes.
YIELD: About 1 cup.

Tapenade

This is a traditional Provençale hors d'oeuvre which classically calls for much more anchovy and no sardines. We like our version better. Good as a dip for raw vegetables, Tapenade can also be spooned over hard-cooked eggs and served with French bread, or spread on bread and topped with sliced hard-cooked eggs as a sandwich.

1 can tuna (7 ounces), with oil
1 can anchovy fillets (2 ounces), with oil
1 can skinless and boneless sardines (3¾ ounces) with oil
¼ cup capers

2 large cloves garlic, chopped
20 pitted ripe olives
⅓ cup olive oil
¼ teaspoon pepper
⅛ teaspoon dry mustard
1 tablespoon lemon juice
¼ cup cognac

Combine tuna, anchovies, sardines, capers, garlic, and olives in a bowl. Put this mixture in a blender, about one-third at a time, and blend until just smooth. You may have to turn off the blender occasionally to stir the mixture down with a rubber spatula. Gradually add the olive oil, using one-third of the oil in each batch. When mixture is all blended, turn into a bowl. Stir in pepper, dry mustard, lemon juice, and cognac.
YIELD: About 3 cups.

Spreads

Roquefort Spread

½ pound Roquefort cheese
1 3-ounce package cream cheese
¼ cup butter

1 tablespoon grated onion
2 tablespoons cognac
¼ cup chopped toasted almonds

Have cheeses and butter at room temperature. Beat together until smooth and well combined. Add grated onion and cognac. Turn into serving dish and sprinkle with almonds. Chill several hours. Serve with crackers and melba toast.
YIELD: About 2 cups.

Turkey Spread

2 cups ground turkey meat and
  skin, lightly packed
1 medium onion, minced
2 hard-cooked eggs, minced
½ cup ground almonds
Salt and pepper

Dash hot pepper sauce
2 tablespoons cognac
Enough mayonnaise to bind
¼ cup pitted green olives,
  sliced

Combine all ingredients except mayonnaise and olives. Add just enough mayonnaise to form a fairly stiff mixture. Turn into a serving bowl. Garnish with sliced olives and chill.
YIELD: About 3 cups.

Mush-Rum Spread

¼ cup butter
1 pound fresh mushrooms,
  finely chopped
1 large onion, minced
¼ cup chicken broth
¼ cup Jamaica rum
½ clove garlic, crushed

½ teaspoon salt
2 tablespoons flour
2 tablespoons sherry
¼ teaspoon grated nutmeg
Dash of Tabasco
2 hard-cooked eggs, coarsely
  chopped

Melt butter in a large skillet. Sauté mushrooms with minced onion over low heat until delicate brown. Add chicken broth, rum, garlic, salt, and flour to mushrooms. Stir over low heat just until boiling. Add sherry, nutmeg, and Tabasco. Simmer 5 minutes longer. Refrigerate several hours. Just before serving, add the eggs, mixing lightly. Serve with melba toast or sesame crackers.
YIELD: 1½ cups.

Pâtés

Shrimp Pâté

3 tablespoons Pernod
2 tablespoons lemon juice
1 pound cooked shrimp, shelled and deveined
½ teaspoon dry mustard

Dash of Tabasco sauce
¼ teaspoon nutmeg
½ cup butter, softened
Salt and freshly ground black pepper to taste

Combine Pernod, lemon juice, shrimp and seasonings. Put about ¾ cup at a time into container of an electric blender. Buzz blender on and off to get mixture just coarsely chopped. Tamp down with spatula between buzzings. When all of mixture has been blended, fold into the softened butter, add salt and pepper. Transfer to a mold or bowl and chill. Serve with bread fingers or toast.
YIELD: About 3 cups.

Bourbon Pâté

¾ cup corn oil
1 small onion, chopped
1 pound chicken livers
1½ cups chicken broth
2 tablespoons sherry
½ teaspoon paprika
⅛ teaspoon nutmeg

½ teaspoon salt
⅛ teaspoon pepper
1 clove garlic, minced
½ cup bourbon
1 envelope unflavored gelatin
1 cup chopped toasted walnuts

Heat oil in a large frying pan; add onion and chicken livers and cook 10 minutes, stirring occasionally. Add ¾ cup broth, sherry, paprika, nutmeg, salt, pepper and garlic. Cook 5 minutes. Remove from heat and add bourbon. Soften gelatin in remaining ¾ cup broth; cook over boiling water until dissolved. Place half of chicken-liver mixture in electric blender and blend until smooth. Repeat with remaining half. Stir broth-gelatin mix and walnuts into chicken-liver mixture. Turn into 5- or 6-cup mold. Chill until firm.
SERVES: 8.

Walnut Chopped Liver

4 tablespoons salad oil
1 small onion, finely chopped
1 pound chicken livers
1 teaspoon salt
⅛ teaspoon pepper

2 tablespoons Scotch whisky
2 tablespoons mayonnaise
½ cup chopped toasted
  walnuts

Sauté onion in oil very slowly until soft but not brown. Remove onions and most of oil from pan and set aside. Sauté livers in remaining oil until just pink inside. Remove from heat and put through fine blade of food chopper. Add onions, oil, and remaining ingredients and beat with a fork until well blended. Chill.
SERVES: 8.

San Juan Liver Pâté

1 3¼-ounce can liver pâté
3 tablespoons finely chopped
  chives

1 teaspoon chopped parsley
2 tablespoons Gold Label rum

Blend all ingredients well. Chill. Serve on toast squares.
SERVES: 4.

Mushroom Liver Pâté

¼ pound mushrooms, sliced
2 teaspoons butter
½ pound goose liverwurst
2 teaspoons chopped chives
½ teaspoon soy sauce

½ cup sour cream
2 tablespoons cognac
⅛ teaspoon pepper
½ teaspoon Dijon mustard

Sauté mushrooms in butter over low heat. Have liverwurst at room temperature. Mash and blend with mushrooms and remaining ingredients. Turn into serving dish and chill.

YIELD: About 2 cups.

Country Pâté

1 pound boneless pork	1½ teaspoons salt
1 pound boneless veal	¼ teaspoon pepper
½ pound sausage meat	½ teaspoon thyme
1 small onion, finely chopped	2 cloves garlic
3 tablespoons cognac	1 pound fresh pork fat or salt
¾ cup dry white wine	pork

Cut pork and veal in pieces and put through a food grinder twice, using the finest blade. Put into a bowl, add sausage meat and chopped onion, and mix well. Combine cognac, wine, salt, pepper, and thyme, and pour over the meat. Cover the bowl tightly and refrigerate for at least 12 hours.

Preheat oven to 375°F. Remove meat from refrigerator. Put garlic through a press, add to the meat and stir the entire mixture thoroughly. Cut pork fat into very thin slices and use most of them to line bottom and sides of a 2-quart mold, overlapping them slightly. (If using salt pork, first simmer slices in water for 10 minutes to reduce saltiness.) Pack meat into mold and arrange the remaining slices of pork fat on top. Cover tightly with aluminum foil. Set the mold into a shallow pan and pour in boiling water to about halfway up the side of the mold.

Bake for two hours or until the pâté shrinks slightly from the sides of the mold. Remove from oven and pan of water. Loosen the foil and set the mold on a rack to cool to room temperature. Now put a heavy plate or pan on top of the mold, set a weight on it, and refrigerate for at least a day before serving. This will keep about a week in the refrigerator.

SERVES: 12 to 16.

Pâté en Croûte

Filling:

½ pound boneless veal steak, sliced

½ pound ham, sliced ⅛ inch thick

¼ cup brandy

1 pound ground veal

¼ pound sausage meat

2 eggs

¾ teaspoon salt

⅛ teaspoon garlic powder

⅛ teaspoon onion powder

¼ cup heavy cream

Pastry:

2⅓ cups sifted flour

½ teaspoon salt

¾ cup butter

3 hard-cooked egg yolks, mashed

2 eggs

2 tablespoons milk

Filling: Cut veal and ham into strips 1½ inches wide. Place in a shallow dish, pour over the brandy, and marinate for 30 minutes. Mix thoroughly the ground veal, sausage meat, eggs, salt, garlic and onion powders, and cream. Refrigerate until ready to use.

Pastry: Sift flour with salt into a bowl. Add butter, cut into small pieces, and hard-cooked egg yolks. Cut into flour until crumbly. Add the 2 unbeaten eggs, one at a time, mixing until blended. Work dough until smooth and refrigerate until ready to use.

Assembly: Roll out three-quarters of the dough on a lightly floured board until about ⅜ inch thick. Make it about 1 inch larger all around than the bottom and sides of the pan you're using. (The traditional pan is a special oval springform called a "croûte mold." If you don't have one, use a 9- x 5-inch loaf pan.) Butter mold lightly and dust with flour. If you are using the loaf pan, first grease pan, line with foil, butter and flour the foil. Fit pastry into the buttered, floured pan, letting it lap 1 inch over the sides of the pan. Pat about one-quarter of the ground meat mixture into the bottom of the pan; then arrange a layer of veal and ham strips. Repeat layers, ending with ground meat. Pour any leftover marinade over.

Roll out the remaining pastry, lay over the meat-filled pan, and pinch edges together. If desired, cut designs from pastry trimmings and set on top. Make a slit in the top for steam to escape. Roll a piece of aluminum foil into a cone and push into the slit, like a chimney, to keep juice from boiling over. Brush top crust lightly with milk.

Bake in hot oven, preheated to 450°F., for 10 minutes. Reduce heat to moderate 350°F., and bake 1 hour and 20 minutes longer. Let cool and serve at room temperature.

YIELD: 8 servings.

Hot Hors d'Oeuvres

Salisbury Beef Balls

1 pound ground beef chuck
1 tablespoon salad oil
1 can (8 ounces) tomato
 sauce
½ bay leaf, crumbled
Salt and pepper to taste
¼ cup bourbon

Shape beef into small balls. Heat oil, add beef balls, and cook over low heat until browned on all sides. Drain off drippings. Pour tomato sauce over meatballs. Stir in bay leaf, salt, and pepper. Cover and cook over low heat for 10 minutes. Stir in bourbon and continue cooking over low flame for 5 minutes more. Serve on cocktail picks.
SERVES: 8.

Canadian Meat Pie (Tourtière)

Pastry:
½ pound butter
¼ pound cream cheese
2¼ cups flour
½ teaspoon salt
1–2 tablespoons ice water

Filling:
1 pound ground veal
1 pound ground pork
2 slices lean salt pork, diced

1 tablespoon oil
1 tablespoon butter
1 large onion, chopped
1 clove garlic, minced
¼ cup beef stock or bouillon
½ teaspoon marjoram
1 teaspoon salt
¼ teaspoon pepper
⅓ cup chopped parsley
2 tablespoons Canadian
 whisky

Pastry: Blend the butter and cream cheese together and mix in the flour and salt. Add a little water, if necessary, to make the pastry form a ball. Refrigerate while preparing filling.

Filling: Combine veal, pork, and salt pork. Heat the oil and butter and sauté onion and garlic until transparent but not brown. Add the meat mixture and cook for 5 minutes, stirring and mixing. Add the beef stock, marjoram, salt, and pepper. Remove from heat and add the parsley and Canadian whisky. Cool to room temperature.

Preheat oven to 375°F. Divide the pastry to make a top and bottom crust for a 9-inch pie pan. Roll out the bottom crust about ¼ inch thick and place in pan. Add the filling and cover with the top crust. Press the edges of the crusts together and flute them. Make two vents in the top. Bake for 45 minutes. Reduce the heat to 350°F. and bake 35 to 40 minutes longer, or until crust is browned and meat is done. This may be served hot but is generally eaten cold.

SERVES: 10 as an appetizer.

Sausage De-Lights

½ pound pork cocktail
   sausages
¼ cup soy sauce
¼ cup brown sugar

2 tablespoons catsup
¼ cup Gold Label Puerto
   Rican rum, warmed

Brown sausages over medium heat and pour off fat in pan. Add soy sauce, brown sugar, and catsup. Cover pan and cook for about 10 minutes. Ignite rum and pour over sauce in pan. Spoon sauce over sausages until flames die out. Serve on cocktail picks.

SERVES: 4 to 6 as hors d'oeuvres.

Chicken Roll-Ups

1 cup cooked chicken, very
  finely chopped (or turkey)
½ teaspoon salt
¼ teaspoon sugar
⅛ teaspoon pepper
2 tablespoons chopped chives

1 tablespoon soy sauce
1 tablespoon salad oil
1 tablespoon Scotch whisky
15 slices thin-sliced white
  bread (approx.)
Oil for frying

Combine chopped chicken with salt, sugar, pepper, chives, soy sauce, salad oil, and Scotch. Refrigerate for about an hour.

Remove crusts from bread slices. Carefully roll each slice with a rolling pin until very thin. Cut each slice in half. Place about a teaspoon of chicken mixture at the narrow edge of each piece of bread and roll up. Cover with waxed paper and refrigerate for at least a half hour. Heat oil to 350°F. Brown "Roll-Ups" on all sides. Serve immediately.

YIELD: About 30.

EGGS
AND
CHEESE
CHAPTER
5

Glazed French Toast Pie

This unusual French toast—crunchy on the outside and custardy within—is made with a *single* thick slice of bread, *cut horizontally* from a large, round French or Italian loaf. It is served in pie-shaped wedges. It takes a little handling, but it's worth the effort.

Round French or Italian bread,
   about 7 inches in diameter
4 eggs
1 cup milk
1 tablespoon sugar
¼ teaspoon salt
½ teaspoon vanilla

1 tablespoon oil
1 tablespoon butter

Glaze:
2 tablespoons sugar
1 tablespoon bourbon
⅛ teaspoon cinnamon

Using a serrated bread knife, cut the bottom crust off the bread. Now cut another slice, 1 inch thick, parallel to the first. (You can use the bottom crust for bread crumbs and the top for garlic bread or croutons.) Beat eggs, milk, sugar, salt, and vanilla. Place the inch-thick bread slice in a 9-inch-square baking pan and pour the egg mixture over. Let it stand for 20 minutes, turning once, or until the liquid is absorbed. (The preparation to this point can be done the night before. Just cover "pie" and refrigerate.)

Now heat oil and butter in a large skillet. (If you have an electric frypan, heat to 375°F.) Carefully lift the bread slice into the skillet and sauté the first side until golden, about 3 minutes. Turn and add a little more oil and butter if needed.

If you find it difficult to turn the toast, lift it out onto a dinner plate. Cover with a second dinner plate and flip over to get the sautéed side uppermost. Now slide it back into the pan. Cook the second side until brown, 3 to 4 minutes. Meanwhile, combine sugar, bourbon, and cinnamon for the glaze.

Lift toast from skillet onto a heatproof platter. Spoon the glaze evenly over the entire surface. Place under broiler for about 3 minutes or until the topping has glazed. *Watch carefully to see that it doesn't burn.* Cut into wedges and serve as is or with syrup, honey, or preserves.
SERVES: 4.

46

Pain Perdu

3 eggs
¾ cup milk
1 teaspoon sugar
½ teaspoon salt
Dash of nutmeg

1 tablespoon Cointreau
6 thin slices of stale
  French bread
2 tablespoons butter
Confectioners' sugar

Beat the eggs slightly. Stir in the next 5 ingredients. Dip slices of bread, one at a time, into mixture. Heat butter and brown bread slices on both sides. Sprinkle with confectioners' sugar.
SERVES: 3 to 4.

Eggheads

Country cousin to Eggs Benedict. For the late, leisurely breakfast or luncheon.

½ pound cream cheese
3 ounces Gruyère cheese
  (3 triangles), cut up
3 tablespoons milk
3 tablespoons bourbon

4 English muffins, split and
  toasted
4 thin slices ham, lightly grilled
4 poached eggs

Combine cream cheese, Gruyère cheese, and milk in the top of a double boiler. Set over simmering water and cook, stirring often, until melted and blended. Add bourbon and cook 3 minutes longer.

Top each English muffin with a slice of ham and a poached egg. Pour sauce over and serve immediately.
SERVES: 4.

Eggs Foo Yung Gin

Just what you thought it was—an omelet the Chinese way, tanged with gin.

¼ cup chopped onions
¼ cup chopped mushrooms
1 tablespoon salad oil
1 cup canned Chinese
    vegetables, drained
¾ cup diced cooked shrimp,
    chicken or pork
1 tablespoon soy sauce
2 tablespoons gin
1 teaspoon salt

½ teaspoon sugar
4 eggs
Oil for frying

Sauce:
½ cup chicken broth or
    bouillon
1 teaspoon soy sauce
2 teaspoons cornstarch
1 tablespoon cold water

Sauté onions and mushrooms in 1 tablespoon of the oil for about 2 minutes. Add drained Chinese vegetables, shrimp (or chicken or pork), soy sauce, gin, salt, and sugar. Mix well and heat for a minute. Remove from fire and let cool for about 10 minutes.

Meanwhile prepare sauce. Bring chicken broth and soy sauce to a boil. Lower flame. Mix cornstarch with cold water and stir into sauce until it thickens. Hold over very low heat.

Beat eggs thoroughly. Add vegetable-meat mixture. Heat 2 teaspoons of oil in a frying pan. When oil is hot, pour in about a quarter of the egg mixture. Cook until eggs are slightly browned on one side. Turn and brown the other side. Remove to a warm serving dish and set aside. Repeat, adding oil to pan as necessary, until eggs are all cooked. Pour sauce over pancakes and serve immediately.
YIELD: 4 servings.

Chicken Liver Omelet

¼ cup oil
1 onion, finely chopped
2 mushrooms, sliced
8 chicken livers
2 tablespoons Scotch whisky
½ teaspoon salt
⅛ teaspoon pepper

¼ teaspoon marjoram
6 eggs
½ cup sour cream, at room
    temperature
1 tablespoon chopped parsley
¼ to ½ cup hot chicken
    bouillon

Heat oil in a heavy skillet and sauté the onion until tender. Add the mushrooms and cook 3 minutes. Increase the heat, add the chicken livers, and cook quickly until browned on all sides. Add the Scotch and stir to loosen the browned bits in the pan. Add salt, pepper, and marjoram. Keep warm over the lowest possible heat.

In a separate pan, make an omelet with the eggs. Remove the chicken-liver pan from the heat, add the sour cream and chopped parsley. Use half the chicken-liver mixture to fill the omelet. Add enough hot bouillon to the remaining chicken-liver mixture to make a sauce to pour over the omelet.
SERVES: 4.

Savory Stuffed Eggs

12 hard-cooked eggs
2 tablespoons mayonnaise
1 small can boneless and skinless sardines, drained and
  mashed
¼ cup finely chopped chives

Dash Tabasco
½ teaspoon lemon juice
Salt and pepper to taste
Gin
Chopped chives for garnish

Carefully cut each egg in half lengthwise and remove yolk. Mash the yolks and blend with mayonnaise. Add sardines, chives, Tabasco, lemon juice, salt, and pepper. Add enough gin to make a good consistency.

Place a good teaspoon of the mixture in each egg-white half (or pipe through a pastry tube). Top each with additional chopped chives. Chill well.
SERVES: 12.

Cheddar Soufflé on Toast

1 tablespoon butter
2 teaspoons flour
⅓ cup hot milk
1 teaspoon kirsch

⅓ pound sharp cheddar
  cheese, grated
1 egg yolk
1 egg white, stiffly beaten
Thinly sliced white bread

Melt butter in a saucepan; remove pan from heat and stir in flour. Gradually add hot milk and cook sauce over low heat, stirring constantly, until it is thick and smooth. Add kirsch and cheese, and cook, stirring, until cheese is melted. Remove pan from heat, thoroughly mix in the egg yolk, and allow mixture to cool. Fold in stiffly beaten egg white.

Toast bread slices. Mound 2 to 3 tablespoons of cheese mixture on each slice. Place under broiler until cheese puffs up and is lightly browned. Watch carefully to prevent burning. Serve at once.
SERVES: 3 or 4.

Swiss Fondue

½ pound Swiss Gruyère cheese	½ teaspoon salt
1 tablespoon flour	⅛ teaspoon pepper
1 clove garlic, split	Pinch of nutmeg
1 cup dry white wine	3 tablespoons kirsch
	French or Italian bread

Grate cheese and dredge with flour. Rub an earthenware or enameled pan with garlic. Pour in wine; set over low heat until just below boiling. Add cheese gradually, stirring with a fork. Keep stirring until the cheese is melted and starting to bubble. Add salt, pepper, nutmeg, and kirsch, and stir thoroughly. Remove bubbling fondue from heat and set on a hot plate or tray to keep warm.

Have bread cut in bite-size pieces, each with some crust on it. Spear bread cubes on long forks and dip into fondue.
SERVES: 4.

Croquemonsieur

The French version of a ham and cheese sandwich, sautéed in butter.

4 ounces Gruyère cheese	1 tablespoon cognac
¼ cup milk	4 slices boiled ham
1 teaspoon melted butter	8 slices cracked-wheat bread
2 teaspoons soy sauce	Butter for frying
1 teaspoon mustard	

Grate cheese and mix with the milk, butter, soy sauce, mustard, and cognac until it is of spreading consistency. Make 4 sandwiches, using one-fourth of the cheese mixture and a slice of ham for each. Sauté in butter until golden on each side. Serve at once.
SERVES: 4.

SOUPS

CHAPTER
6

Double Consommé, Metaxa

Classically, this recipe would take cognac. The Metaxa provides an interesting change of taste.

1 egg white
2 teaspoons cold water
1 eggshell

2 quarts chicken or beef stock
2 tablespoons Metaxa

Beat egg white lightly with cold water. Add to stock along with broken eggshell. Bring stock to a boil over low heat and boil for two minutes. Strain through several thicknesses of cheesecloth.

Bring the clarified consommé to a boil over high heat until reduced to about half its original quantity. Add Metaxa and simmer over low heat for about 3 minutes.

SERVES: 4.

Applejack Glazed Onion Soup

3 tablespoons butter
2 large Spanish onions, thinly
  sliced
1 small clove garlic, finely
  minced
¼ cup applejack
1 quart beef or chicken broth

Salt and pepper to taste
4 thin slices toasted French
  bread
4 slices Swiss cheese
Grated Parmesan cheese
Paprika

In soup pot, melt butter and add onion and garlic. Sauté slowly, stirring frequently, until onions are a deep yellow. Add applejack and cook for about 5 minutes. Add broth, salt, and pepper, and simmer for 15 to 20 minutes. Pour soup into 4 ovenproof soup bowls. Preheat oven to 400°F. Float a slice of bread on top of each soup portion. Place a slice of cheese on bread. Sprinkle generously with Parmesan cheese and dust with paprika. Place soup bowls in oven. Bake about 20 minutes or until top is well browned.

SERVES: 4.

Bean Soup Flambé

1 large onion, chopped
1 clove garlic, minced
1 tablespoon salad oil
1-pound can pork and beans in
tomato sauce
3 cups water

1 teaspoon salt
¼ teaspoon black pepper
¼ teaspoon oregano
¼ teaspoon dry mustard
3 tablespoons bourbon,
warmed

Sauté onion and garlic in oil until golden. Add beans, water, salt, pepper, oregano, and mustard. Simmer 1 hour. Transfer soup to a tureen or serving bowl. Ignite bourbon in a large ladle and lower flame into soup. When flames die, stir and serve.
SERVES: 6.

Purée Indienne Flambé

1 can condensed green pea
soup
1 can condensed tomato soup
2 soup cans water

1 medium apple, peeled, cored
and finely diced
¼–½ teaspoon curry powder
¼ cup applejack, warmed

Blend soups in saucepan with water until smooth. Add apple and curry powder. Heat, stirring occasionally. Just before serving, pour applejack into a large ladle, hold over soup, and ignite. Lower into soup. When flames die, stir and serve.
SERVES: 4 to 6.

Black Bean Soup with Rum

1 can condensed black bean
soup
1 soup can water

1 ounce Gold Label rum
Lemon slices

Combine soup, water, and rum. Heat slowly until just at the boil. Garnish each serving with a lemon slice.
SERVES: 2 to 3.

Plantation Peanut Soup

2 tablespoons butter
½ cup finely chopped celery
1 medium onion, finely
  chopped
1 tablespoon flour
Pinch of curry powder
4 cups chicken stock

2 tablespoons bourbon
½ cup chunk-style peanut
  butter
1 cup milk
¼ cup chopped salted
  peanuts
Paprika

Melt butter in saucepan over low heat. Add celery and onion. Cook until tender but not browned. Add flour and curry powder, and stir until mixture is smooth. Gradually add chicken stock and bourbon, and bring to a boil. Blend in peanut butter and simmer about 15 minutes. Add milk and heat just to boiling point. Garnish each portion with a rounded spoonful of chopped salted peanuts and a light sprinkle of paprika.
SERVES: 6.

Corn-Oyster Chowder

1 can (7 ounces) frozen
  oysters, thawed
2 tablespoons butter
⅛ teaspoon salt
⅛ teaspoon garlic powder

1 jar strained corn (baby food)
1 cup half-and-half (milk and
  cream)
1 tablespoon bourbon

Put thawed oysters (with their liquid), salt, garlic powder, corn, half-and-half, and 1 tablespoon butter in saucepan. Heat quickly. As the edges of the oysters begin to curl, add bourbon. Stir several times and remove from heat. Top with remaining tablespoon of butter.
SERVES: 2.

Scotch Bisque

2 tablespoons quick-cooking
tapioca
1¼ teaspoons salt
⅛ teaspoon pepper
⅛ teaspoon paprika
1 tablespoon minced onion
2 cups milk

2 cups half-and-half (milk and
cream)
1½ cups chopped cooked
shrimp
2 tablespoons butter
2 tablespoons Scotch whisky

In top part of double boiler mix tapioca, salt, pepper, paprika, onion, milk, and half-and-half. Set over boiling water and cook 15 minutes, stirring frequently. Add shrimp and butter, and stir. Reduce heat and simmer 15 minutes longer to blend flavors. Add whisky and stir. Good hot or cold.
SERVES: 4 to 6.

Snappy Red Snapper Soup

This is a detailed recipe, but it is not complicated if you follow directions. It actually breaks down into 3 quite simple steps. We suggest you read the entire recipe before starting.

Fish Stock:
1 red snapper, about 3 pounds
3 pints water
1 medium onion, stuck with
3 cloves
6 peppercorns
½ bay leaf

1½ teaspoons salt
1 tablespoon chopped parsley
1 medium carrot, cut in thin
strips
⅛ teaspoon thyme

Have fish filleted but keep all trimmings—head, fins, bones, etc. Hold fillets out. Place trimmings in kettle with remaining ingredients. Simmer for about 1 hour to reduce. Remove from heat, strain, and reserve. Should make a generous quart.

Tomato and Brown Sauce:

1½ tablespoons flour
¼ cup shortening

1½ cups beef or chicken
  bouillon
1 cup canned tomato purée

Brown flour in shortening over low heat. Gradually add bouillon and tomato purée, stirring constantly. Cover pan and simmer over low heat for about 2 hours, stirring occasionally. Remove from heat and reserve.

Red Snapper Soup:

¼ cup diced onion
½ cup diced celery
1 green pepper, diced
2 tablespoons butter
1 quart strained fish stock

1 pint tomato and brown
  sauce
¾ cup blended whiskey or
  bourbon
Red snapper fillets, diced

Sauté onions, celery, and green pepper in butter. When vegetables are soft, add stock and bring to a boil. Add tomato and brown sauce and whiskey, and bring to a boil again. Add diced red snapper and cook until fish is tender, about 12 minutes.
SERVES: 12.

Fish Bowl

2 onions, chopped
3 ribs celery, chopped
1 large carrot, peeled and
  sliced
½ cup olive oil
2 cloves garlic, crushed
  through garlic press
2 cups clam juice
2 cups water
1 cup dry white wine
2 tablespoons Pernod or
  Ricard

1 pound halibut fillet, cut in
  bite-sized chunks
½ cup green peas, fresh or
  frozen
6 sprigs parsley, coarsely
  chopped
¾ pound raw shrimp, shelled
  and deveined
½ teaspoon thyme
Salt and pepper to taste

Cook onion, celery and carrot in oil until onion is tender but not brown. Add garlic, clam juice, water, wine, Pernod, halibut, peas, and parsley. Simmer over low heat 15 minutes. Add shrimp, thyme, salt, and pepper. Simmer about 10 minutes longer.
SERVES: 4 to 6.

Bloody Mary Soup

1 medium onion, diced
3 celery ribs, diced
2 tablespoons butter
2 tablespoons tomato purée
1 tablespoon sugar
5 cups tomato juice

1 tablespoon salt
2 teaspoons Worcestershire
sauce
¼ teaspoon pepper
1 tablespoon lemon juice
4 ounces vodka

Sauté onions and celery in butter until light brown. Add tomato purée and sugar. Sauté one minute. Add tomato juice. Simmer 8 minutes. Add remaining ingredients. Strain. Serve either hot or well chilled.
SERVES: 6.

Gazpacho Cocktail

5 tomatoes
2 cloves garlic, cut in quarters
½ cup chopped onion
1 cucumber, peeled and cubed
½ green pepper, seeded and
chopped
¼ cup olive oil

2 tablespoons wine vinegar
1 cup bread cubes
1 teaspoon salt
½ cup tomato juice
½ cup chipped ice
½ cup gin

Peel tomatoes and dice directly into a bowl so that no juice is lost. Put all ingredients except tomato juice, ice, and gin into the bowl. Whirl mixture in blender, 2 cups at a time, for 10 to 15 seconds. Watch blending operation very carefully. A little coarseness is desirable for texture, and the mixture can become too liquid in just an instant. After blending, stir in tomato juice and chipped ice. Chill thoroughly. Before serving, add gin and set out bowls of garnishes: chopped hard-cooked eggs, chopped scallions, chopped cucumber. If you have the equipment, nest individual soup bowls in bed of ice. SERVES: 6.

Picnic Soup

1 can condensed beef bouillon
  or broth
1 12-ounce can vegetable juice
  cocktail

3 ounces gin
Pinch of garlic powder
Ice cubes
6 thin slices lemon

Shake all ingredients with ice until chilled. Strain into Old-Fashioned glasses or bouillon cups. Garnish with slice of lemon. SERVES: 4.

Minted Green Pea Soup I

1 tablespoon butter
2 tablespoons chopped onion
2 tablespoons chopped celery
1 clove garlic, minced
4 cups chicken stock
½ package frozen green peas
2 parsley sprigs

¼ teaspoon basil
⅛ teaspoon thyme
4 cups milk or half-and-half
  (approximately)
1 teaspoon salt
⅛ teaspoon white pepper
2 ounces crème de menthe

Melt butter in a large saucepan and sauté onion, celery, and garlic until they start to turn golden. Add chicken stock, peas, parsley, basil, and thyme. Simmer the soup until the peas are tender. Purée in a blender or push through a fine sieve. Add enough milk to give desired consistency. Stir in salt, pepper, and crème de menthe. Taste and correct seasonings. Add more crème de menthe if desired. Chill thoroughly before serving. SERVES: 8 to 10.

Minted Green Pea Soup II

1 teaspoon butter
1 shallot, minced
½ clove garlic, minced
1 cup chicken broth
Pinch basil
Pinch thyme

1 can condensed green pea
  soup
1½ cups half-and-half (half
  milk and cream)
Salt and pepper to taste
2 tablespoons crème de menthe

Sauté shallot and garlic in butter until soft but not brown. Add chicken broth, basil, and thyme; bring to a boil and simmer 2 minutes. Blend in green pea soup and half-and-half. Add salt and pepper if desired. Strain. Chill for at least 4 hours. Stir in crème de menthe. You can use more or less, depending on how you like it.
SERVES: 4.

Spiced Cherry Soup

1 pound can red sour pitted
  cherries
1½ teaspoons cornstarch
⅔ cup apple juice
1 tablespoon cherry liqueur
2-inch cinnamon stick

¼ teaspoon powdered ginger
1 large, tart apple, peeled and
  cubed
½ cup sugar
1 cup yogurt

Strain cherry liquid into saucepan and reserve cherries. Mix cornstarch with apple juice and add to cherry liquid. Add cherry liqueur, cinnamon stick, ginger, and apple cubes. Bring to boil and cook for 5 minutes, stirring constantly. Remove from heat, add cherries and sugar. Chill. Just before serving, fold in yogurt.
SERVES: 4.

FISH
AND
SHELLFISH
CHAPTER
7

The two well-seasoned seafood sauces following complement shrimp, lobster, crab meat, oyster, or clam cocktails. Handsomely.

Zippy Seafood Cocktail Sauce

½ cup chili sauce
½ cup catsup
½ teaspoon dry mustard
½ teaspoon salt

1 tablespoon horseradish
¼ teaspoon black pepper
1 tablespoon bourbon

Mix first 6 ingredients together well. Stir in bourbon. Chill before serving.
YIELD: About 1 cup.

Seafood Sauce Aromatique

½ cup olive oil
3 shallots, sliced
1 teaspoon Dijon mustard
1 teaspoon soy sauce
1 teaspoon tarragon

½ teaspoon freshly ground
black pepper
¼ cup Pernod
2 tablespoons lemon juice
Few sprigs parsley

Combine all ingredients in the blender and blend 30 seconds. Refrigerate to chill and mellow.
YIELD: About 1 cup.

Here are three versions of ceviche, the classic Latin-American raw-fish appetizer. The lime juice and spirits coagulate the protein, or "cook" the tender bay scallops as they marinate.

64

Ceviche à la Gibson

1 pound bay scallops	3 tablespoons tiny pickled
1 cup water, very cold	onions, with a little of
3 teaspoons salt	their liquid
Juice of 3 fresh limes	⅛ teaspoon white pepper
1½ ounces gin	Paprika
½ ounce dry vermouth	

Cover scallops with salted water. Let stand for an hour. Rinse and dry. Put scallops in small bowl. Cover with lime juice, gin, and vermouth for 3 to 4 hours. Add other ingredients, except paprika. Mix. Serve very cold, in small dishes or martini glasses. Sprinkle top with paprika.

SERVES: 8.

Ceviche Mary

1 pound bay scallops	Several dashes Tabasco
Juice of 2 limes	¼ teaspoon salt (or to taste)
1 ounce vodka	2 teaspoons dried minced
	onions
Sauce:	⅛ teaspoon garlic powder
½ cup catsup	1½–2 ounces gin or vodka
2 teaspoons horseradish	

Rinse and dry scallops. Marinate in lime juice and 1 ounce vodka in refrigerator for 3 to 4 hours. Make up sauce a couple of hours before serving time, and refrigerate.

Sauce: Combine remaining ingredients and mix. Taste and correct seasonings. Sauce should be fairly sharp and just a little saltier than normal, to allow for blandness of scallops.

To serve, drain scallops well. Combine with sauce. Serve very cold, in small dishes or cocktail glasses, as appetizer. Garnish with stuffed olive or lime wedge. To use as hors d'oeuvres with drinks, arrange on large plate, with picks.

SERVES: 8 as appetizer; 16 as hors d'oeuvres.

Daiquiri Ceviche

1 pound bay scallops
Juice of 3 limes
1 ounce white Jamaica rum

½ teaspoon sugar
2 ripe avocados, peeled and diced

Rinse scallops in cold water. Drain and dry. Marinate in lime juice, sugar and rum for 3 to 4 hours. Add avocado dice and mix gently.

To serve, skewer 1 scallop and 1 piece of avocado on a pick and salt lightly. Serve with drinks.

SERVES: 16.

Coquille St. Jacques

¾ pound scallops
½ cup clam juice
¼ cup light rum
¼ cup water
1 sprig parsley
2 tablespoons chopped onion
½ bay leaf
Pinch thyme
½ teaspoon salt
Dash pepper

¼ teaspoon sugar
¼ pound sliced mushrooms
3 tablespoons butter
1 tablespoon lemon juice
2 tablespoons flour
¾ cup light cream
½ cup buttered soft white bread crumbs
2 tablespoons grated Parmesan cheese

If using sea scallops, cut them in quarters. In a saucepan, combine clam juice, rum, water, parsley, onion, bay leaf, thyme, salt, pepper, and sugar. Bring to a boil. Add scallops, lower heat, and simmer until tender, 5 to 7 minutes. Remove scallops from pan, strain broth and reserve.

Sauté mushrooms in 1 tablespoon butter until golden. Add lemon juice and set aside. Melt remaining 2 tablespoons butter in a pan and add flour. Gradually stir in ¾ cup of reserved broth and ¾ cup light cream. Cook until smooth and thickened, stirring constantly. Add scallops and mushrooms. Spoon mixture into individual scallop shells or ramekins, top with crumbs, and sprinkle with cheese. Preheat oven to 400°F. and bake 10 minutes or until crumbs are golden.

SERVES: 2 to 4.

Oysters Rockefeller

1 dozen oysters on the half shell
1 tablespoon minced green
  onion
1 small clove garlic, minced
1 tablespoon chopped parsley
2 tablespoons butter
Salt

Freshly ground pepper
1 tablespoon anchovy paste
2 tablespoons finely chopped
  cooked spinach
2 tablespoons Pernod
⅓ cup bread crumbs

Carefully remove oysters from shells and drain. Wash shells and put an oyster in each. Place shells on shallow baking pans. Mix green onion, garlic, parsley, and 1 tablespoon butter: put a little of this mixture on each oyster. Sprinkle each oyster with a little salt and a grind of pepper. Combine anchovy paste, spinach, and Pernod. Top each oyster with some of this mixture. Sprinkle with bread crumbs and dot with remaining tablespoon of butter.

Bake in oven preheated to 450°F. for about 8 minutes. Serve immediately.

SERVES: 2.

Bourbon Shrimp and Mushrooms

¼ cup butter
½ pound mushrooms, sliced
1 pound shrimp, cooked,
  shelled, and deveined
2 tablespoons lemon juice
1 tablespoon minced parsley

1 clove garlic, finely minced or
  put through garlic press
½ teaspoon salt
⅛ teaspoon pepper
⅛ teaspoon Tabasco
¼ cup bourbon

Melt butter; add mushrooms and cook over medium heat until tender. Add shrimp and other ingredients, and cook just until heated through. Serve with rice.
SERVES: 2 to 3.

Sautéed Shrimp Glasgow

⅓ cup salad oil
2 cloves garlic, finely minced
   or put through garlic press
1 tablespoon onion, finely
   minced
Salt and pepper to taste

¼ teaspoon dried thyme
1 pound raw shrimp, peeled
   and deveined
2 teaspoons lemon juice
2 tablespoons Scotch whisky

Heat oil in deep skillet. Add garlic and onion, and cook over low heat until translucent. Add salt, pepper, and thyme, and cook for 1 minute. Add shrimp, lemon juice, and Scotch. Cook shrimp for 6 minutes or more, depending on size, stirring frequently. Be careful not to overcook. Serve with lots of crusty French or Italian bread to sop up the sauce.
SERVES: 2 to 3.

Orange and Walnut Shrimp

1 pound shrimp, peeled and
   deveined
2 tablespoons sweet butter
1 tablespoon salad oil
1 clove garlic, pressed
¼ teaspoon tarragon
¼ cup dry white wine
¼ cup triple sec

2 tablespoons frozen orange-
   juice concentrate
1 seedless orange, peeled
   and sectioned
Salt
Pepper
¼ cup walnuts, chopped and
   toasted

Halve shrimp lengthwise. Heat butter and oil in a large skillet, and sauté shrimp 2 minutes. Add garlic, tarragon, wine, triple sec, orange-juice concentrate, and orange sections. Sauté 2 minutes

more, stirring frequently. Add salt and pepper to taste. Serve over rice. Sprinkle each portion with walnuts.
SERVES: 2 to 3.

Butterfly Shrimp Hollandaise

2 pounds large shrimp
½ cup butter
½ teaspoon salt
⅛ teaspoon pepper
1½ tablespoons chopped
  shallots (or green onions)

1½ tablespoons chopped
  fresh tarragon (or parsley)
⅓ cup Pernod, warmed
1½ cups Hollandaise sauce

Shell shrimp and split down the back. Melt butter in a large skillet over medium heat, and sauté shrimp until pink—3 to 4 minutes. Add salt, pepper, shallots, and tarragon. Stir, add Pernod, and ignite. Continue stirring until flames die out. Add Hollandaise and remove from heat immediately. Serve at once.
SERVES: 4 to 6.

Shrimp Kabobs

1 pound raw jumbo shrimp
¼ cup olive oil
2 tablespoons bourbon
¼ teaspoon thyme
½ teaspoon salt

⅛ teaspoon pepper
¼ pound prosciutto, sliced
2 tablespoons dry bread
  crumbs (approx.)
2 lemon wedges

Peel and devein shrimp. Combine oil, bourbon, thyme, salt, and pepper, and marinate shrimp in this mixture about an hour. Drain the shrimp and reserve the marinade. Preheat broiler. Wrap each shrimp in a small slice of prosciutto. Thread the shrimp on 2 skewers. Broil, turning frequently, until shrimp are browned and prosciutto fat is melted (about 5 or 6 minutes). Sprinkle with bread crumbs and broil 1 minute longer. Meanwhile, heat reserved marinade. Serve with lemon wedges and marinade.
SERVES: 2.

Lobster à l'Américaine

3 lobsters, about 1 pound each
2 tablespoons butter
2 tablespoons olive oil
½ cup chopped onion
½ cup chopped celery
½ cup chopped carrot
1 clove garlic, minced
1 bay leaf

2 tablespoons minced parsley
½ teaspoon thyme
2 tablespoons cognac, warmed
1 cup dry white wine
1 cup chicken stock or
  bouillon
2 cups peeled, seeded, and
  diced tomatoes

Split the lobsters and remove the dark intestinal vein and the sac in the head. Reserve the tomalley and coral, if any. Remove the claws and crack. (Or have your fishman do all of this just before you plan to use the lobsters.) Cut the tail meat, shell and all, into 1-inch sections. Heat butter and oil in a large skillet. Add onion, celery, carrot, bay leaf, parsley, and thyme. Cook until wilted. Add lobster pieces and cracked claws, and cook, turning frequently, until the shells turn red. Add cognac and flame. Add wine, chicken stock, and tomatoes to the pan and simmer 15 minutes. Remove lobsters from sauce. Extract meat from claws and place in body cavity. Put lobsters in a warm serving dish and keep hot. Cook sauce in pan until slightly reduced and thickened. Stir in tomalley and coral, and taste for seasoning. Strain sauce, heat to boiling, and pour over lobsters. Serve at once.
SERVES: 6.

Lobster aux Aromates

Prepare the vegetable base (*brunoise*) in advance:
1 carrot
1 rib celery
1 small onion
2 leeks, white part only
3 tablespoons butter
½ bay leaf

1 tablespoon chopped parsley
1 teaspoon fresh tarragon (or
  ¼ teaspoon dry)
⅛ teaspoon rosemary
⅛ teaspoon thyme

Finely chop vegetables. Melt butter in a large skillet, add vegetables and herbs and sauté over low heat for about 15 minutes, or until half-cooked.

2½ pounds live lobsters
3 tablespoons salad oil
¼ cup cognac
2 cups heavy cream
1 teaspoon salt
⅛ teaspoon pepper

¼ cup sherry
1 teaspoon cognac
1 teaspoon chopped fresh
   tarragon (or ¼ teaspoon
   dry)

Rinse lobsters. Place in a bowl, shell side up. Plunge point of a heavy French knife through center of lobster's back, between the two large claws. Allow liquid to drain into bowl. Cut off all claws and crack the 2 large ones.

Turn lobster on its back. Split lengthwise. Remove dark intestinal vein running down the center and the small sac in the head. (An accommodating fish dealer will handle the above for you. Remind him to save body liquid.) Remove green tomalley from body cavity and add to lobster liquid. Reserve for sauce.

Heat oil in a large skillet. Add lobster bodies, meat side down, and claws. Turn after 2 minutes. Cook two minutes longer, add cognac, and ignite. When flames have died, add vegetable *brunoise* (above) and turn lobsters. Cook about 3 minutes longer and add cream, salt, pepper, and sherry. Turn lobsters again, cover pan, and cook for 15 minutes.

Remove lobsters and large claws from sauce. Extract claw meat and place in body cavity. Keep warm while finishing sauce.

Stir lobster liquid and tomalley into sauce. Cook for about 5 minutes or until reduced to the consistency of heavy cream. Strain sauce and add a teaspoon of cognac. Taste for seasoning and correct if necessary. Pour sauce over lobster, sprinkle with chopped tarragon. Serve with rice.
SERVES: 2.

Lobster Thermidor

6 cooked lobster tails
2 tablespoons sherry
2 tablespoons brandy

Sauce:
½ cup butter
¼ cup flour
1 teaspoon salt

Pinch nutmeg
Pinch paprika
1½ cups half-and-half (milk
   and cream)
1 egg yolk, lightly beaten
⅓ cup grated Parmesan
   cheese

Remove lobster meat from shells, keeping shells intact. Cut lobster into pieces. In large bowl, mix lobster with sherry and brandy; cover; set aside. Wash and dry lobster shells; set aside.

Sauce: Melt butter in large saucepan; remove from heat. Stir in flour, salt, nutmeg, and paprika. Gradually stir in half-and-half. Bring to boil, stirring constantly; reduce heat, and simmer several minutes. Stir some of hot mixture into egg yolk; pour back into saucepan. Add lobster meat. Cook, stirring, over low heat, until sauce is thickened and lobster is heated through.

Preheat oven to 450°F. Fill shells with lobster mixture, piling high. Sprinkle with grated Parmesan cheese. Place filled shells on a baking sheet. Bake until cheese is melted and tops are golden brown, about 8 to 10 minutes.

SERVES: 6.

Lobster Hermitage

½ pound butter
4 cups cooked, sliced lobster
   meat
Salt and pepper to taste
Juice of 1 large lemon

1 cup heavy cream
⅓ cup cognac, warmed
3 tablespoons anisette, warmed
¼ teaspoon paprika
4 cups cooked rice

Melt butter in a skillet over medium heat. Add lobster meat and shake pan over flame just until mixture is warm. Don't allow butter to burn. Stir in salt, pepper, and lemon juice. Add heavy cream, reduce heat, and cook just to the boiling point, stirring frequently.

Turn into a heatproof serving dish. At the table add cognac and anisette. Ignite and spoon over rice while still aflame. Sprinkle with paprika before serving.
SERVES: 4.

Deviled Crab Flambé

1 pound cooked crab meat,
    fresh or frozen
1 small onion, grated
½ teaspoon dry mustard
⅓ cup mayonnaise
2 tablespoons chopped
    pimento

½ teaspoon salt
⅛ teaspoon pepper
2 tablespoons grated
    Parmesan cheese
¼ cup bourbon, warmed

Pick over crab meat to remove all bits of shell and cartilage. Combine crab meat, onion, mustard, mayonnaise, pimento, salt, and pepper. Mix well and turn into a greased shallow casserole. Sprinkle with cheese. Broil in a preheated oven 3 to 4 inches below flame until lightly browned and heated through—about 5 minutes. When serving, ignite bourbon and pour over casserole.
SERVES: 4.

Creamed Crab Meat and Mushrooms

1 pound cooked crab meat,
    fresh or frozen
¼ cup butter
2 cups sliced mushrooms
¼ cup chopped pimento
1 tomato, peeled and sliced
1 tablespoon minced onion

4 tablespoons flour
2 cups half-and-half (milk
    and cream)
Salt and pepper to taste
¼ cup applejack
1 tablespoon minced chives

Pick over crab meat to remove all bits of shell and cartilage. Melt the butter in a large skillet. Add mushrooms and cook over moderate heat, stirring, five minutes. Add pimento, tomato, and onion. Cook one minute. Blend in flour. Add half-and-half, stirring constantly. Add crab meat, salt, and pepper. Stir in applejack. Heat until bubbling. Sprinkle with chives before serving.
SERVES: 4.

Crab Meat Fancy

1 pound cooked crab meat, fresh or frozen	½ teaspoon salt
½ cup butter	⅛ teaspoon pepper
6 scallions, finely chopped	¼ teaspoon tarragon
1 green pepper, finely chopped	1 tablespoon minced parsley
¼ cup dry sherry	⅓ cup cognac, warmed

Pick over crab meat to remove all bits of shell and cartilage. Sauté scallions and green pepper in butter until soft. Add crab meat and stir gently. Add sherry, salt, pepper, and tarragon. When the crab meat is heated through, add parsley. Ignite cognac and pour over. Serve over toast or rice.
SERVES: 4.

Broiled Marinated Swordfish

Swordfish steak, 1 inch thick (about 1 to 1½ pounds)	¼ teaspoon thyme
2 tablespoons lemon juice	½ teaspoon salt
⅓ cup salad oil	⅛ teaspoon pepper
1 tablespoon bourbon	¼ teaspoon sugar
2 tablespoons chopped parsley	Dash of Tabasco
1 clove garlic, finely minced or pressed	2 tablespoons melted butter

Place swordfish steak in a deep dish. Combine all other ingredients *except butter* and pour over fish. Marinate for at least 1 hour, turning at least once.

Preheat oven to broil temperature. Remove fish from marinade. Broil 2 inches below source of heat, 3 minutes on the first side. Turn, baste with marinade, and broil 5 minutes longer. Pour melted butter over and serve immediately.
SERVES: 3 to 4.

Salmon Broil

Salmon steak, about an inch thick
1½ tablespoons butter, melted
¼ cup bread crumbs
⅛ teaspoon garlic powder
Grind of black pepper
1 tablespoon Scotch whisky

Preheat broiler at highest heat. Wipe salmon steak with damp paper towel and pat dry. Oil broiler pan lightly. Brush a little of the melted butter on each side of the salmon and place in pan. Mix rest of butter, seasonings, and Scotch into crumbs. Pat half of the crumb mixture on the top of the salmon. Place pan under broiler, about 2 inches below the flame. Broil for 3 minutes. Turn salmon carefully with spatula. Pat on remainder of crumb mixture and broil 5 minutes longer. Serve immediately.
SERVES: 2.

Filet of Sole au Whiskey

2 pounds filet of sole
1 teaspoon butter
1 teaspoon chopped shallots
½ teaspoon salt
⅛ teaspoon pepper
½ cup fish stock or clam juice
¼ cup blended whiskey
¼ cup butter
¼ cup sliced sautéed mushrooms

Butter a skillet with 1 teaspoon of butter. Add shallots, salt, and pepper. Lay the filets of sole over the shallots. Pour over fish stock

and whiskey. (Liquid should be enough to cover. If it isn't, add more fish stock.) Simmer over low heat for 15 minutes. Remove fish from pan and keep warm. Cook pan liquid until reduced by half. Add ¼ cup butter, bit by bit, stirring constantly. Pour sauce over fish and add sliced mushrooms.
SERVES: 4.

Variation:

Filet of Sole Tullamore

The same as for Filet of Sole au Whiskey, but substitute 3 tablespoons Irish Mist liqueur for blended whiskey.

Chinese Steamed Fish

1 whole sea bass, about 3 pounds	2 tablespoons soy sauce
3 tablespoons gin	2 tablespoons salad oil
1 teaspoon grated fresh ginger root	2 tablespoons chopped parsley
3 scallions cut in 2-inch pieces	1 clove garlic, crushed
	½ teaspoon salt

Have sea bass scaled and cleaned but left whole. Place the fish on a shallow heatproof dish. Mix remaining ingredients and pour over the fish. Put a rack in a large saucepan and set the dish on it. Carefully pour boiling water into the saucepan to the level of the rack. Cover tightly and steam for about 20 minutes over medium heat. Watch carefully so that fish doesn't overcook.
SERVES: 4.

Striped Bass with Fennel

1 whole cleaned striped bass, about 2 pounds	3 tablespoons melted butter
1 teaspoon salt	1 cup dried fennel stalks
¼ teaspoon pepper	⅓ cup ouzo, warmed
	1 tablespoon lemon juice

Sprinkle fish inside and out with salt and pepper and rub with 2 tablespoons melted butter. Break 2 of the fennel stalks in pieces and put inside cavity of fish.

Broil fish about 8 minutes on each side. Place remaining fennel stalks on a heatproof platter and arrange broiled fish on top. Ignite ouzo and pour over fish. When flames have died out, pour mixture of lemon juice and remaining tablespoon of butter over the fish and serve at once.

SERVES: 2 to 3.

Zarzuela de Mariscos
Spanish Seafood Stew

1 pound halibut, cut in
 1½-inch pieces
3 tablespoons olive oil
1 pound shrimp, shelled and
 deveined
2 tablespoons Spanish brandy,
 warmed
1 medium onion, chopped
1 garlic clove, crushed

1 pimento, diced
2 tomatoes, peeled and diced
¼ cup blanched almonds,
 ground
1 teaspoon salt
½ cup dry white wine
1 pound mussels in shell,
 well scrubbed
1 tablespoon minced parsley

Sauté the halibut in olive oil until golden. Add the shrimp and cook about 2 minutes, or until lightly pink. Add the brandy and set aflame. When flame has gone out, add onion, garlic, pimento, and tomato. Cook until onion is soft. Add the almonds and salt, and cook 2 minutes longer. Add the wine, mussels, and parsley. Cover and simmer until the mussels open. (Discard any that do not open.) Serve in soup plates over toasted French bread.

SERVES: 4 to 6.

BEEF
CHAPTER
8

Les Halles Tartar Steak

½ pound lean top round,
  ground twice
1 tablespoon cognac
1 raw egg yolk
2 tablespoons finely chopped
  onion

2 tablespoons anchovy fillets,
  chopped
1 hard-cooked egg
Salt
Pepper
Worcestershire sauce

Mix meat and cognac together and shape into one large patty. Place on a large, flat dish. Make a depression in the top of the meat and carefully put in the raw egg yolk. Arrange onion, anchovy fillets, hard-cooked egg (separated into sieved yolk and chopped white) in separate piles around the meat. At the table, toss all the ingredients together and add salt, pepper, and Worcestershire sauce to taste. Serve with dark rye bread.
SERVES: 2.

Meatballs Stroganoff

1½ pounds ground lean beef
¼ cup bourbon
1 teaspoon salt
⅛ teaspoon pepper
1 egg, slightly beaten
⅓ cup fine dry bread crumbs
2 tablespoons salad oil
¼ pound mushrooms, sliced

1 medium-sized onion, sliced
1 medium-sized green pepper,
  sliced
½ cup boiling water
1 beef bouillon cube
1 cup sour cream, at room
  temperature

Combine beef, bourbon, salt, pepper, egg, and crumbs; mix well. Shape into 1-inch balls. Heat oil; add meatballs and brown on all sides. Add mushrooms, onion, and green pepper, and cook 5 minutes. Combine boiling water and bouillon cube; stir well. Add to beef mixture in pan.

Cover and cook over low heat for 20 minutes. Remove from heat. Add a little of hot sauce to cream. Then stir cream mixture into pan. If necessary, reheat over low flame. Serve at once over rice or noodles.
SERVES: 4.

Meatballs Kingston

Meatballs:
1 pound ground beef
1 egg, slightly beaten
3 tablespoons dry bread
   crumbs
½ teaspoon salt
¼ teaspoon pepper
3 tablespoons minced onion
2 tablespoons oil
⅓ cup chicken broth
9-ounce can pineapple chunks,
   drained

Sweet-Sour Sauce:
3 tablespoons cornstarch
¼ cup sugar
3 teaspoons soy sauce
3 tablespoons vinegar
2 tablespoons water
¼ cup Jamaica rum
⅓ cup chicken broth
1 medium-sized green pepper,
   cut into strips

Combine beef, egg, bread crumbs, salt, pepper, and onion, and shape into small balls. Heat oil over medium flame and brown the meatballs. Remove meatballs from skillet and drain on paper towels. Leave 1 tablespoon fat in skillet. Add chicken broth and pineapple. Simmer for 5 minutes.

Meanwhile, combine all *sauce* ingredients, except green pepper, and mix until smooth. Add to pineapple and broth in skillet, and cook until thickened, stirring often. Add meatballs and green pepper, and cook 5 to 10 minutes longer. Serve with rice.
SERVES: 4.

Teriyaki Meatballs

2 slices bread
2 tablespoons water
1 pound ground beef
1 egg, lightly beaten
1 tablespoon onion juice
½ teaspoon MSG
½ teaspoon salt
1 tablespoon oil
3 tablespoons soy sauce

½ cup beef stock or bouillon
2 tablespoons gin
1 teaspoon sugar
2 cloves garlic, crushed
1 slice fresh ginger, crushed
   through garlic press
1 tablespoon cornstarch
2 tablespoons cold water

Cut bread in small pieces and pour water over. When bread is thoroughly moistened, squeeze water out and add to ground beef. Add egg, onion juices, ¼ teaspoon MSG, and salt. Mix thoroughly and form into small meatballs. Brown quickly in oil. Drain off any fat in the pan after the meatballs have browned.

Add soy sauce, stock, gin, sugar, garlic, ginger, and ¼ teaspoon MSG. Cover pan and simmer for about 12 minutes. Mix cornstarch and cold water, and add to pan. Stir constantly until sauce boils up and thickens.

SERVES: 4 (8 as an hors d'oeuvre).

Swedish Meatballs

1 pound ground beef	¼ teaspoon pepper
½ pound ground veal	¼ teaspoon nutmeg
½ pound ground pork	¼ cup oil
⅓ cup finely chopped onion	1¼ cups beef stock or
2 tablespoons butter	bouillon
1 cup soft bread crumbs	2 tablespoons flour
1 cup milk	3 tablespoons aquavit
2 eggs, slightly beaten	1 cup sour cream, at room
1½ teaspoons salt	temperature

Mix together beef, veal, and pork. Sauté onions in butter until golden. Soak bread crumbs in milk. Add sautéed onions, eggs, soaked crumbs, salt, pepper, and nutmeg to the meat and mix well. Shape into small balls and sauté in oil until browned. Shake the pan often to brown on all sides. Add 1 cup stock to pan, bring to a boil, cover, and simmer for 15 minutes. This can be done ahead of time.

Just before serving, combine flour with ¼ cup stock and stir into pan. Add aquavit. Cook, stirring constantly, until mixture comes to a boil. Simmer 5 minutes. Add a little of the hot pan juices to the sour cream and then stir the sour-cream mixture back into the pan. Cook over low heat just until heated through.

SERVES: 6 to 8 (16 as an hors d'oeuvre).

Bourbon-Burgers

1 pound ground beef chuck or
   round steak

2 ounces bourbon, chilled

Preheat a heavy frying pan and sprinkle lightly with table salt. Mix bourbon into meat thoroughly, and form into 4 patties. Grill 4 or 5 minutes on each side. Served with spiced peach half.
SERVES: 2.

Special Cheeseburgers

1½ pounds ground beef
½ teaspoon onion salt
½ teaspoon garlic salt
¼ teaspoon pepper

4 tablespoons crumbled blue
   cheese
¼ cup Scotch whisky, warmed

Combine beef, onion salt, garlic salt, and pepper. Mix lightly and shape into 8 patties, about 3 inches in diameter. Sprinkle blue cheese in the centers of 4 patties. Top with remaining 4 patties. Press edges to seal. Broil or panbroil with medium flame, about 5 minutes on each side. Arrange cheeseburgers on warmed flameproof serving dish. Pour whiskey over meat. Ignite and serve.
SERVES: 4.

Steak Lomond

1 sirloin steak, about
   3 pounds
1 teaspoon whole black
   peppercorns, crushed
2 tablespoons vinegar

2 tablespoons olive oil
1 teaspoon sugar
3 tablespoons Scotch whisky,
   warmed

Rub crushed pepper over steak and marinate in oil and vinegar 3 to 4 hours at room temperature. Broil to desired degree of doneness and remove to hot platter. Sprinkle with sugar, pour on whisky, and flame.
SERVES: 4 to 6.

Steak au Poivre

Sirloin steak, about 1½ inches
   thick
2 teaspoons crushed
   peppercorns
2 tablespoons butter

2 tablespoons olive oil
¼ cup dry white wine
¼ cup beef stock
¼ cup cognac

Press crushed peppercorns into both sides of the steak. Heat butter
and oil in a large heavy skillet. Sear steaks over high heat, about
2 minutes each side. Reduce heat to medium and cook about 8 to 10
minutes each side for medium-rare. Transfer the steak to a hot
serving platter.

Add white wine, stock, and cognac to the pan. Stir over medium
fire to deglaze pan. Reduce contents to one-third and pour over
steak.

SERVES: 4.

London Broil, Kentucky Style

1 8-ounce can tomato sauce
2 tablespoons chopped chives
¼ teaspoon salt
⅛ teaspoon pepper
¼ teaspoon celery salt

¼ teaspoon garlic powder
2 tablespoons bourbon
1 medium flank steak
¼ pound mushrooms, sautéed

Combine tomato sauce, chives, salt, pepper, celery salt, garlic powder, and bourbon; mix well. Add steak and mushrooms, and marinate 2 hours, turning meat occasionally. Drain steak and pat dry;
reserve mushroom-bourbon mixture. Broil steak 4 to 5 minutes each
side for medium-rare. While steak is broiling, heat bourbon mixture
just to boiling. Slice steak across grain, on the diagonal, and serve
with bourbon sauce.

SERVES: 4.

Tomato Beef

2 tablespoons salad oil
1 large sweet onion, sliced and
separated into rings
½ pound mushrooms, sliced
1 clove garlic, crushed
¼ cup blended whiskey or
bourbon

Shoulder steak, cut 1 inch
thick, about 2 pounds
Salt
¼ teaspoon pepper
2 or 3 firm tomatoes, cut in
quarters

Heat oil in large skillet. Add onion, mushrooms, and garlic. Cook slowly. Add whiskey and continue cooking until onion is transparent.

Cover the bottom of another large, heavy skillet with salt. Heat over medium-high flame. Pat steak dry with paper towels and lay in skillet. Cook about 3 minutes on each side. It should be well browned. Now slice steak on the diagonal, as for London Broil. The center will be almost raw. Put the steak slices and juices into the skillet with the onions and mushrooms. Add pepper and tomato quarters. Cook about 3 minutes, just until steak slices turn pink and tomato quarters are heated through. Do not overcook.
SERVES: 4 to 6.

Sirloin Scallops in Cognac

1½ pounds boneless sirloin
Flour
3 tablespoons clarified butter[1]
1 tablespoon tomato purée

1 teaspoon salt
1 teaspoon A.1. sauce
¼ cup minced parsley
3 tablespoons cognac

Slice beef into small, flat pieces as for veal scallopini. It helps to get beef semifrozen before cutting. Flour sirloin scallops lightly. Sauté quickly in hot butter, about 30 seconds on each side. Remove meat to a hot serving platter and keep in a warm place. Now work quickly. Add tomato purée, salt, A.1., and parsley to pan. Heat

[1] *Clarified butter:* Melt butter over low heat, making sure it does not brown. Gently pour off the clear, golden liquid, leaving the milky residue in the pan.

through, then add cognac. Swirl in pan until warmed and mixed. Pour pan sauce over the meat. Serve at once with hot cooked rice. SERVES: 4.

Beef and Bourbon

2 pounds round steak, about
  ½ inch thick
1 tablespoon salad oil
1 teaspoon lemon juice
1 clove garlic, crushed
¼ teaspoon oregano
¼ teaspoon basil
⅛ teaspoon pepper
2 tablespoons oil or bacon
  drippings

⅓ cup bourbon
½ teaspoon sugar
1 teaspoon salt
1 can (1 pound) boiled white
  onions, drained
1 tablespoon capers
¼ pound mushrooms, sautéed
1 medium green pepper, cut
  into strips
12 cherry tomatoes

Cut steak into narrow strips. Marinate for 1 hour in mixture of 1 tablespoon oil, lemon juice, garlic, oregano, basil, and pepper. Heat 2 tablespoons oil over medium heat in a large skillet. Add meat strips and cook, stirring, until they start to lose color. Reduce heat and add bourbon, sugar, and salt. Cook 5 minutes. Add remaining ingredients and cook for 5 minutes until everything is heated through. SERVES: 6 to 8.

Steak Mandarin

1 flank steak, about
  1½ pounds
¼ cup salad oil
3 tablespoons soy sauce
2 tablespoons gin
1 clove garlic

1 slice fresh ginger root,
  size of a nickel
1 teaspoon sugar
¾ cup beef stock or bouillon
2 tablespoons cornstarch
¼ cup cold water

If flank steak is partly frozen, it will be easier to slice. Cut the flank steak in half, lengthwise. Using a slanting stroke, cut across the short end into thin slices. Combine soy sauce and gin in a small bowl. Squeeze garlic and ginger root through a garlic press, into the soy sauce. Add sugar. Dissolve cornstarch in the cold water.

Heat oil for 2 minutes in a large skillet over medium-high heat. Add meat slices and stir quickly with a fork until meat starts to lose color, about 2 minutes. Add soy-sauce mixture and stir well. Add stock. When liquid comes to boil, add cornstarch mixture. Stir constantly until it boils again and the sauce is thickened. Serve immediately over hot, cooked rice.
SERVES: 4.

Roast Beef Oriental

3 pounds roast beef, eye round
 or sirloin tip
½ cup soy sauce
2 teaspoons ground ginger
3 large cloves garlic, cut
 in half

1 medium onion, cut in
 thick slices
1 teaspoon sugar
¼ cup bourbon
1 tablespoon salad oil

Place roast beef in large bowl. Mix other ingredients, except oil, and pour over meat. Marinate for 24 hours, turning meat occasionally. Take out of marinade 2 hours before roasting. Pat dry and rub oil over roast. Preheat oven to 300°F. Place meat on rack and roast at 20 minutes to the pound for medium-rare. (Best to use a meat thermometer and cook to desired degree of doneness as indicated on thermometer.)
SERVES: 6 to 8.

Beef à la Mode

4 pounds boneless beef roast
1 tablespoon salt
Freshly ground pepper
2 medium carrots, finely
 chopped
2 ribs celery, chopped
2 medium onions, finely
 chopped
¼ cup chopped parsley
1 teaspoon marjoram

2 cloves garlic, minced
1½ cups dry red wine
3 tablespoons olive oil
¼ cup brandy
3 tablespoons salad oil
1 cracked veal knuckle or
 beef bone
½ cup bouillon
1 tablespoon cornstarch
2 tablespoons sherry

Rub meat with salt and pepper, and place in a large enamel or earthenware bowl. Mix together the carrots, celery, onions, parsley, marjoram, and garlic, and sprinkle around and over the meat. Pour over wine, olive oil, and brandy. Refrigerate for at least 24 hours, turning the meat several times.

Remove the meat from the marinade, drain, and pat dry thoroughly with paper towels. Heat the salad oil in a Dutch oven or deep casserole that can be used both on top of the range and in the oven. Brown the meat well on all sides; pour off excess fat.

Add the wine marinade, including the chopped vegetables, veal knuckle, and bouillon. Bring to a simmer, cover, and place in moderately slow oven, 325°F., for 3 hours, or until meat is tender.

Transfer meat to a platter and keep warm. Remove and discard bones. Skim fat off the liquid in the casserole and then strain into a saucepan, pressing the liquid out of the vegetables. Discard vegetables. You should have about 2 cups of gravy. Bring to a boil and then blend in a paste of cornstarch and sherry. Cook until thickened, stirring constantly.

Slice meat and arrange on a platter. Spoon part of the sauce over the meat and serve the rest in a sauceboat or bowl.
SERVES: 8.

Ragout au Whiskey

2½ pounds lean beef, cut in
   2-inch cubes
¼ cup flour
⅛ teaspoon pepper
2 tablespoons oil
½ cup chopped onion
1 clove garlic, crushed

1 8-ounce can tomato sauce
½ cup water
¼ cup straight rye whiskey
1 teaspoon salt
½ teaspoon sugar
½ teaspoon basil

Dredge beef cubes in mixture of flour and pepper, and brown in oil over medium heat. Do not crowd the pan, and add more oil if needed. Remove beef cubes from pan as they brown. Add onions and garlic to pan and cook until soft. Return meat to pan; add remaining in-

gredients. Cover and simmer over low heat for 1½ to 2 hours, or until meat is tender.
SERVES: 4 to 6.

NOTE: If you want to emphasize the rye-whiskey flavor, add 2 tablespoons more to pan when ragout is done. Return to a boil and cook uncovered for 2 minutes.

Beef Bourguignon

2 dozen small white onions
4 tablespoons oil
3 pounds chuck, cut in
  2-inch cubes
2 tablespoons minced shallots
2 tablespoons minced carrots
2 tablespoons flour
2 cups dry red wine
1 cup beef stock or bouillon

3 tablespoons cognac
½ teaspoon thyme
½ teaspoon marjoram
1 bay leaf
2 teaspoons salt
¼ teaspoon pepper
1 clove garlic, crushed
2 tablespoons butter
½ pound mushrooms, sliced

Heat oil in a large, heavy casserole or Dutch oven. Add onions and cook until they are well browned, stirring often. Remove from pan and set aside.

Add beef cubes, a few at a time, to brown well on all sides. Remove as they brown completely. When all the beef is browned, add shallots and carrots to pan and cook slowly until lightly gold. Sprinkle with flour and stir constantly until flour browns. Be careful to avoid burning. Add wine, stock, and cognac, and stir until smooth. Add thyme, marjoram, bay leaf, salt, pepper, and garlic. Bring to a boil. Add meat. Cover and cook over very low heat for about 3 hours or until meat is tender.

While meat is cooking, heat butter and sauté mushrooms quickly until brown. About a half hour before the meat is done, add browned onions and mushrooms.
SERVES: 6 to 8.

Beef Stew Kill Devil

6 strips bacon, cut in quarters
2½ pounds lean beef, cut in
   2-inch cubes
2 tablespoons flour
¼ teaspoon pepper
1 teaspoon salt
1 cup beef stock or bouillon

⅔ cup Gold Label Puerto
   Rican rum
2 cups sliced carrots
12 small onions
½ teaspoon thyme
5 cloves
1 bay leaf
6 peppercorns, crushed

Fry bacon strips in a large skillet just until crisp. Drain off all but 2 tablespoons fat. Dredge beef cubes in mixture of flour, salt, and pepper. Brown on all sides in fat remaining in skillet. Place quartered bacon strips in a casserole; add browned beef cubes. Preheat oven to 300°F. Pour out any fat remaining in skillet and add stock and ⅓ cup rum. Stir over low heat until all the brown bits are loosened. Pour over meat in casserole. Add other ingredients, including remaining ⅓ cup rum. Cover casserole and place in oven. Bake for 2 hours or until meat is tender.
SERVES: 4 to 6.

Roman Beef Roll

1½-pound round steak slice,
   ½ inch thick
½ pound ground pork
¼ pound prosciutto ham
¼ cup grated Parmesan
   cheese
1 egg, lightly beaten
½ teaspoon salt
⅛ teaspoon pepper
¼ cup chopped parsley

1 tablespoon olive oil
1 tablespoon salad oil
1 medium onion, chopped
1 clove garlic, finely minced
3 tablespoons brandy
½ cup dry red wine
2 tablespoons tomato paste
½ teaspoon oregano
½ teaspoon basil
1 cup beef stock or bouillon

Pound steak with a mallet until it is ¼ inch thick.

Mix together ground pork, ham, cheese, egg, salt, pepper, and parsley. Spread the mixture on the flattened steak; roll up tightly like a jelly roll, and turn in the ends to seal. Tie securely with a string. Heat olive and salad oil in a skillet and brown the roll on all sides. Add onion and garlic, and sauté until soft. Add brandy and wine and simmer until nearly evaporated. Stir in tomato paste, oregano, basil, and stock. Simmer 45 minutes.

To serve, remove the roll from the sauce and cut into 1-inch slices. Pour the sauce over slices and serve with noodles.
SERVES: 4.

Creamed Chipped Beef, Scotch

2 tablespoons minced onion	1 cup milk
2 tablespoons minced celery	3 tablespoons Scotch whisky
¼ pound sliced mushrooms	1 cup sour cream, at room
4 tablespoons butter	temperature
½ pound chipped beef	Cooked rice or hot toast
2 tablespoons flour	Paprika

Sauté onion, celery, and mushrooms in butter until lightly browned. Add beef and cook about 2 minutes more. Sprinkle with flour, stir. Slowly add milk and whisky. Simmer over low heat, stirring constantly, until thick and smooth. Add a little of the sauce to sour cream. Stir mixture back into pan. Keep stirring until hot, but do not allow to boil. Spoon over rice or slices of hot toast. Dust with paprika, for color.
SERVES: 4.

PORK
AND
HAM
CHAPTER
9

Fresh Ham Jamaica

Whole fresh ham, about
  10 pounds
1 teaspoon salt
¼ teaspoon pepper
¼ teaspoon ginger
¼ teaspoon ground cloves
1 clove garlic, crushed

4 bay leaves
1½ cups Jamaica rum
4¾ cups water
⅔ cup lime juice
½ cup brown sugar, firmly
  packed
2 tablespoons flour

Slash skin of ham diagonally to form diamond pattern, each about 2 inches. Combine salt, pepper, ginger, cloves, and garlic. Rub into skin and slashes. Place ham on a rack in a large roasting pan and lay bay leaves on top. Pour ¾ cup rum and ¾ cup water into pan.

Preheat oven to 325°F. Roast ham for about 5 hours or until meat thermometer registers 180°F. After about 2½ hours of roasting, combine ¾ cup rum, lime juice, and brown sugar. Set about a third of this mixture aside. Baste roast twice with the other two-thirds.

Remove meat from oven and keep warm. Skim most of the fat off the pan drippings. Stir in flour and bring to a boil. Add 4 cups of water and reserved basting mixture. Taste for seasoning. Add more salt, pepper, and sugar if necessary. Cook until smooth and thickened, and serve with meat.

SERVES: 10.

Jack Rose Pork

6 pounds pork loin roast
¾ cup applejack
1 teaspoon salt
¼ teaspoon pepper
⅛ teaspoon nutmeg

⅛ teaspoon ground cloves
6 large potatoes
6 large cooking apples
½ cup brown sugar
¼ teaspoon cinnamon

Marinate pork in applejack 3 hours, turning several times. Drain

94

and reserve marinade. Rub pork with mixture of salt, pepper, nutmeg, and cloves.

Preheat oven to 325°F. Place pork on a rack in a roasting pan and roast for 2 hours. Remove from oven and pour off all fat into a flat baking pan. Return pork to oven for another half-hour.

Meanwhile, peel and quarter potatoes and boil in salted water for 5 minutes. Drain and turn in fat so that all sides are coated. Sprinkle with salt and pepper to taste. Roast for 45 minutes along with the pork.

Now peel, core, and thinly slice apples. Remove pork from the oven and pour off excess fat. Place sliced apples all around the roast and sprinkle with mixture of brown sugar and cinnamon. Ignite reserved marinade and pour over apples. Return the roast to the oven until pork has reached an internal temperature of 180°F. on a meat thermometer, about a half-hour longer, and apples are soft and potatoes browned and tender.
SERVES: 6.

Pork with Mandarin Sauce

2 cups roast pork, cut in long, thin strips (julienne)

Sauce:
1 tablespoon cornstarch
½ cup orange juice
¼ cup gin
¼ cup orange liqueur
4 teaspoons soy sauce

1 teaspoon vinegar
2 teaspoons honey
¼ teaspoon Chinese five-flavor spice (or a pinch each ginger, cloves, cinnamon)
¼ teaspoon pepper
½ teaspoon garlic powder

Put cornstarch into a saucepan. Slowly add orange juice and stir until smooth. Add other sauce ingredients. Cook about 5 minutes over medium heat, stirring constantly, until thickened. Add pork strips and cook about 3 minutes more until heated through. Serve over rice.
SERVES: 4.

Julienne of Pork with Water Chestnuts

1½ pounds boneless pork loin
4 tablespoons oil
5-ounce can water chestnuts,
   drained and sliced
2 tablespoons soy sauce
¼ cup beef stock or bouillon

3 tablespoons bourbon
  whiskey
2 teaspoons sugar
½ teaspoon salt
½ pound mushrooms, sliced
1 tablespoon cornstarch
2 tablespoons water

Cut pork in julienne strips and brown in 2 tablespoons oil in a large skillet. Add water chestnuts, soy sauce, stock, whiskey, sugar, and salt. Bring to a simmer and cook for about 10 minutes, or until meat is tender. In another skillet, sauté mushrooms in remaining 2 tablespoons oil. Add to pork mixture and cook 3 minutes longer. Combine cornstarch and cold water to a smooth paste and stir in. Bring to a boil, stirring until thickened. Serve with rice.
SERVES: 4.

Char Siu
Chinese Barbecued Pork

1½ pounds boneless pork loin
⅛ teaspoon Chinese five-
  flavor spice
¼ teaspoon paprika
¼ teaspoon pepper
½ teaspoon salt

1 teaspoon sugar
1 teaspoon honey
2 cloves garlic, crushed
2 tablespoons soy sauce
1 teaspoon vinegar
1 tablespoon full-bodied rum

Cut pork loin, lengthwise, into strips about 1 inch thick. Combine remaining ingredients. Marinate pork strips in this mixture for several hours.

Preheat oven to 350°F. and line a large shallow baking pan with aluminum foil. Lay pork strips in the pan and add marinade. Roast 40 minutes to an hour, turning and basting strips often. The pork is done when it is well browned and crusty. Slice strips crosswise to serve.
SERVES: 8 as an hors d'oeuvre.

Cordial Pork Chops

4 large pork chops
1 teaspoon salt
½ teaspoon dry mustard
⅛ teaspoon pepper

¼ cup orange marmalade
4 tablespoons tomato paste
2 tablespoons minced onion
½ cup orange liqueur

Remove fat from meat. Grease a skillet with some of the trimmed fat and brown the chops on both sides over medium-high heat. Combine salt, mustard, pepper, marmalade, tomato paste, and onion. Spread on both sides of chops. Place chops in an ovenproof casserole, cover, and bake for 1 hour in oven preheated to 300°F. Baste occasionally and turn chops after a half-hour. Ten minutes before chops are done, pour over ¼ cup orange liqueur.

At serving time, place chops on a heated platter. Add remaining liqueur to sauce in casserole. Place over low heat and scrape brown particles from bottom and sides of dish. Stir until gravy is smooth. Pour over chops and serve at once.
SERVES: 2.

Orange-Pineapple Spareribs

2 sides lean spareribs, about
   5 pounds
½ cup orange liqueur
½ cup soy sauce
½ cup honey

1 cup canned crushed pineapple, drained
1 lemon, thinly sliced
2 teaspoons ginger
½ cup vinegar
4 cloves garlic, crushed

Place spareribs in a large dish. Combine other ingredients and pour over spareribs. Marinate ribs for at least a half-hour, turning once. Preheat oven to 325°F. Remove ribs from marinade, put in a shallow baking pan and place in oven. During baking, baste several times with marinade. Turn ribs once. Bake 1 to 1½ hours until meat is tender.
SERVES: 4 to 6.

Apricot-Glazed Baked Ham

1 canned cooked boneless
ham, about 8 pounds
1 can peeled apricot halves,
drained
1 cup brown sugar, firmly
packed

⅓ cup juice drained from
apricots
¼ cup plus 2 tablespoons
apricot brandy
2 tablespoons lemon juice
1 tablespoon dry mustard

Place ham, fat side up, on a rack in a baking pan. Combine brown sugar, apricot juice, ¼ cup apricot brandy, lemon juice, and dry mustard. Spoon over ham. Bake in oven preheated to 325°F. Baste with pan drippings every 20 minutes. Bake for 2½ hours. Remove from oven and arrange apricot halves over top. Sprinkle with 2 tablespoons apricot brandy and bake 10 to 15 minutes longer.
SERVES: 15.

Calvados Glaze for Virginia (Smithfield) Ham

This is a cold-cut or hors d'oeuvre rather than a main-dish ham.

Cooked half Smithfield ham,
6 to 7 pounds
¼ cup Calvados
¼ cup apple juice

¼ cup light corn syrup
¼ cup brown sugar
½ teaspoon ground ginger

Preheat oven to 400°F. Mix ingredients together. Brush on ham. Bake ham 20 to 25 minutes, basting two or three times.
　　Cool to room temperature before slicing. Slice very thin.
SERVES: 20.

Fruitcake-Stuffed Ham

1 ready-to-eat ham (10 to 12
pounds), boned[1]
4 cups fruitcake, crumbled
½ cup chopped walnuts

½ cup bourbon (for the
stuffing)
Granulated sugar
¼ cup warmed bourbon
for flaming

[1] This is a job for your butcher. Ask him to bone the ham, leaving just a piece of the knuckle at the base of the shank.

Preheat oven to 350°F. Combine fruitcake and walnuts. Put 2 tablespoons of bourbon and one-quarter of the cake-nut mixture in blender container. Blend only until everything is finely chopped. Repeat until all the cake, nuts, and bourbon are blended. Stuff ham with this mixture and tie it securely. Wrap the ham in foil and place it on a rack in a roasting pan. Bake about 2 hours (12 minutes per pound).

Remove ham from oven and strip foil. Sprinkle the ham with sugar. Increase oven temperature to 500°F. and put the ham back to glaze, about 5 minutes. Remove strings. Ignite ¼ cup bourbon and spoon over ham. Serve in fairly thin slices, with some filling accompanying each portion.

SERVES: About 16 to 20 depending on size of ham.

NOTE: This makes an exciting buffet item. Serve at room temperature and slice as thin as you can.

Baked Irish Ham Clonmel

Irish ham	2 tablespoons brown sugar,
1 quart cider	firmly packed
½ cup Irish whiskey	2 tablespoons lightly browned
	flour

Cook Irish ham according to package (or butcher's) directions. Remove rind, place ham in a roasting pan, and pour over mixture of cider and ⅓ cup Irish whiskey.

Bake in 375°F. oven, basting frequently, for about 1½ hours or until outside is golden. Mix sugar, flour, and a small amount of cider to a paste and spread evenly over ham. Sprinkle remaining whiskey over and return to oven for 10 to 15 minutes until well browned.

SERVES: 12 to 16 depending on size.

Ham Steak with Rum-Raisin Sauce

1 tablespoon raisins	½ cup pineapple juice
1 tablespoon brown sugar	Ham steak, about 1 pound
1 teaspoon ginger	¼ cup Gold Label rum

Preheat oven to 350°F. Put raisins in a small bowl and pour boiling water over. Let stand several minutes, then drain. Mix brown sugar and ginger to a paste in a little pineapple juice. Spread mixture on both sides of ham, place in a baking pan, and sprinkle with raisins. Combine remaining pineapple juice and rum, and pour around ham in pan. Bake for 30 minutes. Remove ham to a serving dish and pour over pan juices.
SERVES: 2 or 3.

Jambalaya

½ pound shrimp, cooked,
   shelled and deveined
3 tablespoons oil
1 cup chopped onions
2 cloves garlic, crushed
2 cups diced, cooked ham
¼ cup Scotch whisky
½ cup shrimp broth
   (or water)
1 8-ounce can tomato sauce

¾ cup water
2 cups beef bouillon
½ teaspoon basil
¼ teaspoon marjoram
¼ teaspoon thyme
¼ teaspoon paprika
¼ teaspoon pepper
½ teaspoon salt
1 cup raw rice

If shrimp is cooked at home, save cooking liquid.

Heat oil in a large casserole and slowly cook onion and garlic until soft. Add remaining ingredients, *except rice and shrimp,* and bring to a boil. Slowly add rice and return to a boil. Cover casserole, reduce heat, and simmer 20 minutes. Add shrimp, cover pan, and cook 5 minutes longer.
SERVES: 4.

Brandied Ham Loaf

2 cups ground cooked ham
1½ cups soft bread crumbs
2 eggs, slightly beaten
2 tablespoons minced onion
⅛ teaspoon pepper

¾ cup milk
6 tablespoons brandy
2 tablespoons minced parsely
¼ teaspoon dry mustard
2 tablespoons brown sugar

Mix ham, crumbs, eggs, onion, pepper, milk, 4 tablespoons brandy, parsley, and dry mustard. Pack into a greased 9x5 loaf pan.

Preheat oven to 350°F. Bake about 50 minutes. Remove from oven and turn out on a platter. Pat brown sugar over loaf. At serving time, warm two tablespoons brandy and put in a ladle. Set the brandy alight and pour over the ham loaf.

SERVES: 4.

VEAL
LAMB
VARIETY MEATS
CHAPTER
10

Veal

Veal Amandine Flambé

1½ pounds veal scallops
2 tablespoons flour
½ teaspoon salt
¼ teaspoon pepper
¼ teaspoon garlic powder

2 tablespoons grated
  Parmesan cheese
¼ teaspoon basil
2 to 3 tablespoons butter
½ cup blanched almonds
⅓ cup cognac, warmed

Dip veal scallops into flour mixed with salt, pepper, garlic, cheese, and basil. Heat butter and sauté scallops quickly. Add blanched almonds and shake the pan well. At the last moment, ignite cognac and add to pan. Serve with buttered noodles.
SERVES: 4.

Veal Scallops Zurich

1½ pounds veal scallops
6 tablespoons butter
3 tablespoons minced shallots
1 tablespoon lemon juice
3 tablespoons warmed cognac

4 tablespoons flour
½ teaspoon salt
¼ teaspoon white pepper
1 cup chicken stock
1 cup heavy cream

Cut veal into 1-inch strips. Heat butter in a large skillet. Add shallots and cook 2 minutes. Add veal. Cook for 1 minute. Add lemon juice. Measure cognac into a ladle and ignite. Pour over meat in pan. When flame has died, sprinkle flour, salt, and pepper over veal. Add stock and cream. Cook over low heat, stirring constantly, until mixture comes to a boil and thickens. Cook two more minutes. Serve immediately, with noodles.
SERVES: 4.

Scallopini Chinamartini

1½ pounds veal scallops,
   pounded ⅛ inch thin
3 tablespoons flour
¼ teaspoon salt
⅛ teaspoon pepper
¼ teaspoon garlic powder
3 tablespoons oil

¼ pound mushrooms,
   quartered
2 tablespoons onions, minced
2 tablespoons Chinamartini
   liqueur
3 tablespoons blended whiskey
1 tablespoon butter

Dredge veal scallops in mixture of flour, salt, pepper, and garlic powder. Brown quickly in oil over medium-high heat, about 2 minutes each side. Remove from pan and keep warm.

Add mushrooms and onion to pan. Sauté 1 minute. Add Chinamartini and whiskey. Lower heat and cook about 4 minutes more, or until onion is transparent. Return veal scallops to pan and cook about 2 minutes longer on each side. Arrange veal and mushrooms on a platter. Add butter to pan juices and swirl around until melted. Pour over veal and serve immediately with hot rice.
SERVES: 4.

Veal Scallops Framboise

1½ pounds veal scallops
1 tablespoon oil
1 tablespoon butter
1 tablespoon minced shallots
1 clove garlic, minced

2 tablespoons framboise
⅓ cup white wine
¼ pound mushrooms, sautéed
Salt and pepper to taste

Pound veal scallops between sheets of waxed paper, flattening to ⅛-inch thickness. Heat oil and butter and brown scallops on both sides. Remove from pan. Add shallots and garlic and cook over low heat until just soft. Add framboise to pan and ignite. When flames have died, loosen all browned bits still adhering to the pan. Add wine and cook until it has reduced by half. Add mushrooms, veal scallops, and salt and pepper. Cook just until heated through.
SERVES: 4.

Parsleyed Veal Chops

2 pounds veal chops
2 tablespoons oil
½ teaspoon salt
¼ teaspoon pepper

¼ teaspoon garlic powder
2 tablespoons kirsch, warmed
½ cup finely chopped parsley
½ cup cream

Heat the oil in a heavy skillet and brown the chops lightly on both sides. Season with salt, pepper, and garlic powder. Continue cooking them over low heat, turning once or twice, for 20 to 25 minutes. Pour the kirsch over and ignite. When flames have died down, place chops on a heated serving platter and keep hot. Add the chopped parsley to the juices in the skillet and, with a spoon, loosen all the browned bits in the pan. Add 3 tablespoons of pan gravy to the cream, then stir mixture slowly back into pan. Heat through but do not boil. Pour the sauce over the chops and serve immediately. SERVES: 4 to 6.

Veal and Water Chestnuts

2 tablespoons butter
2 tablespoons salad oil
2 pounds boneless veal, cut in
    1-inch cubes
2 cloves garlic, crushed
1 medium onion, finely
    minced
1 teaspoon salt
¼ teaspoon pepper
⅛ teaspoon MSG

1 pound mushrooms,
    quartered
1 cup chicken stock
    or bouillon
⅛ teaspoon nutmeg
1 bay leaf
1 can water chestnuts,
    thinly sliced
¼ cup gin
1 cup sour cream, at room
    temperature

Preheat oven to 350°F. Heat butter and oil in a heavy skillet. Brown the veal cubes lightly on all sides. Add the garlic and onions toward the last to sauté along with the meat. Sprinkle with salt, pepper, and

MSG. Place the lightly browned veal in a casserole with a cover. (Use a casserole that can go in the oven and on top of the stove.)

In the same skillet used for the meat, quickly sauté the mushrooms, stirring to cook evenly. Add the mushrooms to the meat. Deglaze the frying pan with a little of the stock. Add to the casserole and pour in the remaining stock. Add nutmeg, bay leaf, and water chestnuts. Stir and cover and place in the oven. Cook, covered, until the meat is tender, about 1 hour and 15 minutes. Add gin, stir, and cook uncovered for 15 minutes longer. Remove casserole from oven. Spoon out 2 or 3 tablespoons of the pan juices and stir into the sour cream. Now add sour-cream mixture to pan. Place over low heat on top of the stove and stir. Cook just until sauce is heated through. SERVES: 6.

Lamb

Lamb Pericles

6-pound leg of lamb	1 bay leaf
⅔ cup Metaxa	¼ teaspoon thyme
¼ cup olive oil	1 teaspoon salt
1 clove garlic, crushed	¼ teaspoon pepper
¼ cup minced shallots	⅓ cup sherry
⅛ teaspoon cinnamon	1 tablespoon flour

Marinate lamb for about 4 hours in mixture of ⅓ cup Metaxa, olive oil, garlic, shallots, cinnamon, bay leaf, thyme, salt, and pepper. Turn occasionally.

Preheat oven to 350°F. Place lamb in a roasting pan and roast about 3 hours, or until meat shows internal temperature of 170°F. on a meat thermometer. Baste frequently with marinade.

Remove meat to a warm platter. Skim fat from pan juices, add ⅓ cup Metaxa and ⅓ cup sherry to pan. Cook for 5 minutes, stirring to loosen all the browned bits in the pan. Sprinkle with flour and

simmer for 5 minutes longer, stirring constantly. Taste for seasoning, pour into warm sauceboat and serve with meat.
SERVES: 6 to 8.

Roast Lamb Café

5- to 7-pound leg of lamb 2 cloves garlic, crushed
¼ cup coffee liqueur ⅛ teaspoon pepper

Combine coffee liqueur, garlic, and pepper, and brush over meat. Let stand about 2 hours before roasting. Preheat oven to 325°F. Roast 30 to 35 minutes per pound for medium-rare, or until meat thermometer registers 170°F. Do not overcook.
SERVES: 6 to 8.

Lamb with Currant Sauce

5- to 6-pound leg of lamb ⅓ cup orange juice
Salt and pepper 1 tablespoon wine vinegar
¾ cup applejack ½ teaspoon dry mustard
1 cup red-currant jelly ½ teaspoon ginger

Preheat oven to 350°F. Rub lamb with salt and pepper, and place in a roasting pan. Roast for 2½ to 3 hours (about 30 minutes per pound), or until lamb reaches internal temperature of 170°F. on a meat thermometer.

After lamb is in the oven, combine ¼ cup applejack and remaining ingredients in a small saucepan and bring to boil. Use sauce as a baste, every 15 minutes, during last hour of roasting.

Take roast out of oven and skim fat off pan juices. Warm remaining ½ cup of applejack. Pour a little over the meat and set aflame. Continue basting with remainder of applejack until flames die out.

Remove meat to a warm platter. Pour pan juices into a warm sauceboat and pass with meat.
SERVES: 6 to 8.

Lamb Steaks Chausseur

1 tablespoon chopped onion	¼ cup dry white wine
1 tablespoon salad oil	1 tablespoon brandy
½ cup sliced mushrooms	4 lamb steaks, cut from leg
1 cup tomato sauce	1 teaspoon salt
1 beef bouillon cube, crushed	⅛ teaspoon pepper

Sauté onion in oil until soft. Add mushrooms and sauté 3 minutes more. Stir in the tomato sauce and bouillon cube. Add wine and brandy and simmer until sauce has thickened, about 15 minutes.

Sprinkle steaks with salt and pepper. Grease a skillet with some of the fat cut from the lamb. Heat pan and brown steaks on both sides. Add the sauce. Cover and simmer until tender, about 25 minutes.
SERVES: 4.

Sosaties

2 pounds boneless lamb, cut from leg	2 teaspoons sugar
	2 teaspoons honey
Salt and pepper	2 tablespoons chutney
1 large onion, thinly sliced	½ cup water
1 clove garlic, minced	½ cup beef bouillon
2 tablespoons oil	½ cup Scotch whisky
2 teaspoons curry powder (or to taste)	2 teaspoons cornstarch
	2 teaspoons cold water

Cut meat into 1½-inch cubes, place in a china or earthenware bowl, and sprinkle with salt and pepper. Separate onion slices into rings and sauté lightly with garlic in oil. Add curry powder, sugar, honey, chutney, water, bouillon, and Scotch. Bring to a boil. Simmer for 2 or 3 minutes. Cool and pour over meat. Let meat marinate overnight.

When ready to cook, remove meat from marinade, pat dry, and arrange on skewers. Broil for 4 minutes on one side, turn, and broil

3 minutes longer. Heat marinade and stir in cornstarch mixed with cold water. Cook, stirring, until sauce is slightly thickened. Serve meat with rice, with sauce poured over.
SERVES: 4 to 6.

Lamb Shanks Gibson

6 lamb shanks	1 to 2 cloves garlic, minced
½ cup gin	¼ teaspoon thyme
4 tablespoons vermouth	¼ teaspoon basil
4 tablespoons salad oil	1 teaspoon salt
1 medium onion, chopped	¼ teaspoon freshly ground pepper

Marinate lamb shanks 4 hours in the refrigerator in mixture of gin, vermouth, oil, onion, garlic, and seasonings. Turn frequently for even flavoring. Place shanks on a rack in an open roasting pan. Roast in oven preheated to 350°F. for about 1 hour, or until tender, basting frequently with the marinade.

Remove lamb to a heated serving platter and keep warm. Skim excess fat from pan juices. Add marinade to the pan, plus enough water to make 1 cup of liquid. Cook, stirring in the brown bits in the pan, until well blended. Strain sauce into a heated gravy boat.
SERVES: 6.

Variety Meats

Chicken Livers Hoisin

1 pound chicken livers	2 tablespoons Hoisin sauce
¼ cup flour	2 tablespoons bourbon
¼ teaspoon salt	1 clove garlic, crushed
⅛ teaspoon pepper	1 teaspoon soy sauce
¼ teaspoon paprika	½ cup chicken bouillon
3 tablespoons oil	

Dredge chicken livers in flour seasoned with salt, pepper, and paprika. Heat oil in large skillet over medium-high heat. Quickly brown chicken livers, about 1 minute on each side. Lower heat. Add remaining ingredients and bring to a boil. Simmer for about 2 minutes longer.
SERVES: 2 to 3.

Chicken-Liver Spaghetti

¼ cup oil
1 pound chicken livers, cut in half
1 medium-size onion, chopped
2 cans (8 ounces each) tomato sauce

1 teaspoon sugar
1 teaspoon Worcestershire sauce
⅓ cup bourbon
1 teaspoon salt
¼ teaspoon pepper
1 pound thin spaghetti

Heat oil and brown chicken livers quickly on each side. Remove from pan. Reduce heat, put onions in pan, and cook until soft, but not brown. Stir in tomato sauce, sugar, Worcestershire sauce, bourbon, salt, and pepper. Cook uncovered, over low heat, 15 minutes, stirring occasionally. Add chicken livers and cook 5 minutes longer.

Meanwhile, prepare spaghetti according to package directions. Drain and arrange on serving platter. Remove sauce from heat and pour over spaghetti.
SERVES: 4.

Spicy Rumaki

½ pound chicken livers
½ pound bacon (approx.)
1 small can water chestnuts, drained

2 tablespoons ginger-flavored brandy
1 clove garlic, pressed
⅓ cup soy sauce

Separate livers. Halve the bacon slices and cut water chestnuts in three crosswise slices. Combine ginger-flavored brandy, garlic, and soy sauce. Dip livers in this mixture, coating well. Pair each liver piece with a slice of water chestnut, and surround with a bacon slice. Fasten with a toothpick. Bake on a rack in a shallow pan, in oven preheated to 400°F., for about 20 minutes, or just until bacon is crisp.

SERVES: 4 to 6 as an hors d'oeuvre.

Calf's Liver au Whisky

8 slices calf's liver, ¼ inch
   thick
¼ cup Scotch whisky
¼ cup oil
4 medium onions, sliced thin

2 small carrots, sliced
¼ cup flour
1 teaspoon salt
¼ teaspoon pepper

Place liver slices in a shallow platter and pour Scotch over them. Leave for 20 minutes, turning liver once. Sauté sliced onions and carrots in the oil until they are tender, then remove and keep hot.

Drain liver, saving liquid. Pat liver pieces dry and coat both sides in flour mixed with salt and pepper. Sauté for about 3 minutes on each side over moderate heat, then remove liver to a hot platter, to be garnished with the hot vegetables. Meanwhile, add reserved liquid to pan in which the liver cooked, and simmer, stirring over moderate heat until sauce is hot and all the browned bits in the pan are mixed into the sauce. Spoon sauce over the liver.

SERVES: 4.

Veal Kidneys Flambé

2 veal kidneys
¼ cup butter
2 tablespoons Armagnac,
   warmed

¼ teaspoon dry mustard
1 teaspoon lemon juice
Salt and pepper
¼ cup heavy cream

Remove all fat and membranes from kidneys. Slice thin, trimming away the hard core. Heat butter; add kidney slices and sauté very quickly on each side. Cover the pan, lower the heat, and cook a minute or two longer. Add the Armagnac, ignite, and shake the pan. When the flames have gone out, transfer the kidneys with a slotted spoon to a warm plate.

Turn the heat up under the pan and cook the pan juices for 1 minute. Add the mustard and lemon juice. Return the kidneys to the sauce. Salt and pepper to taste, and add the cream. Heat through, but do not boil.

SERVES: 2.

Smoked Tongue in Blackberry-Raisin Sauce

1 smoked tongue, 4 pounds
   approx.
1 medium onion
2 whole cloves
1 leek
2 cloves garlic
2 sprigs parsley
4 peppercorns
2 teaspoons salt

Sauce:
½ cup raisins
1 cup water
¾ cup blackberry jelly
¼ cup blackberry-flavored
   brandy
3 tablespoons lemon juice

Put the tongue in a large pot; cover with cold water. Add the onion stuck with cloves, leek, garlic, parsley, peppercorns, and salt. Bring to a boil and simmer, covered, for 2 to 3 hours, until tongue is tender and the skin slips off easily. Remove the skin and the cartilage and small bones.

Sauce: Simmer raisins in the water for several minutes, or until they are plumped. Drain off the water and stir in jelly, blackberry-flavored brandy, and lemon juice. Heat the sauce slowly, stirring constantly, until the jelly melts and the sauce is well blended. Do not let it boil.

Slice the tongue and heat the slices slowly in the sauce.

SERVES: 6 to 8.

Tripes à la Mode de Caën

2 pounds honeycomb tripe,
   cut in 2-inch squares
2 onions, chopped
2 large carrots, chopped
2 leeks, white part only, split
1 bay leaf
1 rib celery, with top
3 sprigs parsley
2 calf's feet, split

1 teaspoon salt
¼ teaspoon pepper
½ teaspoon thyme
1½ cups dry white wine
1½ cups chicken stock
¼ cup Calvados
¼ pound beef suet, sliced
  ⅛ inch thick

This is a good dish to make the day before you plan to use it. Tripe is parboiled when you buy it, but be sure to wash it thoroughly. Use a heavy 4-quart casserole with a tight cover. Preheat oven to 300°F. Place the onions, carrots, leeks, bay leaf, celery, and parsley in the casserole. Put the tripe squares and calf's feet on top and sprinkle with salt, pepper, and thyme. Add the wine, stock and Calvados. If the liquid doesn't cover the meat, add a little more stock. Place the slices of beef fat on top. Take a double thickness of heavy aluminum foil and put over the top of the casserole. Fold it down against the sides and tie tightly. Put cover on top. Bake for 8 to 10 hours.

Uncover the casserole and skim off as much fat as possible. Put the tripe in another casserole. Remove calf's feet, cut off as much meat as possible, and add to the tripe. Strain the liquid and discard the vegetables. Pour over the tripe and cool to room temperature. Chill until ready to use. Remove the congealed fat from the top. Bring to a boil and serve very hot on heated plates.
SERVES: 4.

POULTRY
CHAPTER
11

Chicken

Baked Chicken Florentine

3½–4-pound roasting chicken
½ pound fresh spinach
2 teaspoons salt
1 tablespoon butter
½ pound mushrooms, finely
  chopped
½ cup chopped parsley
2 cloves garlic, crushed
2 teaspoons basil
⅔ cup dry bread crumbs

¼ teaspoon pepper
1 egg, slightly beaten
⅓ cup grated Parmesan
  cheese
1 tablespoon flour
4 tablespoons oil
½ cup chopped onion
⅓ cup bourbon
⅓ cup dry white wine
½ cup tomato juice

Wash chicken inside and out, and pat dry. Wash and drain spinach. Add ½ teaspoon salt and cook, covered, in only the water that clings to the leaves, just until wilted. Drain and coarsely chop. Set aside. Melt butter in a large skillet. Add mushrooms, parsley, 1 clove garlic, and 1 teaspoon basil. Sauté for about 5 minutes. Add the spinach, bread crumbs, 1 teaspoon salt, ⅛ teaspoon pepper, and cook 5 minutes longer. Set aside to cool. When cooled, add egg and Parmesan cheese.

Fill bird with this mixture and skewer or lace shut. Sprinkle chicken with mixture of flour, ¼ teaspoon salt and ⅛ teaspoon pepper. Heat oil in a casserole and brown chicken on all sides. Remove from casserole. Add onion, 1 teaspoon basil, and 1 clove garlic. Sauté 5 minutes. Add bourbon, wine, tomato juice, and ¼ teaspoon salt. Cook for 5 minutes. Return chicken to casserole and cover.

Place in oven preheated to 325°F. and bake for about 1½ hours or until tender. Baste several times. Remove chicken to a heated

platter. Skim fat off top of gravy and pour into a sauceboat to serve with chicken and stuffing.
SERVES: 6.

Stuffed Squabs Metaxa

6 squabs
3 medium onions
3 carrots
3 ribs celery
½ cup plus 2 tablespoons
butter
½ cup chopped scallions
3 cups toasted bread crumbs
1 clove garlic, crushed
2 tablespoons finely chopped
celery

1 tablespoon chopped parsley
½ cup pine nuts (or chopped
blanched almonds)
1 teaspoon salt
⅛ teaspoon pepper
⅛ teaspoon marjoram
3 tablespoons Metaxa
1 cup chicken stock
Hot cooked rice
½ cup dry white wine

Cut onions, carrots, and celery ribs into thin julienne strips. Sauté in ½ cup butter, stirring often, for about 5 minutes. Transfer to a large roasting pan with a cover.

To make the stuffing, sauté scallions in 2 tablespoons butter. Add crumbs, garlic, chopped celery, parsley, pine nuts, salt, pepper, marjoram, and Metaxa. Fill birds with mixture and close openings with toothpicks or small skewers. Preheat oven to 450°F. Place squabs on top of vegetables and roast for 20 minutes. Reduce oven heat to 300°F. Add chicken broth and cover pan. Roast another 30 minutes, basting frequently.

Remove squabs from roasting pan and scoop out vegetables with a slotted spoon. Arrange birds and vegetables on the hot rice. Add white wine to pan juices. Cook over high heat for about 3 minutes to reduce liquid slightly. Pour into a sauceboat.
SERVES: 6.

Chicken and Kumquats

2 whole 2-pound broilers
6 tablespoons orange liqueur
4 tablespoons brandy
1 teaspoon pepper
3 tablespoons butter

4 teaspoons juice from
preserved kumquats
½ cup drained preserved
kumquats

Brush chickens with mixture of 3 tablespoons orange liqueur and 1 tablespoon brandy, and refrigerate for several hours. Remove and pat dry. Sprinkle chicken inside and out with salt and pepper. Heat butter until it bubbles and brown chickens on all sides.

Mix remaining 3 tablespoons orange liqueur and 3 tablespoons brandy. Place chickens in baking dish and brush with liqueur-brandy mixture. Bake for 50 minutes at 350°F., brushing chickens twice with liqueur-brandy mixture. After 50 minutes, add kumquat juice to remaining liqueur-brandy mixture. Brush chickens with this mixture and continue baking 15 minutes longer. Arrange chickens on a warm platter and garnish with kumquats.
SERVES: 4.

Broiled Rock Cornish Hen

6 Rock Cornish hens, split
down the back
4 tablespoons melted butter
½ teaspoon salt
¼ teaspoon pepper

½ teaspoon marjoram
1 pound mushrooms, sliced
4 tablespoons butter
¼ cup cognac

Open birds flat. Brush with melted butter and sprinkle with salt, pepper, and marjoram. (Any remaining butter will be used for basting.) Preheat broiler to 450°F. Broil the birds skin side down, 3 inches below the flame, for 10 to 12 minutes. Turn and continue to broil for another 10 to 12 minutes, or until the skin is golden and the birds are done. Baste them frequently with melted butter.

Meanwhile sauté mushrooms in 4 tablespoons butter until golden.

Add cognac. Arrange the birds on a heated platter and pour mushroom and cognac sauce over.
SERVES: 6.

Bourbon-Smothered Chicken

3-pound frying chicken,
   quartered
½ teaspoon salt
⅛ teaspoon pepper
½ cup melted butter
1 medium tomato, peeled and
   seeded
4 medium mushrooms
4 sprigs parsley

2 green onions
1 small carrot
1 small rib celery
1 small clove garlic
½ teaspoon salt
⅛ teaspoon pepper
1 tablespoon brown sugar,
   firmly packed
¼ cup bourbon

Preheat oven to 350°F. Sprinkle the chicken with salt and pepper, and place in a shallow baking pan. Brush with melted butter. Bake 45 to 50 minutes, or until tender.

Meanwhile, coarsely chop the tomato, mushrooms, parsley, green onions, carrot, celery, and garlic. Combine with salt, pepper, brown sugar, and bourbon. Place in a blender, about a cup at a time, and blend until smooth. Pour this mixture over the chicken and bake 10 minutes longer.
SERVES: 4.

Chicken Flamed with Bay Leaves

2 whole broilers, 2 pounds
   each
2 teaspoons salt
1 teaspoon pepper
½ cup butter
1¾ cups chicken broth

⅓ cup lemon juice
1 small box whole bay leaves
½ lemon, thinly sliced
½ cup blended whiskey,
   warmed

Season chickens with salt and pepper inside and out. Truss as for roasting. Melt butter in a large casserole or Dutch oven. Brown chickens well on all sides over medium-high heat. Arrange chickens breast side up. Add chicken broth and lemon juice. Cover and simmer for a half-hour or until tender.

Place both chickens on a large heatproof platter. Surround with bay leaves and garnish breasts with lemon slices. Ignite whiskey and pour over chicken and bay leaves. As the whiskey flames, the fragrance of the bay leaves is released.

SERVES: 4.

Chicken Hunter's Style

3-pound chicken, cut up
4 tablespoons olive oil
2 green onions, chopped
1 clove garlic, crushed
½ pound mushrooms, sliced
4 medium tomatoes, peeled,
    seeded, and chopped

1½ teaspoons salt
¼ teaspoon pepper
½ cup dry white wine
¼ cup chicken stock
¼ cup brandy

Heat oil in a large skillet and brown chicken pieces. Place browned chicken pieces in an ovenproof casserole. Preheat oven to 350°F. Put green onions, garlic, mushrooms, and tomatoes in skillet. Cook for 5 minutes. Add salt, pepper, wine, chicken stock, and brandy, and bring just to a boil. Pour contents of skillet over chicken. Cover casserole and bake for 45 to 60 minutes.

SERVES: 4.

Poulet Valle d'Auge

A classic of Normandy where the great Calvados is made.

2 broilers (about 2½ pounds
    each), cut up
¼ cup butter
2 cups diced, peeled tart
    apples
4 shallots, minced
½ cup Calvados

1 cup cream
2 tablespoons lemon juice
1½ teaspoons salt
¼ teaspoon pepper
2 teaspoons cornstarch
1 tablespoon cold water

Heat butter in a heavy skillet and sauté chicken pieces until lightly browned. Remove pieces from the pan and keep warm. Preheat oven to 375°F. Add apples and shallots to skillet, sauté for about 3 minutes, and then transfer to an ovenproof casserole. Place the chicken pieces on top. Pour off fat from the skillet, add Calvados, and swirl it around over high heat for a minute or two, scraping the bottom of the pan to loosen all the browned bits. Pour over the chicken.

Cover the casserole and bake for 30 minutes. Add the cream, lemon juice, salt, and pepper, and bake uncovered for another 30 minutes, or until the chicken pieces are tender. Remove the chicken pieces to a serving platter and keep warm. Combine cornstarch with the water and stir the paste into liquid in the casserole. Cook on top of stove over moderate heat, stirring constantly until sauce thickens. Pour into a heated sauceboat and serve with chicken.
SERVES: 4.

Chicken Flamed with Gin

2 broilers (about 2½ pounds
   each), cut up
1 teaspoon salt
¼ teaspoon dry mustard
6 tablespoons salad oil
1 clove garlic

¼ pound mushrooms, sliced
8 pitted black olives, cut
   in half
¼ cup gin, warmed
1 tablespoon cornstarch
1½ cups chicken stock

Season the chicken pieces with salt and dry mustard. In a heavy skillet, heat oil with the clove of garlic, removing the garlic before it burns. Sauté the chicken pieces, transferring them to a large shallow baking pan as they are browned. Keep warm in a low oven, 200°F.

Add mushrooms and olives to the skillet and sauté lightly. Remove the chicken from the oven and sprinkle with sautéed mushrooms and olives. Ignite gin and pour over the chicken pieces. When the flames die down, return the pan to the oven.

Mix the cornstarch with a little of the chicken broth to a smooth paste. Combine remaining broth with drippings in the frying pan.

Heat slowly, stirring in cornstarch mixture. Stir until smooth and clear. Adjust seasoning.

Remove pan from oven; pour sauce around the chicken and cover the pan with aluminum foil. (Be careful not to burn your fingers.) Raise oven heat to 350°F. Return pan to oven and bake for a half-hour. Uncover, baste with sauce in the pan, and bake 15 minutes longer, or until chicken is tender.

SERVES: 4.

Coq au Vin, au Cognac

4-pound roasting chicken, cut
   in serving-size pieces
¼ cup flour
1½ teaspoons salt
¼ teaspoon pepper
2 tablespoons oil
4 tablespoons butter
3 tablespoons cognac, warmed
12 small white onions, peeled

12 mushroom caps
2 cups red wine (approx.)
1 teaspoon sugar
1 bay leaf
½ teaspoon thyme
1 tablespoon finely chopped
   parsley
1 clove garlic, crushed

Dredge chicken pieces in flour mixed with salt and pepper. Heat butter and oil in a large skillet and brown chicken pieces. Transfer to a Dutch oven or casserole. Pour cognac over chicken pieces and ignite.

Sauté onions and mushroom caps in skillet for about 5 minutes, or until slightly golden. Add to chicken pieces in casserole. Rinse skillet thoroughly with about ½ cup of wine and pour over chicken. Add sugar, bay leaf, thyme, parsley, and garlic to casserole. Add enough wine barely to cover chicken.

Cover casserole and simmer over low heat for about 45 minutes to an hour, or until chicken is tender.

SERVES: 6 to 8.

Chicken Benedictine

2 broilers (2 pounds each),
 cut up
1 teaspoon salt
¼ teaspoon black pepper
⅓ cup olive oil
1 clove garlic, crushed
6 small green onions, chopped

½ cup cooked ham, diced
24 small mushroom caps,
 halved
½ teaspoon oregano
⅓ cup dry white wine
2 tablespoons B&B

Season chicken pieces with salt and pepper. Heat oil in a large, heavy skillet over medium flame. Sauté chicken pieces quickly until golden on all sides. Turn down the heat and add garlic, chopped green onions, ham, mushroom caps, oregano, white wine, and B&B. Stir. Cover the pan and simmer for about 25 minutes, or until the chicken is tender.

Remove the chicken to a hot platter. Turn up the heat under the skillet a little, and let the wine sauce reduce to about half. Then pour this over the chicken and serve.
SERVES: 4.

Pineapple Chicken

2 broilers (about 2 pounds
 each), cut up
¼ cup lime juice
¼ cup flour
1 teaspoon salt
¼ teaspoon pepper
3 tablespoons olive oil
3 tablespoons butter

1 medium onion, finely
 chopped
1 cup drained crushed
 pineapple
2 tomatoes, peeled, seeded
 and chopped
3 tablespoons currants
¼ cup Gold Label rum

Rub the chicken pieces with lime juice and sprinkle them lightly with flour seasoned with salt and pepper. In a flameproof casserole, brown the chicken on all sides in olive oil and butter. Add onion and cook for 5 minutes, stirring occasionally. Add pineapple, to-matoes, and currants. Stir well, cover, and cook the chicken over low heat for about 1 hour, or until tender. Stir in rum and cook 5 minutes longer, uncovered. Serve the chicken from the casserole. SERVES: 4.

Scotched Chicken Breast Amandine

2 chicken breasts, split and
  left on the bone
2 tablespoons butter
2 tablespoons salad oil
½ cup slivered almonds

½ teaspoon salt
1 tablespoon finely minced
  onion
3 tablespoons Scotch whisky,
  warmed

Place butter and oil in a heavy skillet over low heat. Add almonds and cook for 5 minutes. Remove almonds from pan. Put onions in pan and sauté for 3 minutes. Add chicken and sauté for about 40 minutes, turning occasionally. Pour Scotch over and ignite. When flames have died out, remove chicken from pan. Sprinkle each portion with sautéed almonds. SERVES: 2.

Baked Chicken

4 whole chicken breasts,
  left on bone
4 tablespoons Scotch whisky
½ cup fine dry bread crumbs
½ teaspoon salt

⅛ teaspoon MSG
½ teaspoon paprika
⅛ teaspoon pepper
¼ cup sour cream

Split chicken breasts in half and remove skin. Pour 2 tablespoons Scotch into a shallow pan. Place chicken breasts, flesh side down, in this pan. Spoon Scotch over backs. Marinate 1 hour, basting occasionally.

Preheat oven to 350°F. Combine bread crumbs with salt, MSG,

paprika, and pepper. Add remaining 2 tablespoons of Scotch to sour cream.

Pat chicken pieces dry with paper towels. Spread sour cream over each piece of chicken, front and back. Dip chicken pieces in seasoned bread crumbs. Shake off excess crumbs. Place on an oiled shallow pan and bake for 1¼ hours.
SERVES: 4.

Chinese Foil-Wrapped Chicken

1 large raw chicken breast
1 tablespoon soy sauce
1 tablespoon bourbon
1 tablespoon Worcestershire
   sauce
1 teaspoon sugar
1 clove garlic, crushed

3 thin slices fresh ginger root
2 tablespoons sesame oil or
   salad oil
3 scallions, sliced
Lightweight aluminum foil,
   cut in 6-inch squares
Oil for deep-frying

Have chicken breast slightly frozen. Remove skin and bones. Cut chicken into slices, about 1 inch x 1 inch x ½ inch. Combine soy sauce, bourbon, Worcestershire, sugar, garlic, and ginger root. Marinate chicken slices in this mixture 15 to 20 minutes. Put a drop of oil on each square of foil. Place a slice of chicken and a piece of scallion in the center of each square. Fold each square of foil as described below. Heat oil to 375°F. and fry packages, a few at a time, for 5 minutes, turning occasionally. Drain and serve.
SERVES: 4 as an hors d'oeuvre.

Folding the foil:
1. Place square of foil 6 inches x 6 inches on table with one of the corners pointing toward you.
2. Take bottom corner and fold toward top. Distance from fold to corner should be about 3½ inches.
3. Fold each side corner toward the center to make an envelope about 3 inches across the bottom.
4. Fold bottom of envelope over on itself.
5. Tuck in flap.

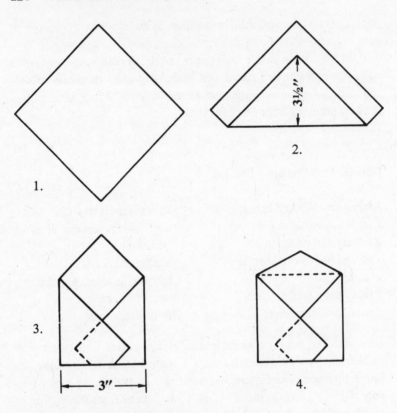

Chicken Croquettes Pojarski

4 whole chicken breasts
2 cups soft bread crumbs
½ cup milk
1 teaspoon salt
1½ tablespoons gin

¼ pound butter
1 egg yolk
¼ cup flour
¼ teaspoon pepper

Skin and bone chicken breasts and discard any gristle. Grind the chicken meat twice, using a fine blade. Soak the bread in the milk, then squeeze it dry. Combine the chicken meat, crumbs, ½ teaspoon salt, gin, and 2 tablespoons butter. Mix thoroughly. Stir in egg yolk and combine well.

Spread a large piece of waxed paper on your working surface and dampen. Turn the chicken mixture out on the waxed paper and form into 12 small, flat cakes. Spread flour, mixed with pepper and ½ teaspoon salt, on another length of waxed paper. Dip each croquette into the flour on both sides. Heat the remaining butter in a large skillet and sauté croquettes until golden brown on each side. This takes careful handling or croquettes can fall apart.
SERVES: 4 to 6.

Chicken à la King, Curaçao

2 tablespoons butter
½ pound mushrooms, sliced
1 small onion, chopped
4 tablespoons flour
1½ cups milk
½ teaspoon salt

⅛ teaspoon pepper
⅛ teaspoon garlic powder
1 tablespoon chopped parsley
1 tablespoon chopped pimento
2 cups diced, cooked chicken
½ cup curaçao

Sauté mushrooms and onion in butter for 10 minutes. Remove from fire. Blend in flour. Return to fire. Add milk slowly, stirring constantly, until thickened. Add salt, pepper, garlic powder, parsley, pimento, and chicken. Cook slowly, covered, for 10 minutes. Remove cover. Stir in curaçao and cook 5 minutes longer. Serve on hot toast points.
SERVES: 4.

Duck and Goose

Duckling Bigarade

4½-pound dressed duckling
Salt and pepper
2 seedless oranges

½ cup brandy
½ cup orange juice

Preheat oven to 325°F. Wash duck inside and outside with cold water and dry thoroughly. Rub with salt and pepper. Using a vegetable peeler, remove just orange part of the peel from the oranges. Cut peel in very thin strips, cover with water. Bring to a boil and boil for three minutes. Drain and reserve for sauce. Cut one orange in quarters and put in cavity of duck. Finish peeling second orange, section, and reserve.

Place the duck on a rack in a shallow roasting pan. Roast for 30 minutes and drain the fat from the pan. Baste with mixture of brandy and orange juice every 20 minutes. Roast about 2½ hours. Remove from pan. Take orange pieces out of the cavity and discard. Keep duck warm.

Skim fat from pan juices. Bring to a boil. Add reserved orange peel and sectioned orange. Taste for seasoning. Carve duck and arrange pieces on a warmed platter. Pour sauce over.

SERVES: 4.

Brandied Duckling with Bing Cherries

4½-pound dressed duckling	1 can (1-pound size)
Salt and pepper	Bing cherries
1 clove garlic, crushed	2 tablespoons kirsch
½ cup brandy	2 tablespoons lemon juice
½ cup cranberry juice	

Preheat oven to 325°F. Wash duck inside and outside with cold water and dry thoroughly. Rub with salt, pepper, and garlic. Place the duck on a rack in a shallow roasting pan. Roast for 30 minutes and drain the fat from the pan. Baste with mixture of brandy and cranberry juice every 20 minutes. Roast about 2½ hours. Remove duckling from pan and keep warm. Drain juice from can of cherries, reserving ½ cup. Skim fat from pan juices. Add reserved cherry juice, kirsch, lemon juice, and salt and pepper to taste. Bring to a boil. Add cherries. Simmer 5 minutes. Carve duckling. Pour a little sauce over and serve the rest in a sauceboat.

SERVES: 4.

Roast Duck Isabella

5-pound dressed duck
Salt and pepper
¾ cup Gold Label rum
¾ cup water
2 tablespoons butter
2 tablespoons olive oil
1 medium onion, finely
   chopped

1 clove garlic, minced
½ pound mushrooms, sliced
1 tablespoon Spanish paprika
2 tablespoons flour
½ cup chicken broth
½ cup white wine
2 tomatoes, peeled, seeded
   and chopped

Preheat oven to 325°F. Wash duck inside and outside with cold water and dry thoroughly. Rub with salt and pepper. Place the duck on a rack in a shallow roasting pan. Roast for 30 minutes and drain the fat from the pan. Combine ½ cup rum and ½ cup water and baste duck with this mixture every 20 minutes. Roast about 2½ hours, until browned and tender. Remove from oven and keep warm.

When duck has cooked about 1 hour, start to make the sauce. Heat 1 tablespoon butter and 1 tablespoon olive oil in a large skillet. Add onions and garlic, and sauté over low heat until golden. Add remaining butter and oil and sliced mushrooms. Cook for 5 minutes. Blend in paprika and flour. Add broth and wine, stirring until mixture comes to a boil. Simmer for about 20 minutes. Taste for seasoning and add salt and pepper as needed. Skim fat from pan in which duck was roasted. Add ¼ cup rum with ¼ cup water to pan and bring to a boil to loosen all the browned bits in the pan. Add this to the sauce. Carve duck and arrange pieces on a warmed platter. Pour a little sauce over and serve remainder in a sauceboat.
SERVES: 4.

Broiled Honey-Glazed Duckling

2 4-pound ducklings,
   quartered
⅔ cup honey
½ cup Cointreau

1 teaspoon dry mustard
¼ teaspoon garlic powder
½ teaspoon salt

Trim the duck pieces of any surplus skin or fat. Preheat broiler to 350°F. Combine honey, Cointreau, dry mustard, garlic powder, and salt. Brush each piece with this mixture.

Place the pieces, skin side down, on the broiler rack. Set the rack about 4 inches below the heat. Broil for 20 minutes and then raise heat to 400°F. Baste with honey-Cointreau mixture. Continue broiling for 20 minutes. Turn duck pieces over so that they are skin side up. Baste with honey-Cointreau mixture and broil 15 minutes longer. Turn heat to 450°F. and broil 5 minutes longer.
SERVES: 6.

Duck with Green Olives

4-pound duckling, quartered
½ teaspoon salt
3 tablespoons salad oil
3 tablespoons gin
1 cup chicken broth
1 cup dry white wine

2 teaspoons tomato paste
1 teaspoon butter
1 teaspoon flour
12 pitted green olives, rinsed
½ teaspoon salt
¼ teaspoon pepper

Trim the duck pieces of any surplus skin or fat. Sprinkle with salt. Heat oil in a large skillet. Brown duck pieces on all sides. Add 2 tablespoons gin, set afire, and shake pan until flames go out. Cover skillet and reduce heat. Cook, turning pieces occasionally, until tender, about 1 hour.

When duck is tender, remove from pan and keep warm. Drain off fat in pan. Add chicken broth, wine, tomato paste, and 1 table-spoon of gin. Bring to a boil and simmer for 10 minutes. Knead butter and flour together and add to gravy a little at a time. (Will make thin sauce. If you want the sauce thicker, increase the flour and butter in equal proportions.) Cook, stirring, until smooth and thickened. Add olives and duck pieces, and simmer for 5 minutes.
SERVES: 3 to 4.

Vermont Duck Casserole

4 large cooking apples
2 tablespoons applejack
1 teaspoon grated orange rind
½ cup white wine
½ pound mushrooms
1 tablespoon grated onion
½ teaspoon salt

¼ teaspoon pepper
½ teaspoon marjoram
2 tablespoons butter
2 cups cooked duck meat, sliced
½ cup bread crumbs
1 teaspoon butter

Peel apples and slice into a bowl. Combine applejack, orange rind, and wine, and pour over apples. Marinate for two hours. Wipe the mushrooms with a damp cloth and slice.

Drain the apples and reserve the marinade. Arrange them in the bottom of an ovenproof casserole with a tight cover. Cover with the sliced mushrooms. Sprinkle with grated onion, salt, pepper, and marjoram. Dot with 2 tablespoons butter. Place slices of duck meat on top and pour over apple marinade. Cover casserole and bake in an oven preheated to 350°F. After 35 minutes, check to see if apples are soft. (If they still seem a little firm, bake 5 minutes longer.) Remove cover of casserole and sprinkle with bread crumbs mixed with 1 teaspoon butter. Brown under the broiler.
SERVES: 6.

Roast Goose with Gin Sauce

1 goose, good size
1 teaspoon pepper
2 large onions
20 juniper berries (approx.)

2 tablespoons cornstarch
2 cups chicken broth
½ cup gin
½ cup currant jelly

Sprinkle goose with salt and pepper inside and outside. Peel onions and remove center bulb. Stuff each onion with 10 juniper berries and put onions inside cavity of goose. Preheat oven to 350°F.

Prepare goose for oven, then place on a rack breast side down. Cover bottom of roasting pan with cold water; make sure it does not reach up to the rack. For the first 2½ hours of roasting, add water to the pan as it evaporates. Roast bird uncovered for about 2 hours; then turn and roast breast side up for another 2 hours. Remove goose from oven and take onions out of the body cavity. Place bird on another roasting rack and pan, and return to the oven for 30 minutes to crisp the skin.

Pour off drippings from first pan and skim most of fat. Return drippings to pan. Blend cornstarch with a little of broth and add to pan. Gradually add remaining broth, stirring to loosen all the browned bits clinging to pan. Add gin and currant jelly. Simmer for about 15 minutes, stirring often. Taste for seasoning. Serve in a sauceboat with the goose.

SERVES: 6.

Turkey

Turkey with Walnut-Bourbon Dressing

1½ cups chopped onion	⅛ teaspoon pepper
2 tablespoons butter	1 cup bourbon
½ cup chopped walnuts	1 egg, beaten
5 cups soft bread crumbs	½ teaspoon poultry seasoning
½ teaspoon salt	1 12-pound turkey

Sauté onions in butter until soft but not browned. Combine onions, walnuts, bread crumbs, salt, pepper, ¾ cup bourbon, egg, and poultry seasoning. Mix well. Fill turkey cavity with mixture. Secure openings. Place on rack in shallow roasting pan. Preheat oven to 325°F. Combine melted butter with remaining ¼ cup bourbon and use as baste. Roast turkey about 4½ hours, or until meat thermometer registers 190°F. Brush turkey with butter-bourbon mixture often during roasting period.

SERVES: 8.

Brandied Chestnut Stuffing

2 pounds chestnuts
4 cups chicken broth
1 onion, chopped
1 clove garlic, minced
2 ribs celery, chopped
2 tablespoons butter
½ pound ground veal

1 tablespoon chopped parsley
½ teaspoon thyme
½ teaspoon marjoram
1½ teaspoons salt
¼ teaspoon pepper
2 cups soft bread crumbs
½ cup brandy

With a sharp knife, slit the shells of chestnuts on the rounded side. Put them in a pan with water to cover and bring water to a boil. Remove the pan from the stove and, without draining the water, take the chestnuts from the pan, one at a time; peel off shells and inner skins while the nuts are still hot. Cook the chestnuts in chicken broth for about ½ hour, or until tender. Chop chestnuts. Reserve broth for basting turkey.

Sauté onions, garlic, and celery in butter until soft but not browned. Add veal, parsley, thyme, marjoram, salt, and pepper. Sauté gently over moderate heat for 5 minutes, stirring constantly. Add bread crumbs, and toss to mix in thoroughly. Add the chopped chestnuts and brandy, and mix well. If too dry, add some of reserved chicken broth.

YIELD: Enough for a small to medium-sized turkey.

Apricot-Sausage Turkey Stuffing

1 cup cooked dried apricots
1 pound sausage meat
1 medium onion, finely
    chopped
1 clove garlic, minced
2 tablespoons salad oil

8 cups soft bread crumbs
¼ cup apricot-flavored
    brandy
1 teaspoon salt
¼ teaspoon pepper
½ teaspoon marjoram

Drain apricots, reserving liquid in which they were cooked. Cut cooked apricots into slivers.

Sauté sausage meat until most of the fat has been released. Drain off fat. Sauté onion and garlic in oil until soft but not browned. Combine with apricot slivers, sausage meat, bread crumbs, salt, apricot-flavored brandy, pepper, and marjoram. If too dry, add some of the reserved liquid in which the apricots were cooked. Toss until well mixed.

YIELD: Enough for a 10-pound turkey. Double recipe for stuffing a big tom turkey.

NOTE: For an unusual baste, use a mixture of melted butter and apricot-flavored brandy, brushed on periodically during roasting.

GAME
CHAPTER
12

Game recipes very often include spirits at some point in the preparation. They are used in marinades, as part of the cooking liquid, for flaming, in stuffings, sauces or garnishes. It's been apparent for a long time to hunters and other devotees of game that spirits modify or complement the forthright flavors of wild meat.

Well-Sauced Venison

2 pounds venison, ground
2 cloves garlic, finely chopped
1 tablespoon minced onion
2 teaspoons salt
½ teaspoon pepper

1 tablespoon butter
1 tablespoon oil
¼ cup bourbon, warmed
¼ cup red wine

Mix venison with garlic, onion, salt, and pepper. Form into patties. Heat butter and oil in a large skillet. Sauté patties about 4 to 5 minutes on each side, or until well browned on outside but still moist inside. Pour bourbon over and set aflame. When the flames have died, place venison patties on a warmed platter. Add wine to pan to deglaze; stir to pick up bits. Pour pan sauce over venison burgers and serve immediately.
SERVES: 4.

Grilled Venison au Cognac

2 venison steaks, cut ¼ inch
   thick
3 tablespoons butter
3 tablespoons cognac

¼ cup heavy cream
¼ cup veal or chicken stock
Salt and pepper to taste

Brown steaks in butter over high heat, about 2 to 3 minutes each side. Pour off butter, add cognac to hot pan, and ignite. Shake the pan until flames die. Remove steaks from pan, but keep hot.

136

Reduce heat under pan. Add the cream and cook about 3 minutes, stirring often. Add veal stock, salt and pepper, and cook 2 or 3 minutes longer, until thickened. Pour sauce over steak and serve at once.
SERVES: 2.

Rabbit Daniel Boone

2 fryer rabbits (each about
  2½ pounds), cut in
  serving pieces
1½ teaspoons salt
¼ cup flour
½ cup butter
2 tablespoons warm bourbon
½ cup minced green onion
¼ cup minced parsley

1 pound mushrooms, sliced
2 tablespoons Dijon-style
  mustard
2 cups half-and-half (milk
  and cream)
2 tablespoons lemon juice
3 egg yolks, slightly beaten
1 teaspoon salt

Sprinkle rabbit pieces with salt, then dust with flour, shaking off excess. Melt 5 to 6 tablespoons of butter in a large skillet, and sauté rabbit. Transfer pieces to a 4-quart casserole as they become browned. Add the warm bourbon to the last rabbit piece in the frying pan and set afire. Add this piece, along with the pan juices, to the casserole and keep warm. Preheat oven to 375°F.

Meanwhile, cook the onion, parsley, and mushrooms in remaining butter (adding a little more if needed) until onion is soft but not browned. Blend in the mustard, half-and-half, and lemon juice, and bring to a boil. Pour over the rabbit in the casserole. Cover and bake about 45 to 55 minutes, or until rabbit is tender enough to pierce easily.

Drain liquid from casserole into the skillet and boil 1 minute. Blend some of the hot liquid with egg yolks, then return mixture to pan. Cook over low heat, stirring constantly, until sauce is thickened; do not boil. Add salt. Pour sauce over rabbit.
SERVES: 6 to 8.

Marinated Lapin

1 rabbit, cut in serving pieces	Bay leaf
2 cups red wine	¼ teaspoon thyme
½ cup salad oil	1 sprig parsley
5 tablespoons cognac	1 teaspoon peppercorns
1 carrot, sliced	1 teaspoon salt
1 clove garlic, minced	3 tablespoons flour
2 medium onions, chopped	3 tablespoons seedless raisins
3 cloves	

Place rabbit pieces in a large glass or enameled bowl. Pour over a marinade made of red wine, ¼ cup salad oil, ¼ cup (4 tablespoons) cognac, carrot, garlic, onions, cloves, bay leaf, thyme, parsley, peppercorns, and salt. Let stand 24 hours, turning pieces occasionally.

Remove the rabbit from the marinade and dry each piece. Strain the marinade into a saucepan and heat. Put remaining ¼ cup of oil in a heavy casserole or Dutch oven and heat. Brown rabbit pieces, a few at a time, on all sides. When all of them have been sautéed, dust with flour and add the hot marinade. Cover tightly and simmer for about 1¼ hours.

Soak the raisins for 1 hour in the remaining tablespoon of cognac with just enough warm water added to cover. Add raisins to pan and cook 1 minute before serving.

SERVES: 4.

Scotch Pheasant

1 pheasant, cleaned and quartered	¼ cup hot water
4 tablespoons butter	½ teaspoon salt
½ cup Scotch whisky	¼ teaspoon pepper
¾ cup chicken broth	1 cup sour cream, at room temperature
1 tablespoon cornstarch	

Sauté pheasant quarters in butter over medium heat. Turn frequently until a rich, golden brown on both sides. Pour Scotch whisky over and cook 5 minutes or until whisky has evaporated. Add broth, cover pan, and lower heat. Simmer until tender.

Remove pheasant pieces to a serving platter and keep warm. Mix cornstarch with a little cold water and stir into skillet juices. Cook until thickened, stirring constantly. Add hot water, salt, and pepper to sour cream. Reduce heat under skillet and stir in sour-cream mixture. Heat only until sauce begins to simmer. Pour over pheasant pieces on platter and serve at once.

SERVES: 2 to 4.

Grape-Stuffed Pheasants

¾ cup butter
½ teaspoon thyme
¼ cup gin
1 tablespoon salt
⅛ teaspoon pepper

2 pheasants (about 3 pounds each), well cleaned
2 pounds seedless grapes
1 cup coarsely chopped walnuts

Melt the butter and mix in thyme, gin, salt, and pepper. Rub the birds inside and out with the seasoned butter. Mash half of the grapes and mix with whole grapes, nuts, and remaining seasoned butter. Stuff each bird with this mixture. Skewer openings shut, and truss. Wrap any remaining stuffing in aluminum foil.

Preheat oven to 425°F. Place birds on a rack in an open roasting pan and roast for 15 minutes. The foil-wrapped stuffing can be placed in the roasting pan beside the birds. Baste with drippings, reduce to 350°F., and continue to roast for 40 minutes more, or until birds are tender. Baste every 10 minutes with drippings.

SERVES: 8.

VEGETABLES

CHAPTER
13

Near East Asparagus

The seasoning is Oriental, but the cooking method is simple braising, rather than Chinese stir-fry. Flavor and texture, however, are definitely Oriental.

1 pound fresh asparagus (or
   1 package frozen)
2 tablespoons water
1 tablespoon oil
1 tablespoon gin

1 teaspoon soy sauce
¼ teaspoon garlic powder
Pinch of sugar
Salt and pepper to taste

Cut off whitish ends of fresh asparagus, then trim off tough outside skin with a vegetable peeler. Peel from just below the tip and go all the way down. Wash well to remove sand.

Put cleaned asparagus (or package of frozen asparagus) into a large skillet. Add remaining ingredients, cover, and cook over low heat about 10 minutes, or until asparagus is tender but still crisp. SERVES: 3 to 4.

Black Beans with Rum

1 pound dried black beans
1 medium onion, sliced
1 clove garlic, minced
1 bay leaf
¼ teaspoon oregano
1 celery rib, chopped
2 tablespoons chopped parsley
¼ pound salt pork, cut in
   chunks

6 cups cold water
1 tablespoon butter
1 tablespoon flour
1 tablespoon salt
¼ teaspoon pepper
¼ cup Jamaica rum
1 cup sour cream

Cover beans with cold water and refrigerate, covered, overnight. Next day, drain and put into a large kettle. Add onion, garlic, bay leaf, oregano, celery, parsley, salt pork, and water. Bring mixture to boiling point; reduce heat, cover pan, and simmer about 2 to 2½

142

hours, or until beans are tender. Stir occasionally during cooking. Drain beans, reserving liquid. Place beans in a 2-quart casserole.

Preheat oven to 350°F. Melt butter in a small saucepan. Remove from heat and stir in flour, salt, pepper, and 2 cups reserved bean liquid. Cook over low heat, stirring, until mixture bubbles. Stir in rum and pour mixture over beans in casserole. Bake, uncovered, 30 to 40 minutes. Remove from oven and serve with sour cream. SERVES: 6.

Way-Out Beans

4 cans Boston-style
  baked beans
¾ teaspoon dry mustard
½ cup chili sauce

1 tablespoon molasses
⅓ cup brandy
¼ cup finely chopped onion

Preheat oven to 350°F. Place everything in a 2-quart casserole or baking dish, mix, and bake for one hour.
SERVES: 8 to 10.

Beets in Orange Sauce

1-pound can small whole beets
½ cup orange juice
2 tablespoons lemon juice
2 tablespoons orange liqueur
1 teaspoon grated orange rind

2 tablespoons sugar
1 tablespoon cornstarch
½ teaspoon salt
2 tablespoons cold water
2 tablespoons butter

Combine orange juice, lemon juice, orange liqueur, and orange rind, and bring quickly to a boil. Mix sugar, cornstarch, salt, and cold water. Add to hot liquid and cook over low heat, stirring constantly, until thickened. Add drained beets and butter and heat through.
SERVES: 4.

Canadian Carrots

1 pound young carrots
2 tablespoons butter
2 tablespoons maple syrup

3 tablespoons Canadian whisky

Scrape carrots and cut crosswise in diagonal slices. Cook in boiling salted water for about 10 minutes, or until tender. Drain. Melt butter in skillet, add maple syrup, carrot slices, and Canadian whisky. Cook over low heat for about 5 minutes or until carrots have absorbed pan liquids and are glazed. Shake pan occasionally to keep carrots from sticking.
SERVES: 4.

Three Spirit Walnut Carrots

A more or less happy collaboration almost foundered on this recipe. The distaff preference was for Calvados—"more delicate." An emphatic vote for bourbon was cast by the male contingent, with a hedge for the spiciness of Galliano.

1 bunch young carrots
  (about 1 pound)
¾ cup water
½ teaspoon salt
¼ teaspoon sugar

Dressing:
¼ cup butter

2 tablespoons chopped
  walnuts
1 tablespoon bourbon
  (Calvados or Galliano can
  be substituted)
1 teaspoon lemon juice
Salt and pepper to taste

Scrub and pare carrots. Grate coarsely. Put in a large skillet with water, salt, and sugar. Bring to a boil. Cover and cook over low heat about 10 minutes. Shake pan once or twice and watch carefully that carrots don't burn. Add a little more water if necessary. Carrots are done when they are barely tender.

While carrots are cooking, combine butter, walnuts, spirit of your

choice, lemon juice, salt, and pepper. Heat over *very low* flame, so that flavors just blend. Pour dressing over cooked carrots, stir lightly, and serve at once.
SERVES: 4 to 6.

Cointreau-Glazed Carrots

1 jar (or can) whole cooked
   baby carrots, drained
1 tablespoon carrot liquid
1 teaspoon lemon juice

2 teaspoons Cointreau
1 pinch nutmeg
1 tablespoon butter
1 tablespoon brown sugar

Preheat oven to 375°F. Put all ingredients but carrots in shallow baking dish and place in oven until butter melts, about 3 minutes. Now add drained carrots to dish and baste with glaze. Bake 15 to 20 minutes until glaze is almost completely absorbed.
SERVES: 4.

Cauliflower Fritters

¾ cup sifted flour
¼ teaspoon salt
1 egg, separated
⅓ cup beer

2 tablespoons blended whiskey
1 cauliflower
Oil for frying

Sift flour and salt into a bowl. Add beaten egg yolk, beer, and blended whiskey. Stir until smooth. Cover and refrigerate for 2 or 3 hours.

Separate cauliflower into flowerets and boil in salted water to cover for 10 minutes. Drain and cool.

When ready to fry, beat egg white until stiff and fold into batter. Heat oil in an electric skillet or deep-fryer to 375°F. Dip the flowerets into the batter and fry a few at a time until golden.
SERVES: 4 to 6.

Green Beans Sesame

2 packages frozen French-
   style green beans
1 teaspoon salt
2 tablespoons water
2 tablespoons oil

1 tablespoon gin
2 teaspoons soy sauce
¼ teaspoon sugar
2 tablespoons toasted
   sesame seeds

Place frozen green beans in a large skillet. Add salt, water, and oil, and cover. Cook over low heat until beans are just tender, about 10 minutes. Remove from heat. Place in a serving bowl and add remaining ingredients. Stir well. Refrigerate for several hours.
SERVES: 4 to 6.

Bourbon-Walnut Mushrooms

1 pound large mushrooms
2 tablespoons chopped onion
1 tablespoon oil
½ pound ground beef
½ teaspoon salt
⅛ teaspoon pepper

2 tablespoons chopped parsley
¼ cup chopped walnuts
¼ cup bourbon
2 eggs, lightly beaten
⅓ cup bread crumbs
1 tablespoon butter

Clean mushrooms with a damp paper towel. Remove and chop stems. Lightly sauté onions in oil. When golden, add beef and 2 tablespoons chopped mushroom stems. (Any remaining mushroom stems can be sautéed in a little butter and refrigerated for other uses.) Cook, stirring frequently, for 5 minutes. Add salt and pepper. Remove from fire. Stir in parsley, walnuts, bourbon, and beaten eggs. Add bread crumbs until mixture forms a crumbly paste. Mound in mushroom caps. Dust tops with bread crumbs and dot with butter. Bake in oiled pan for 20 minutes in oven preheated to 375°F.
SERVES: 6.

Mushrooms in Cream

1 pound fresh mushrooms
¼ cup butter
1½ tablespoons minced chives
½ teaspoon salt
⅛ teaspoon pepper
¼ cup catsup

1 cup light cream
3 tablespoons Scotch whisky
4 slices toast
⅓ cup coarsely chopped
   toasted walnuts

Wipe mushrooms with damp cloth and slice. Melt butter in skillet. Add mushrooms and chives. Cook over low heat until mushrooms are browned and tender. Stir in salt, pepper, catsup, cream, and Scotch. Heat to serving temperature, stirring frequently. Serve on toast, garnishing each portion with chopped walnuts.
SERVES: 4.

Braised Onion Slices

2 tablespoons olive oil
2 tablespoons butter
4 large onions, peeled and cut
   in 1-inch slices

1 teaspoon salt
½ teaspoon pepper
¼ cup beef bouillon
¼ cup Scotch whisky

Heat oil and butter in a heavy skillet. Add onions and sauté over high heat for 2 minutes. Reduce heat and add salt, pepper, and bouillon. Cover and simmer for 10 minutes, or until just tender. Uncover, add Scotch, and cook 2 or 3 minutes longer.
SERVES: 6.

Flaming Parsnips

1 pound cooked parsnips
½ medium onion, minced
2 tablespoons butter
¼ teaspoon salt
⅛ teaspoon nutmeg

⅛ teaspoon pepper
1 egg, lightly beaten
½ cup milk
1 teaspoon sugar
3 tablespoons light rum, warm

Preheat oven to 375°F. Butter a 1-quart casserole. Rice or mash parsnips and mix well with other ingredients, except sugar and rum. Turn mixture into casserole and bake for about 20 minutes.

Sprinkle parsnip casserole with sugar and 1 tablespoon rum. Ignite rest of rum and pour over.

SERVES: 4.

Minted Peas

1 package frozen peas	1 tablespoon butter
1 teaspoon crème de menthe	

Cook peas according to package directions. Drain. Mix with crème de menthe and butter.

SERVES: 2 to 3.

Bourbon Squash

1 acorn squash	2 tablespoons granulated
Salt	brown sugar
2 teaspoons butter	2 tablespoons bourbon

Cut squash in half and remove seeds. Sprinkle with salt and put 1 teaspoon butter and 1 teaspoon sugar in each half. Preheat oven to 350°F. Place squash halves on a baking sheet and bake for 30 minutes. Pour 1 tablespoon bourbon in each squash half and pierce the flesh with a knife, not cutting through the skin. Cover the whole baking sheet with aluminum foil and bake for another 20 to 30 minutes, depending on size.

SERVES: 2.

Candied Sweet Potatoes

4 medium sweet potatoes	¼ cup water
½ teaspoon salt	2 tablespoons applejack
¾ cup brown sugar, firmly packed	2 tablespoons butter

Cook sweet potatoes until tender, peel, halve, and sprinkle with salt. In a skillet, combine brown sugar, water, applejack, and butter. Bring to a boil. Put potatoes in syrup and cook over low heat, turning occasionally, until syrup is almost completely absorbed and the potatoes are well glazed, 15 to 20 minutes.
SERVES: 4.

Sweet Potato-Rum Soufflé

2 cups warm mashed sweet
  potatoes
½ cup hot milk
¼ cup Gold Label Puerto
  Rican rum
¼ cup butter

½ teaspoon salt
⅛ teaspoon nutmeg
⅛ teaspoon pepper
1 teaspoon grated lemon rind
4 eggs, separated

Add milk, rum, butter, salt, nutmeg, pepper, and lemon rind to mashed sweet potatoes. Beat until smooth and light. Beat egg yolks and stir into sweet-potato mixture; blend well. Cool to lukewarm. Beat egg whites and fold in. Turn into a well-buttered 1½-quart soufflé dish. Bake for 25 minutes in oven preheated to 375°F. until soufflé is well puffed. Serve immediately.
SERVES: 4.

Sweet and Sour Zucchini

6 medium zucchini
2 teaspoons oil
½ teaspoon salt
⅛ teaspoon pepper

2 tablespoons blended whiskey
3 tablespoons wine vinegar
2 teaspoons sugar
¼ teaspoon basil

Scrape zucchini and cut each in half, crosswise. Cut each half in lengthwise slices, ¼ inch thick. Heat oil and fry slices on each side until tender and golden. Stir slices gently from time to time. Sprinkle with salt and pepper, and place in a serving dish. Keep warm. Add whiskey, vinegar, sugar, and basil to the oil in the pan, and bring to a boil. Simmer for 2 minutes. Pour over zucchini and serve. This can also be served cold.

Variation: Substitute anisette for whiskey. Eliminate sugar and basil.

SERVES: 6.

Fiori di Zucchini Fritti
Fried Zucchini Blossoms

2 tablespoons very finely
  minced onion
2 teaspoons butter
2 eggs, separated
⅔ cup milk
1 tablespoon olive oil
1 tablespoon lemon juice
½ teaspoon salt

⅔ cup sifted flour
2 tablespoons grated
  Parmesan cheese
2 tablespoons bourbon
2 dozen large zucchini
  blossoms
¼ cup flour

Sauté onion in butter until golden, and set aside. Beat egg yolks until lemon-colored. Stir in milk, olive oil, lemon juice, salt, and ⅔ cup flour; mix until smooth. Add sautéed onion, Parmesan cheese, and bourbon. Set batter aside for an hour or longer. Just before using, beat egg whites until stiff but not dry and fold into batter.

Wash zucchini blossoms and drain well (best done by shaking each flower and placing on a paper towel). Put ¼ cup flour in a plastic bag and toss flowers in this, a few at a time. Then dip each flower into the batter and deep-fry in salad oil at 350°F. Keep turning until flowers are golden brown. Drain and serve immediately.

SERVES: 4 to 6.

SALADS
AND
SALAD DRESSINGS
CHAPTER
14

Avocado Salad

2 medium-size ripe avocados
½ Bermuda onion
½ cup salad oil
3 tablespoons lemon juice
3 tablespoons blended whiskey

½ teaspoon sugar
½ teaspoon salt
⅛ teaspoon pepper
1 seedless orange

Peel avocados and cut into cubes. Slice onion paper thin and separate into rings. Place in a bowl. Mix all ingredients, except orange, and pour over. Cover bowl and refrigerate for several hours, stirring mixture occasionally. Just before serving, peel and section orange. Add to salad and toss lightly. Serve on bed of shredded lettuce.
SERVES: 4.

Guacamole

1 *ripe* avocado
⅛ teaspoon garlic powder
⅛ teaspoon chili powder,
   or to taste

½ teaspoon salt
1 teaspoon grated onion
1 teaspoon lime juice
1 teaspoon tequila

Peel avocado, remove pit, and mash. Blend in other ingredients and beat until light and creamy. Use as savory cocktail dip or appetizer.

For dip, serve in small bowl along with crackers, Fritos, potato chips, thinly sliced rye bread. For appetizer, serve on bed of lettuce with garnish of tomato wedges.
SERVES: 3 to 4 as an appetizer.

Potato-Green Bean Salad

1 pound new potatoes
1 package frozen cut green
   beans
4 eggs, hard-cooked
1 small can anchovy fillets
¼ cup pitted green olives,
   cut in half
¼ cup pitted black olives,
   cut in half

1 cup dry white wine
2 tablespoons cognac
2 tablespoons lemon juice
¼ teaspoon dry mustard
¼ cup olive oil
½ teaspoon salt
⅛ teaspoon pepper

Cook the potatoes in their jackets until tender. While still warm, skin and cut into thin slices. Cook green beans according to package directions, until just tender. Slice the hard-cooked eggs. Place the anchovies in a colander and rinse under running cold water to remove excess salt.

Place a layer of potatoes in a large salad bowl, add the green beans, another layer of potatoes, the egg slices and anchovies, another layer of potatoes, and finish with the olives. Mix the wine with the cognac and pour over the salad. Refrigerate overnight.

Mix together the lemon juice, dry mustard, olive oil, salt, and pepper. Pour over the salad at serving time.
SERVES: 4.

Potato Salad Provençal

2 pounds new potatoes
1 teaspoon salt
½ teaspoon pepper
¼ cup wine vinegar
1 tablespoon pastis (anise-
   flavored spirit)

2 tablespoons beef bouillon
¼ cup dry white wine
¼ teaspoon dried tarragon
3 tablespoons chopped parsley
½ cup oil

Cook potatoes in their jackets until tender. While still warm, peel

and cut into slices ¼ inch thick. Place in a salad bowl. Combine salt, pepper, vinegar, pastis, bouillon, and wine. Mix until salt dissolves. Add tarragon, parsley, and oil, and mix well. Pour over potatoes and toss gently until all the liquid is absorbed. Taste before serving, to correct salt and other seasoning.
SERVES: 4 to 6.

Summer Tomato Salad

6 beefsteak tomatoes
⅓ cup olive oil
1 teaspoon salt
¼ teaspoon sugar
1 tablespoon finely chopped
   fresh basil (or 1 scant
   teaspoon dried)

1 tablespoon finely chopped
   parsley
1 teaspoon lemon juice
2 tablespoons rye whiskey or
   bourbon

Peel and thinly slice the tomatoes and arrange on a serving dish. Combine remaining ingredients and pour over tomatoes. Refrigerate for about a half-hour before serving.
NOTE: If using dried basil, steep it in the whiskey for about a half-hour beforehand.
SERVES: 4 to 6.

Isle of Rhodes Vegetable Salad

½ cup cooked diced beets
½ cup cooked diced carrots
½ cup cooked peas
½ cup cooked cut string
   beans
2 teaspoons ouzo

1 teaspoon salt
⅛ teaspoon black pepper
½ teaspoon dill weed
   (optional)
3 tablespoons mayonnaise
Lettuce leaves

Although fresh vegetables can be used, drained canned vegetables are quite good in this salad. Place drained beets, carrots, peas, and string beans in a salad bowl. Combine ouzo with seasonings and

mayonnaise, and add to vegetables. Toss lightly. Refrigerate for several hours. Spoon into lettuce cups at serving time. This is delicious with fish or seafood.
SERVES: 4 to 6.

Tangerines Jamaica

Serve with pork, ham or poultry.

1 cup tangerine sections,
  cleaned
½ cup honey
½ cup water
⅓ cup cider vinegar

3 tablespoons Jamaica rum
1½ teaspoons finely chopped
  shallots
1 teaspoon dried rosemary
1 teaspoon soy sauce

Prepare a syrup by boiling honey and water for one minute. Add vinegar, rum, shallots, rosemary, and soy sauce. Bring to a boil.
  Pour syrup over tangerine sections and marinate overnight.

Bloody Mary Aspic

Delicious served with cold seafood.

1½ cups tomato juice
½ teaspoon sugar
1 envelope gelatin
  (1 tablespoon)
1 teaspoon fresh basil or
  ¼ teaspoon dried

1 small bay leaf
1 tablespoon lemon juice
¼ cup vodka
½ teaspoon salt
¼ teaspoon pepper

Mix in a saucepan ¾ cup tomato juice, sugar, gelatin, basil, and bay leaf. Stir over moderate heat until the gelatin dissolves. Remove from heat, strain, and add remaining ¾ cup tomato juice, lemon juice, vodka, salt, and pepper. Pour into a 1-pint ring or other mold and chill until firm.
SERVES: 4.

Blue Cheese Salad Dressing

¼ cup crumbled blue cheese	¼ teaspoon sugar
½ cup salad oil	Dash garlic powder
2 tablespoons wine vinegar	Salt to taste
2 tablespoons brandy	1 tablespoon minced chives

Combine all ingredients and mix until completely blended. Serve with greens, tomatoes or mixed salads.
YIELD: About 1 cup.

Orange-Onion Salad with Blue Cheese Dressing

Make up half of recipe for Blue Cheese Salad Dressing (above) with these modifications: substitute orange liqueur for brandy, and eliminate sugar.

3 navel oranges, peeled and sliced across grain	½ medium-size sweet red onion, sliced very thin
	Lettuce leaves

Combine orange slices and onion slices, separated into rings. Toss with dressing to coat well. Distribute over lettuce leaves on individual salad plates.
SERVES: 4.

Caribe Dressing

1 egg	¼ cup sour cream
2 tablespoons tarragon vinegar	1 tablespoon lemon juice
½ teaspoon salt	1 tablespoon Silver Label rum
1 tablespoon anchovy paste	1 teaspoon sugar
½ clove garlic	2 tablespoons minced chives
1 cup salad oil	2 tablespoons minced parsley

In the container of an electric blender, place egg, vinegar, salt, anchovy paste, and garlic. Add ¼ cup oil, cover the blender, and blend thoroughly about 5 seconds. Without stopping blender, remove cover and gradually pour in remaining oil. Turn off when all the oil has been added. Add remaining ingredients and blend until completely mixed.
YIELD: About 2 cups.

Martini French Dressing

½ cup olive oil or salad oil
1 tablespoon wine vinegar
1 tablespoon dry vermouth
1 tablespoon gin
1 teaspoon salt

½ teaspoon sugar
¼ teaspoon dry mustard
1 clove garlic, squeezed
    through press

Combine all ingredients in a jar with a tight cover. Shake well before using.
YIELD: About ¾ cup.

Loch Lomond Tartar Sauce

1 cup mayonnaise
2 tablespoons finely chopped
    sweet pickle
1 tablespoon minced onion
2 tablespoons minced
    green pepper

2 tablespoons finely chopped
    peeled cucumber (drained)
1 tablespoon finely chopped
    celery
1 tablespoon lemon juice
1 tablespoon Scotch whisky

Combine all ingredients thoroughly and refrigerate. This sauce can be served with fish or seafood or used as a dressing for greens.
YIELD: About 1½ cups.

SAUCES
BASTES
MARINADES
CHAPTER
15

Hoisin Barbecue Sauce

Hoisin sauce, a thick, spicy Chinese seasoning mixture, can be purchased in Oriental specialty shops.

½ cup Hoisin sauce
1 cup honey
½ cup bourbon

1 cup tomato purée
1 clove garlic, minced
1 teaspoon soy sauce

Combine Hoisin sauce, honey, bourbon, tomato purée, garlic, and soy sauce. Use as a marinade for beef, pork, lamb, or shrimp, or serve as a barbecue sauce for ribs. Will keep indefinitely in the refrigerator.
YIELD: About 3 cups.

Spiked Barbecue Marinade and Baste

¼ cup bourbon
¼ cup salad oil
2 tablespoons soy sauce

1 teaspoon Worcestershire
  sauce
2 cloves garlic, finely chopped
¼ teaspoon black pepper

Combine all ingredients and blend thoroughly. Use as marinade for meat or fish: roasts about 24 hours, steaks 4 hours, fish or poultry 2 hours. Refrigerate meat or fish while marinating and turn occasionally. Use marinade as baste during broiling or roasting.
YIELD: About ⅔ cup.

Brandied Seasoning Bouquet

A concentrated seasoning to flavor meats and sauces.

½ pound mushrooms
1 small can anchovy fillets
¼ cup olive oil
4 cloves garlic
¼ cup chopped fresh parsley
1 can tomato paste
½ teaspoon marjoram

½ teaspoon basil
¾ cup salad oil
1 cup beef stock
1 cup dry wine
1 cup brandy
½ teaspoon salt
¼ teaspoon pepper

Cut mushrooms in quarters. Drain oil from anchovy fillets and rinse them in cold water. Pour olive oil in blender container. Add mushrooms, anchovies, garlic, and parsley. Blend until well combined. Pour this mixture into a saucepan and add remaining ingredients. Bring to a boil over low heat, cover, and simmer for 15 minutes. Cool and then refrigerate.

Brush on roasts, pot roasts, steaks, or hamburgers before cooking. Add small quantities to stews, ragouts, spaghetti sauce, etc., while cooking.

YIELD: About 1 quart.

Flaming Mushroom Sauce

For steaks, chops, hamburgers.

1 pound fresh mushrooms	¼ teaspoon pepper
¼ cup butter	¼ cup Gold Label rum,
½ teaspoon salt	warmed

Cut mushrooms in thin slices. Heat butter, add mushrooms, and sauté over medium heat until slightly browned. Add salt and pepper. Remove from heat and bring to table. Pour rum over and ignite. Spoon flaming sauce over meat.

SERVES: 6 to 8.

Sauce Diable

Use with broiled meats and yesterday's cold roast.

¼ cup butter	3 tablespoons minced shallots
6 tablespoons flour	or scallions
2 beef bouillon cubes	⅛ teaspoon pepper
2 cups boiling water	¼ cup cognac
2 sprigs parsley	1 teaspoon Worcestershire
½ small bay leaf	sauce
⅛ teaspoon thyme	

Melt butter in a heavy saucepan over low heat. Add 4 tablespoons of the flour. Cook over moderate heat about 6 to 8 minutes, stirring constantly, until medium brown. Remove from heat and stir in the remaining 2 tablespoons of flour. Dissolve bouillon cubes in boiling water. Gradually stir into the flour mixture. Return to heat and cook until thickened and smooth, stirring constantly. Add parsley, bay leaf, and thyme. Cook over very low heat for about a half-hour, stirring occasionally.

Place shallots, pepper, and cognac in the top of a double boiler. Cook over low heat for about 5 minutes. Add cooked brown sauce and Worcestershire. Cook over simmering water for 15 minutes. Strain into a sauceboat.

YIELD: About 1½ cups.

Sauce Maltaise

An orange-scented Hollandaise to dress asparagus, broccoli and other green vegetables.

½ cup butter	⅛ teaspoon white pepper
3 egg yolks	1½ teaspoons grated orange
2 tablespoons lemon juice	rind
¼ teaspoon salt	2 tablespoons orange liqueur

Heat butter in a small saucepan until frothy, but do not let it brown. Put egg yolks, lemon juice, salt, and pepper into blender container. Cover container and turn on high speed. Immediately remove cover and pour in the hot butter in a slow, steady stream. When all the butter is added, turn off the motor. If the sauce is not to be served immediately, keep warm by setting container into a saucepan containing 2 inches of hot water. When ready to serve, pour into sauceboat and stir in orange rind and orange liqueur.

YIELD: About 1 cup.

Jack's Mornay Sauce

Excellent over poached eggs, fish, pasta.

3 tablespoons butter
3 tablespoons flour
¾ teaspoon salt
2 cups milk
2 egg yolks
2 tablespoons heavy cream

1 tablespoon applejack
2 tablespoons grated
  Parmesan cheese
2 tablespoons grated
  Gruyère cheese

Make a white sauce with butter, flour, salt, and milk. Beat egg yolks and cream together. Stir in ½ cup of the hot white sauce. Pour back into remaining white sauce. Add applejack and Parmesan and Gruyère cheeses. Heat over low heat about 10 minutes.
YIELD: About 2¼ cups.

Fragrant Aspic

For shellfish, poached eggs, chicken breasts, open-faced sandwiches or any handsome dish that would be enhanced by a transparent glaze.

1¾ cups chicken broth
¼ cup tomato juice
2 envelopes unflavored
  gelatin

2 egg whites, slightly beaten
2 eggshells, crushed
1 tablespoon cognac

Combine in a saucepan: broth, tomato juice, gelatin, egg whites, and eggshells. Stir over medium heat until the mixture comes to a full boil. Strain through a sieve lined with a double thickness of tea towel that has been dampened with cold water and wrung dry. When strained, add cognac and stir. Chill until syrupy.

All food to be glazed should be cold. Arrange chilled food on a cake rack set over a baking sheet. Spoon enough aspic over the food to cover it, then chill until set. If more glaze is desired, spoon on a second layer of aspic when the first has set. If aspic has become too firm, warm until it returns to a syrupy consistency.

Leftover aspic can be chilled in a shallow pan, chopped, and used as a garnish.

YIELD: About 1 cup.

PRESERVES
AND
RELISHES
CHAPTER
16

Bourbon-Apple Jelly

1 cup bourbon
1 cup apple juice
3 cups sugar

½ bottle liquid fruit pectin
(3 ounces)

Combine bourbon, apple juice, and sugar in a saucepan. Cook over low heat, stirring often until sugar dissolves. Remove from heat and stir in pectin. Cool and pour into sterilized jelly glasses. Seal with paraffin and put on jar lids.
YIELD: 4 8-ounce glasses.

Apricot-Whiskey Jelly

1½ cups apricot nectar
½ cup blended whiskey
2 tablespoons fresh lemon
    juice

3½ cups sugar
½ bottle liquid fruit pectin
(3 ounces)

Combine nectar, whiskey, lemon juice, and sugar in the top of a double boiler. Place over rapidly boiling water and cook until sugar is dissolved, stirring often. Remove from heat and stir in pectin. Pour into sterilized jars and seal with paraffin. Cover with jar lids.
YIELD: 4 8-ounce glasses.

Crème de Menthe Jelly

1 cup crème de menthe
1 cup water
2½ cups sugar

½ bottle liquid fruit pectin
(3 ounces)
4 fresh mint sprigs

In the top of a double boiler, over rapidly boiling water, combine crème de menthe, water, and sugar. Stir until sugar is dissolved. Remove from heat and stir in pectin. Skim off foam if necessary.
    Plunge mint sprigs into boiling water for one minute. Place 1 sprig

in each of 4 hot, sterilized jelly glasses. Pour jelly into jars. Seal with paraffin.

YIELD: 4 half-pint glasses.

Cranberries Cassis

4½ cups cranberries	¾ cup water
2 medium apples	¼ cup crème de cassis
3 cups sugar	

Wash and drain cranberries. Peel and core apples, and dice coarsely. In a large saucepan, heat sugar with water, stirring constantly until the sugar dissolves. Add the cranberries and apples. Bring the mixture to a boil; reduce the heat to moderate and cook, stirring frequently, for 15 minutes, or until the liquid has a jamlike consistency. Remove the pan from the heat and stir in crème de cassis. Pour into hot, sterilized jars and seal.

YIELD: About 3 pints.

Peach-Almond Conserve

4 pounds firm, ripe peaches	1 cup blanched toasted
48 large dried apricot halves	almonds, coarsely chopped
3 cups light-brown sugar	¼ cup slivered angelica
3 cups granulated sugar	½ cup B&B liqueur
1 teaspoon cinnamon	

Scald the peaches and remove skins and pits. Dice coarsely. Sliver the apricots. Combine peaches, apricots, sugars, and cinnamon in a large pot. Cook over high heat for about 15 minutes, stirring occasionally, until a candy thermometer registers 220°F. or until the juice is thickened and syrupy. (It will thicken more as it cools.) Remove from heat and stir in almonds, angelica, and B&B. Pour into hot, sterilized jars and seal.

YIELD: About 4 pints.

Peach-Rum Jam

3 pounds firm, ripe peaches   5 cups sugar
1 package powdered pectin   ¼ cup Gold Label rum

Scald the peaches and remove skins and pits. Chop finely. Combine with the fruit pectin in a very large saucepan. Place over high heat and bring to a full, rolling boil, stirring constantly. Immediately add all the sugar and stir. Again bring to a full, rolling boil and boil hard for one minute, stirring constantly. Remove from heat; stir in rum. Skim off foam with a metal spoon. Stir and skim for 5 minutes, to cool slightly and distribute fruit. Ladle into hot, sterilized jars and seal at once.

YIELD: 6 to 7 8-ounce jars.

Brandied Cherries

2 pounds sweet cherries   2 cups water
2 cups sugar   Brandy

Soak the cherries in ice water for 30 minutes. Drain and remove the stems carefully. Dissolve the sugar in water and bring to a boil. Cook rapidly for 5 minutes. Add the cherries and bring once more to a boil. Let the syrup boil up 3 times, stirring gently with a long wooden spoon. Fill sterilized jars three-quarters full of fruit and syrup, and let stand to cool. When the syrup is almost cool, fill each jar to the top with brandy. Seal. Turn the jars upside down overnight, then store right side up in a cool, dark place for at least 3 months before using. Marvelous over ice cream, custard and stewed or tinned fruit.

YIELD: About 4 pints.

Grapes in Cognac

2 pounds green seedless grapes   1 teaspoon lemon juice
2 cups sugar   1 cup cognac (approx.)
3 cups water

Wash grapes and remove them from the stems. Bring the sugar, water, and lemon to a boil, reduce heat, and simmer for 10 minutes. Add grapes to the syrup and simmer for about 15 minutes, or until tender. Remove the grapes from the syrup with a slotted spoon and pack into hot, sterilized jars. Continue cooking syrup until it is as thick as honey. Stir in ⅓ cup cognac for each cup of syrup. Pour the syrup over the grapes to fill the jars to overflowing, and seal. YIELD: 3 to 4 pints.

Brandied Peaches

3 pounds firm, ripe peaches   1½ cups water
3 pounds sugar   Brandy

Drop peaches into a large kettle of boiling water. Remove at once and plunge into cool water. Slip off skins, halve, and remove the pits.

Bring sugar and water to a boil and cook for 5 minutes. Add peaches, a few at a time, and cook 5 to 10 minutes, or until they are tender. Lift the peaches out of the syrup with a slotted spoon and pack into hot, sterilized jars.

Continue cooking syrup until it is very thick. Cool syrup, measure, and add an equal amount of brandy. (The amount of brandy is optional. Use less if you like.) Pour brandy-syrup mixture over fruit in jar to the very top. Seal at once.
YIELD: About 4 pints.

Pear Brandy Pears

4½ cups sugar   1 cup pear brandy
1½ cups water   Maraschino cherries, drained
4 pounds firm, ripe pears

Combine sugar and water in a large pot. Bring to a boil over medium heat, stirring constantly, until sugar dissolves. Reduce heat and simmer, uncovered, for 10 minutes.

Meanwhile, cut pears in half, peel, and core. Add to sugar syrup. Simmer, uncovered, 30 to 40 minutes, or until pears are tender. Remove from heat. While pears are cooking, sterilize 4 pint jars and leave in hot water until ready to fill.

Put 2 tablespoons pear brandy into each hot jar. With slotted spoon, lift pears from syrup. Put a maraschino cherry in each pear half. Half-fill jars with pears. Add 1 tablespoon pear brandy to each. Fill jars with rest of pears. Add 1 tablespoon brandy to each. Fill with sugar syrup to within ½ inch of top. Seal at once.
YIELD: 4 pints.

Tutti-Frutti Rum Crock

1 bottle Gold Label rum	Peaches, peeled and pitted
Assorted fruits:	Plums, halved and pitted
Strawberries, hulled,	Apricots, halved and pitted
washed and drained	Pears, peeled and cored
Bing cherries, pitted	Sugar

Tutti-frutti is best started in the late spring, at the beginning of the fresh-fruit season. Begin by pouring the rum into a large crock or jar (at least a gallon). Add fruits in season and *their weight in sugar*. After each addition of fruit and sugar, cover the crock and let it stand in a cool place. Fruits should always be covered by rum, so add more if necessary.

As fruits come into season, add them with *their weight in sugar*. When the crock is full, cover tightly and let it stand in a cool place for 3 months before using.

Rum Butter

This is a delicious spread for biscuits, toast, or crackers. It is best made in small quantities and used within a fairly short time. It should be refrigerated.

½ cup soft butter	¼ cup Jamaica rum
½ cup light-brown sugar,	⅛ teaspoon cinnamon
firmly packed	

Combine butter and sugar in a heavy saucepan and mix until well blended. Stir in rum and cinnamon. Cook over low heat, stirring constantly, until sugar has completely dissolved and mixture sheets from a spoon. Do not overcook.

Pour into a half-pint jar. Cool to room temperature and then refrigerate. NOTE: As the mixture cools, some of the butter may rise to the top. If this happens, stir well with a fork after spread has chilled about a half-hour. It will not separate again.

Vanilla Liqueur

1 vanilla bean	1 pound sugar
½ cup brandy	1 cup water

Split the vanilla bean and cut it into 1-inch lengths. Soak for 3 days in the brandy. Bring sugar and water to a boil. Skim off any scum that rises to the surface. Cook until clear and thick enough to spin a light thread. Strain the vanilla-flavored brandy into the syrup and stir well. Bottle and store in a cool place. Use small amounts of this liqueur as a flavoring for desserts.

YIELD: About 1½ pints.

Kentucky Walnut Sauce

3 cups shelled walnuts	3 tablespoons lemon juice
1½ cups honey	1 teaspoon grated lemon rind
½ cup water	¼ cup bourbon

Cover nuts with boling water, let stand about 5 minutes, and remove the skins. Use a small pointed knife and start at the back of the nut where the skin is broken. Break the nuts into quarters.

Bring honey and water to a boil. Add the nuts and cook gently for 10 minutes, stirring frequently. Add lemon juice and rind and cook 2 minutes longer. Add bourbon and stir well. Pour into sterilized jars and seal. Sauce over puddings, custards, ice cream.

YIELD: 4 or 5 8-ounce jars.

Gin Dandy Catsup

3 pounds prune plums, seeded
1 orange
1 lemon
1 lime
1 green pepper
3 medium onions
1 teaspoon mixed pickling
  spices

6 bay leaves
1 tablespoon salt
2½ cups gin
2 cups red wine vinegar
1 package powdered pectin
¼ cup sugar

Finely chop plums, orange, lemon, lime, pepper, and onions. Add pickling spices, bay leaves, and salt. Bring slowly to a boil; turn heat low and add 1 cup of gin and 1 cup of vinegar. Cook, stirring often, until fruit cooks down. Add a second cup of both gin and vinegar. Continue to cook over low heat, stirring frequently, until cooked down to a rich compote. Remove from heat and put through a food mill. To the remaining pulp, add sugar, powdered pectin, and the last half cup of gin. Stir over low heat until mixture is thick.

Pour into hot, sterilized jars and seal at once. Serve as a sauce with roast pork, baked ham or game. Also good as a dip for cocktail sausages.
YIELD: 3 pints.

Zingy Cranberry Relish

1 can whole-cranberry sauce
1 orange, peeled, diced
¼ teaspoon cinnamon
¼ teaspoon mace

¼ teaspoon nutmeg
½ cup orange juice
¼ cup triple sec

Put all of the ingredients in blender, and blend for one minute. Chill for several hours. Nice served in avocado halves or peach cups.
YIELD: About 3 cups.

PASTRIES
AND
CONFECTIONS
CHAPTER
17

Cakes

Kentucky Pound Cake

1 cup soft butter
1½ cups sifted flour
¼ teaspoon baking soda
1½ cups sugar
2 tablespoons bourbon

1 teaspoon vanilla
5 eggs, separated
⅛ teaspoon salt
1 teaspoon cream of tartar

Grease a 9-inch tube pan with 1 tablespoon of the butter. Dust with flour and shake out excess. Preheat oven to 325°F. Sift flour, baking soda, and ¾ cup sugar into a bowl. Add remaining butter and mix in well. (This is best done with your hands.) Add bourbon, vanilla, and egg yolks, one at a time, mixing until well blended. Beat egg whites with salt until stiff but not dry. Gradually beat in remaining ¾ cup sugar; stir in cream of tartar. Fold beaten egg whites into first mixture until thoroughly blended. Spoon into prepared pan and spread evenly. Rap on table to remove air bubbles. Bake for 1 hour, or until done. Turn off heat and let stand in oven about 10 minutes. Remove to cake rack and let stand 10 minutes longer. Turn out on waxed-paper-covered rack. Cool. Dust with confectioners' sugar at serving time.
SERVES: 12.

Pecan-Whiskey Cake

2 cups finely chopped pecans
1 cup rye whiskey
3½ cups sifted flour
1½ teaspoons baking powder
½ teaspoon salt
½ teaspoon nutmeg

½ teaspoon cinnamon
¼ teaspoon cloves
2 cups butter
2½ cups sugar
8 eggs, well beaten
1 teaspoon vanilla extract

Butter and flour a 10-inch tube pan. Shake out excess flour. Preheat oven to 350°F. Combine pecans and ½ cup whiskey in a small bowl. Let stand. Sift together flour, baking powder, salt, and spices. Cream butter until soft. Gradually beat in sugar until light and fluffy. Add beaten eggs, and beat very well until mixture is thick and fluffy. Stir in flour mixture and mix just until combined. Stir in pecan-whiskey mixture. Pour batter into prepared pan and smooth out. Bake 1 hour and 10 minutes, or until cake tester inserted in center comes out clean. Cool in pan for about 15 minutes. Turn out on cake rack and cool completely. Soak a cloth in remaining ½ cup of whiskey. Wrap cake completely in this cloth and then in foil. Let stand in refrigerator for several days before using.

Orange-Syrup Nut Cake

1 cup butter	½ teaspoon salt
1½ cups sugar	1 cup sour cream
3 eggs, separated	1 teaspoon grated orange rind
2 cups flour, sifted	½ cup chopped walnuts
1 teaspoon baking powder	¼ cup orange juice
1 teaspoon baking soda	⅓ cup orange liqueur

Butter a 9-inch tube pan. Preheat oven to 350°F. Cream butter until soft. Gradually beat in 1 cup of sugar until light and fluffy. Beat in the egg yolks, one at a time. Sift together flour, baking powder, soda, and salt. Add to batter alternately with sour cream, stirring until smooth. Mix in orange rind and nuts. Pour batter into prepared pan and bake for 50 minutes.

Meanwhile, combine remaining half cup of sugar, orange juice, and orange liqueur. Spoon over cake as soon as it is removed from the oven. Cool cake completely before removing from pan.

White Fruitcake

1½ pounds blanched almonds, sliced	4 cups sifted flour
½ pound citron, slivered	6 eggs, separated
¼ pound candied pineapple, slivered	1½ cups butter
¼ pound candied cherries, halved	2 cups sugar
½ pound golden raisins	½ cup milk
	½ cup cognac
	1 teaspoon almond extract

Combine almonds and fruit and sprinkle with ½ cup of flour. Beat egg yolks lightly. Cream butter until soft. Beat in sugar gradually until light and fluffy. Add egg yolks to creamed mixture and beat thoroughly. Combine milk, cognac, and almond extract. Add remaining flour to batter alternately with liquid, blending well after each addition. Add fruit and nut mixture and mix well. Beat egg whites until they hold stiff peaks, then fold into batter.

Butter two 9- x 5-inch loaf pans, line with brown paper, and butter again. Preheat oven to 275°F. Spoon batter into pans and smooth out. Bake about 2¼ hours, or until a cake tester inserted in center comes out clean.

Cool cakes on racks and then remove from pans. Peel off paper. Store in an airtight container for several weeks before using. If desired, cakes can be sprinkled with brandy occasionally.

Dark Fruitcake

1 cup butter
1 cup brown sugar, firmly
   packed
6 eggs, separated
2 cups flour, sifted
1 teaspoon cinnamon
1 teaspoon cloves
½ teaspoon nutmeg
½ teaspoon allspice
½ teaspoon salt
½ pound mixed candied fruit,
   chopped
½ pound candied cherries,
   halved

½ pound seeded raisins
½ pound seedless raisins
½ pound currants
½ pound chopped dates
½ pound shelled walnuts,
   coarsely chopped
1 cup bourbon
2 teaspoons grated orange rind
1 cup orange juice
½ teaspoon grated lemon
   rind
2 tablespoons lemon juice

Beat egg yolks until thick and lemon-colored. Cream butter and sugar together until light and fluffy. Add beaten egg yolks and mix very well. Sift flour with spices. Combine fruits and walnuts and mix with ½ cup of the spiced flour. Mix ⅔ cup of bourbon, grated rinds, and fruit juices together. Add remaining flour to batter alternately with liquid, blending well after each addition. Add fruit and nut mixture and mix well. Beat egg whites until they hold stiff peaks, then fold into batter.

Butter two 9- x 5-inch loaf pans, line with brown paper, and butter again. Preheat oven to 250°F. and set a shallow pan of water in the bottom of the oven. Spoon batter into pans and smooth out. Bake about 3½ hours, or until a cake tester inserted in center comes out clean.

Cool cakes on racks and then remove from pans. Peel off paper. Wrap each cake in a cloth soaked in bourbon. (Add more if necessary.) Wrap individually in 2 layers of foil and seal to make airtight. Age at least a month.

Peach Upside-Down Cake

½ cup butter
1 cup light-brown sugar,
   firmly packed
2 cups sliced canned peaches,
   drained
¼ cup Canadian whisky
2 egg yolks

1 teaspoon lemon juice
1 cup sugar
6 tablespoons hot water
1 cup sifted flour
1½ teaspoons baking powder
¼ teaspoon salt
3 egg whites, stiffly beaten

Melt butter in a 9-inch square pan, and spread brown sugar over. Cover with peaches. Pour whisky over peaches and let stand. Preheat oven to 325°F.

Beat egg yolks with lemon juice until thick and lemon-colored. Add sugar gradually; slowly stir in hot water. Beat until well mixed. Sift flour with baking powder and salt. Add to egg-yolk mixture and mix until batter is smooth. Fold in beaten egg whites. Pour batter over the peaches and bake for ¾ of an hour. Turn out on platter with fruit on top. Serve slightly warm.
SERVES: 6 to 8.

Glazed Applejack Cake

1½ cups sifted flour
1 cup sugar
½ teaspoon salt
1 teaspoon baking soda
½ teaspoon baking powder
1 teaspoon cinnamon
¼ teaspoon ginger
¼ teaspoon nutmeg
½ cup soft butter

1 cup thick, unsweetened
  applesauce
2 eggs

Applejack Glaze:
⅓ cup sugar
5 tablespoons applejack
⅛ teaspoon salt

Butter and flour a 9-inch square pan. Preheat oven to 350°F.

Sift together flour, sugar, salt, soda, baking powder, and spices into a bowl. Put soft butter, applesauce, and eggs into a blender container. Blend until mixture emulsifies and is as thick as mayonnaise. Fold applesauce mixture into dry ingredients and stir only until blended. Do not overmix. Spoon batter into prepared pan and smooth off. Bake 30 minutes. Spoon glaze (below) over cake and bake 5 minutes longer.

Glaze: Combine ingredients and stir well.

Rummy Cream Cake

This cake should be made at least 24 hours in advance of serving.

2 cups sifted cake flour
2 teaspoons baking powder
¼ teaspoon baking soda
¼ teaspoon salt
½ cup butter
1 cup sugar
2 eggs, separated

1 teaspoon grated orange peel
½ cup orange juice
½ cup Gold Label rum
¼ teaspoon almond extract
½ teaspoon vanilla
2 to 3 tablespoons water
½ cup finely chopped walnuts

Whipped-Cream Filling:
2 teaspoons unflavored
  gelatin
2 tablespoons cold water
2 cups heavy cream
½ cup confectioners'
  sugar
⅓ cup Gold Label rum

Chocolate Frosting:
4 squares (oz.) unsweetened
  chocolate, melted
1 cup sifted confectioners'
  sugar
2 tablespoons hot water
2 eggs
6 tablespoons soft butter

Butter two 8- or 9-inch layer-cake pans and line with waxed paper. Preheat oven to 350°F. Sift flour with baking powder, soda, and salt. Cream butter and gradually beat in ¾ cup sugar until fluffy. Beat in egg yolks, one at a time; add orange peel. Blend orange juice with 3 tablespoons rum, almond extract, vanilla. Add alternately with flour to the butter mixture. Beat egg whites until foamy. Add remaining ¼ cup sugar and beat until stiff. Fold into batter. Divide batter between two prepared pans and bake for 25 minutes. Cool layers 5 minutes in pan, then invert on cake racks, peel off paper, and cool. Split each layer crosswise, making 4 thin layers. Mix remaining 5 tablespoons rum with water.

To assemble cake, sprinkle each layer with rum mixture, and spread whipped-cream filling (below) between layers. Spread chocolate frosting (below) over top and sides of cake. Pat walnuts on cake sides. Chill 24 hours before serving.

Filling: Soften gelatin in cold water. Dissolve over hot water. Beat cream in a chilled bowl until it begins to thicken. Add sugar and gradually blend in rum. Slowly pour in gelatin mixture, beating until just stiff enough to hold shape. Use immediately. (This can be made ahead of time and chilled. Mix very well when ready to use.)

Frosting: Beat melted chocolate and sugar together. Gradually add hot water. Beat in eggs, one at a time. Mix in soft butter, beating until smooth.

SERVES: 12.

Lane Cake

Cake:
1 cup butter
2 cups sugar
1 teaspoon vanilla
3¼ cups flour, sifted
3½ teaspoons baking powder
¼ teaspoon salt
1 cup milk
8 egg whites

Lane Filling:
8 egg yolks
1¼ cups sugar
1 teaspoon grated orange rind
½ cup butter
⅓ cup bourbon
1 cup pecans, chopped
¼ teaspoon salt
1 cup flaked coconut
1 cup raisins, finely chopped
1 cup candied cherries,
  quartered

Cake: Butter and flour 3 9-inch layer-cake pans. Preheat oven to 375°F. Cream the butter and gradually add sugar, beating until very light and fluffy. Beat in vanilla. Sift together flour, baking powder, and salt. Stir flour mixture alternately with the milk into the batter. Beat egg whites stiffly and fold in gently. Spoon into prepared pans and bake 20 to 25 minutes. Cool in pans for 10 minutes and then turn onto cake racks until completely cool. Spread Lane Filling (see below) between layers and on top of cake. Cover cake loosely and store in refrigerator for at least 24 hours before using.

Lane Filling: Put egg yolks in the top of a double boiler and beat slightly. Add sugar, butter, and orange rind. Cook over simmering water, stirring constantly until sugar dissolves, butter melts and mixture is slightly thickened. Do not allow water to boil or eggs may overcook. The mixture should be almost translucent. Stir in bourbon and remove from heat. Mix in remaining ingredients. Cool before using.

SERVES: 12.

Chocolate Rum Cake

Cake:
2 squares unsweetened
   chocolate
½ cup water
½ cup butter
1½ cups light-brown sugar,
   firmly packed
3 eggs
1¾ cups sifted cake flour
1½ teaspoons baking powder
½ teaspoon baking soda
¼ teaspoon salt
¼ cup Jamaica rum

Chocolate Rum Frosting:
1½ squares bitter chocolate
3 tablespoons semisweet
   chocolate bits
1 tablespoon butter
1 cup sifted confectioners'
   sugar
1 egg
2 tablespoons milk
2 tablespoons Jamaica rum

Cake: Grease 2 9-inch layer-cake pans. Line with waxed paper and grease again. Preheat oven to 350°F.

Melt chocolate in water over very low heat, stirring constantly. Cool. Cream butter until fluffy. Gradually beat in sugar. Beat in eggs, one at a time, beating well after each addition. Sift flour with baking powder, soda, and salt. Add flour and chocolate alternately to egg mixture, beating until smooth. Stir in rum.

Pour batter into prepared pans. Bake for 20 to 25 minutes. Cool 5 minutes. Turn out on racks and peel off paper. When cool, spread Chocolate Rum Frosting (below) between layers and on top of cake.

Chocolate Rum Frosting: Melt bitter chocolate, semisweet chocolate, and butter over hot water. In a bowl, mix sugar, egg, milk, and rum smoothly together. Stir in melted chocolate and butter mixture. Set bowl in a pan of cracked ice and beat until mixture is thick and fluffy and the color has lightened.
SERVES: 8 to 10.

Cherry-Topped Cheesecake

¾ cup graham-cracker
    crumbs
3 tablespoons melted butter
2 tablespoons sugar
1½ pounds creamed small-
    curd cottage cheese
½ pound cream cheese,
    softened
1 cup sugar

2 tablespoons flour
4 eggs
1 cup heavy cream
¼ teaspoon salt
1 teaspoon vanilla
1 can (16 ounces) prepared
    cherry-pie filling
2 tablespoons kirsch

Mix together graham-cracker crumbs, butter, and 2 tablespoons sugar. Pat evenly into the bottom of a 9-inch spring-form pan. Bake in oven preheated to 350°F. for 8 minutes.

Push the cottage cheese through a sieve or purée in a blender. Beat the cream cheese until light and fluffy. Add the puréed cottage cheese. Combine cup of sugar with flour and gradually beat into the cottage-cheese mixture. Add the eggs, one at a time, beating until smooth. Mix in the cream, salt, and vanilla. Turn into the prepared crumb crust and bake for 1 hour in oven preheated to 325°F. Remove from oven and cool. Refrigerate. At serving time, heat the cherry-pie filling with the kirsch. Spoon hot sauce over individual cheesecake portions.

SERVES: 12.

Double Nut Roll

Nut Roll:
7 eggs, separated
6 tablespoons sugar
¾ cup ground walnuts

Nut Filling:
1 scant cup milk

1½ cups ground walnuts
⅔ cup butter
⅔ cup sugar
2 tablespoons cognac
Granulated sugar
Whipped cream (optional)

Nut Roll: Grease a 15- x 10-inch jelly-roll pan. Line with waxed paper; grease again. Beat egg yolks until very thick and light. (This takes about 10 minutes with an electric beater.) Add sugar gradually and continue beating until mixture is very creamy. Beat egg whites until they hold stiff peaks. Stir about ¼ of the beaten egg whites into the yolks and then gently fold in remainder. Fold in ground walnuts. Pour into prepared pan and bake 30 to 35 minutes.

While the cake is baking, spread a tea towel on a cooling rack. Sprinkle with confectioners' sugar. When cake is removed from oven, invert pan over sugared towel and lift off pan. Gently peel off waxed paper. Roll the cake, starting with the short side, while it is still warm. Use towel to gently push the cake along as you roll. Cover cake with waxed paper and let cool. While cake is cooling, prepare filling.

Nut Filling: Heat milk to the boiling point. Pour over ground nuts and set aside to cool. Cream butter and gradually beat in sugar until light and fluffy. Stir in nut mixture and cognac. Mix thoroughly.

When cake is completely cool, unroll and spread filling evenly over it. Roll again and sprinkle with granulated sugar. Garnish each portion with whipped cream if desired.
SERVES: 8 to 10.

Irish-Coffee Cake

¾ cup water
⅓ cup sugar
1 teaspoon instant coffee
  powder
⅓ cup Irish whiskey
Sponge cake, 8-inch square
  loaf

¾ cup heavy cream
2 teaspoons semisweet
  chocolate bits, melted
1 tablespoon coffee-bean
  candies
1 tablespoon toasted blanched-
  almond slivers

Combine water and sugar and boil for 10 minutes. Stir in instant-coffee powder and Irish whiskey. Remove from fire and cool. Set cake on a large piece of aluminum foil. Drizzle syrup slowly over.

Wrap cake in foil and let stand for several hours until syrup is absorbed. Unwrap and slide onto a serving plate.

Whip heavy cream until stiff and stir in melted chocolate. Spread over top and sides of cake. Garnish with coffee-bean candies and toasted almonds.

SERVES: 6 to 8.

Cassata Siciliana

1½ pounds ricotta or cream-style cottage cheese
½ cup sugar
1 teaspoon vanilla extract
½ teaspoon almond extract
1 ounce semisweet chocolate, grated
½ cup toasted chopped almonds

4 tablespoons diced, mixed candied fruit
1 9-inch sponge cake
6 tablespoons full-bodied rum
3 tablespoons water
1½ cups heavy cream
2 tablespoons halved candied cherries

If you use cottage cheese, push through a sieve before mixing with other ingredients. Combine cheese, sugar, vanilla, and almond extract in a large bowl and beat until light and fluffy. Add the chocolate, almonds, and candied fruit. Mix rum with water. Cut the sponge cake into three layers. Place the bottom layer on a serving plate and sprinkle with 3 tablespoons of rum mixture. Spread with half the ricotta mixture. Cover with the second cake layer and sprinkle that with 3 tablespoons of rum mixture. Spread with remaining ricotta mixture. Top with the third cake layer and sprinkle that with the remainder of the rum mixture. Cover with plastic wrap and chill for several hours.

About an hour before serving, whip the cream and spread it over the top and sides of the cake. (You may whip with a little sugar if you like.) Garnish with the halved candied cherries.

SERVES: 8 to 10.

Yodeler's Torte

Torte:
6 tablespoons fine dry bread
   crumbs (approximately)
4 ounces semisweet chocolate
1⅔ cups whole almonds
1 tablespoon baking powder
½ cup butter
1 cup sugar
6 eggs, separated
2 tablespoons kirsch

Chocolate Glaze:
4 ounces semisweet chocolate
4 tablespoons water
2 tablespoons butter
1 teaspoon kirsch
4 tablespoons sifted
   confectioners' sugar

Torte: Preheat oven to 375°F. Grease an 8-inch spring-form pan. Line bottom of pan with waxed paper and grease again. Sprinkle sides and bottom with about a tablespoon of dry bread crumbs and shake off excess.

Grate or grind the chocolate and almonds very fine and mix with 5 tablespoons of dry bread crumbs and the baking powder. Cream the butter until very light and fluffy. Gradually beat in the sugar. Add unbeaten egg yolks one at a time and mix well after each addition. Add chocolate-almond mixture and mix well. Beat egg whites until they stand in soft peaks, and fold in. Spoon into prepared baking pan and bake 1 hour, or until a cake tester comes out clean. Cool cake and prepare Chocolate Glaze (see below).

When cake has cooled, remove sides of pan. Place the cake on a rack over a waxed-paper-lined tray. Quickly pour all the glaze over the cake at one time. Tip the cake back and forth so that glaze runs off the top and covers the sides. (Don't smooth with a spatula as this dulls the glaze and makes it less attractive.)

Chocolate Glaze: Combine chocolate, kirsch, and water, and place over medium heat until chocolate has melted. Remove from heat and stir in butter. Add the sugar and stir just until smooth. SERVES: 8.

Linzer Torte

1 cup unsalted butter
1 cup sugar
2 egg yolks
2 hard-cooked egg yolks,
  sieved
1 teaspoon grated lemon rind
1 tablespoon lemon juice

2 tablespoons apricot-flavored
  brandy
½ pound almonds, ground
2 cups sifted flour
1 teaspoon baking powder
1 cup apricot jam
Confectioners' sugar

Cream butter and gradually beat in sugar. Add egg yolks, one at a time, beating after each addition. Stir in sieved, hard-cooked egg yolks, lemon rind, lemon juice, and apricot-flavored brandy. Stir in almonds, flour, and baking powder. Work dough with hands until smooth. Divide dough in half and put 1 portion in refrigerator to chill. Press other half of the dough on the bottom and sides of a shallow 9-inch spring-form pan. Have dough thicker on the bottom than on the sides. Spread with ¾ cup apricot jam. Roll or pat remaining dough to a thickness of ⅜ inch. Cut into ½-inch strips and arrange in a crisscross pattern over jam-covered dough. Bake in oven preheated to 350°F. for 45 to 50 minutes or until pale-gold color. Cool and then remove sides of pan. Before serving, fill spaces between strips with remaining ¼ cup jam. Dust with confectioners' sugar.
SERVES: 8.

Sweet Breads

Pain d'Épice

A spicy loaf which is a French holiday favorite. Store several days before using.

1¼ cups honey
1 teaspoon baking soda
1 cup boiling water (approx.)
2 tablespoons anisette
2 tablespoons rum
¾ cup sugar

1½ teaspoons salt
1 teaspoon baking powder
1½ teaspoons cinnamon
3 cups sifted flour
Whole blanched almonds

Butter a 9 x 5 loaf pan, line with waxed paper, and butter the paper. Preheat oven to 350°F. Pour honey into a large mixing bowl. Put baking soda into a half-cup measure and add boiling water to fill. Add to honey along with another half-cup boiling water, anisette, and rum. Stir in sugar, salt, baking powder, cinnamon, and flour. Mix well. Pour batter into prepared pan and decorate top with whole blanched almonds. Bake for 1½ hours, or until a cake tester comes out clean. Let stand in pan for about 5 minutes and then invert on cake rack. Cool, remove paper, and wrap in foil.

Martini Raisin Loaf

½ cup raisins	¾ cup sugar
2 tablespoons gin	3 eggs, well beaten
1 envelope active dry yeast	½ cup lukewarm milk
¼ cup lukewarm water	¼ teaspoon grated lemon rind
3½ cups flour (approx.)	1 teaspoon dry vermouth
1 teaspoon salt	¼ cup soft butter

Stir 1 tablespoon gin into raisins and set aside. Dissolve the yeast in the lukewarm water. Sift flour and salt into a large mixing bowl. Beat together sugar, eggs, milk, 1 tablespoon gin, lemon rind, and vermouth. Add to the flour mixture.

Add yeast mixture to batter and beat until the batter is smooth and elastic. This batter is too soft for kneading, but it can be worked in the bowl with floured hands or with a wooden spoon. If it seems too soft, add a little more flour. Beat in the butter and the raisins.

Place the dough in a greased bowl, cover with a damp towel and set in a warm place to rise until double in bulk. Stir down the dough. Turn into a greased 9- x 5- x 3-inch loaf pan. Cover and let rise in a warm place until doubled in bulk.

Preheat oven to 350°F. Bake 45 minutes. Cool on a rack.

Sugar Nuts

½ cup warm milk (105° to
  115°F.)
1 envelope active dry yeast
2 tablespoons sugar
⅛ teaspoon salt
2 eggs, beaten
1 tablespoon butter, melted

1½ cups sifted flour
2 tablespoons raisins
2 tablespoons chopped citron
1 tablespoon Jamaica rum
Oil for frying
Confectioners' sugar

Place warm milk in bowl, add yeast and sugar; stir to dissolve. Let stand several minutes. Add salt, melted butter, eggs, and flour. Stir until well blended. Add the fruit and rum. Cover and let rise in warm place until doubled. Heat oil, at least 2 inches deep, in heavy pan to 375°F. Drop batter from a tablespoon into the hot fat and fry until golden, turning once. Remove with slotted spoon; drain on absorbent paper. While warm, shake doughnuts in a paper bag with confectioners' sugar to cover completely.
YIELD: 12 to 15.

Sticky Wickets

½ cup warm water (105° to
  115°F.)
2 packages active dry yeast
½ cup sugar
¾ cup milk
2 teaspoons salt
½ cup butter
2 eggs, beaten
4½ cups unsifted flour

Soft butter

Glaze and Filling:
1 cup bourbon
1¾ cups light-brown sugar,
  packed
1 cup pecan halves
¼ cup soft butter
2 teaspoons cinnamon

Pour warm water into a large warm bowl. Sprinkle yeast over water. Add sugar and stir to dissolve. Heat milk just until bubbles form. Stir in salt and butter. Cool to lukewarm. Add to yeast mixture along with eggs and 2 cups flour; beat until smooth, about 2 minutes.

Gradually add remainder of flour, beating until dough is stiff, smooth, and leaves sides of bowl. Turn into a large greased bowl. Brush with soft butter. Cover the bowl with foil; refrigerate for 2 hours. Dough will rise to the top of the bowl.

Glaze and Filling: Preheat oven to 350°F. Grease muffin tins or custard cups for 24 buns. Put into each 1½ teaspoons bourbon, 2 teaspoons brown sugar, and 3 or 4 pecan halves. Roll the dough out on a floured board to a 12- x 24-inch rectangle. Combine remaining bourbon, sugar, butter, and cinnamon to make a paste and spread on dough. Roll up and cut across roll into 24 slices. Place each slice into prepared muffin cups, cover with towel, and set in warm place to rise until double in bulk.

Bake 15 to 20 minutes until browned. Cool on rack 5 minutes before unmolding. Serve warm.

Savarin

½ cup warm water (105° to 115°F.)
1 package active dry yeast
2 tablespoons sugar
½ teaspoon salt
3 eggs
2 cups sifted flour
6 tablespoons soft butter
¼ cup grated orange peel
2 tablespoons currants

Syrup:
2 cups sugar
1 tablespoon grated orange peel
1 cup water
⅓ cup Calvados

Glaze:
½ cup apricot preserves
2 tablespoons orange liqueur

Grease a 1½-quart ring mold. Pour warm water into large warmed bowl. Sprinkle yeast over water. Add sugar and stir until dissolved. Let stand several minutes. Add the salt, eggs, and 1½ cups flour. Beat until smooth. Add butter. Beat until well blended. Beat in rest of flour until smooth. Batter will be thick. Stir in orange peel and currants, mixing well. Turn batter into prepared mold, spreading evenly. Cover with towel; let rise in a warm place, free from drafts, 1 hour, or until savarin has risen to rim of pan, more than double in bulk. Bake in oven preheated to 400°F. for 25 minutes, or until top is golden brown. Cool in pan 5 minutes. Loosen edges and turn out of pan. Cool 5 minutes. Return to pan.

Syrup: While cake is baking, combine sugar, orange peel, and water in a small saucepan. Bring to a boil, then simmer over medium heat for 6 minutes. Add Calvados and remove from heat. Strain before using.

After cake is returned to pan, poke holes in it at 1-inch intervals, using a fork or a thin skewer. Gradually pour some of the hot syrup over the cake. Wait for it to be absorbed and add more, until all the syrup has been used. This will take about an hour.

Glaze: Melt apricot preserves in a small saucepan over low heat. Remove from heat. Stir in orange liqueur. Let stand at room temperature. At serving time, invert savarin onto a round serving platter. Brush top and sides with glaze.

Center of ring may be filled with sweetened whipped cream if desired.

SERVES: 8 to 10.

Baba au Rhum

½ cup warm water (105° to 115°F.)
1 package active dry yeast
2 tablespoons sugar
½ teaspoon salt
3 eggs, beaten
½ cup soft butter
¼ cup Gold Label rum
1¾ cups sifted flour

½ cup chopped candied fruit

Syrup:
1½ cups water
1½ cups sugar
½ lemon, sliced
1 slice orange
¾ cup Gold Label or Jamaica rum

Pour warm water and sugar into a warmed bowl. Sprinkle yeast over. Stir until dissolved. Let stand several minutes. Add salt, eggs, butter, and rum. Mix well. Stir in flour and beat for 1 minute. Stir in candied fruit. Cover and let rise in a warm place until double. Grease 24 small muffin tins. Stir down dough and spoon into pans, filling about ⅔ full. Let rise until batter pokes over rim. Bake in oven preheated to 350°F. for 10 minutes.

Syrup: Bring water, sugar, sliced lemon, and orange to a boil. Simmer 5 minutes. Add rum and remove from fire. Strain.

Let babas cool in pan for about 10 minutes. Remove from pan and arrange on a shallow dish. Pour syrup slowly over. Baste with syrup in dish until each baba has absorbed as much syrup as possible.

YIELD: 24.

Stollen

½ cup chopped candied citron
½ cup chopped candied orange peel
1½ cups seedless raisins
¾ cup blanched almonds, chopped
¼ cup brandy
½ cup warm water (105° to 115°F.)
2 packages active dry yeast

¾ cup warm water
1 teaspoon grated lemon rind
4½ cups sifted flour (approx.)
¼ cup butter
½ cup sugar
¼ teaspoon salt
2 eggs, lightly beaten
½ cup melted butter (approx.)
Confectioners' sugar

Combine citron, orange peel, raisins, and almonds. Stir in brandy. Pour warm water into a warmed bowl. Sprinkle yeast over. Stir until dissolved. Stir in milk, lemon rind and 1½ cups flour. Beat until smooth. Cover with a towel. Let rise in a warm place about 45 minutes, or until double in bulk. While dough is rising, cream butter with sugar and salt. Add creamed butter mixture, beaten eggs, and 3 cups flour to raised yeast mixture. Beat until smooth.

Turn dough onto a lightly floured board. Knead until dough is smooth and elastic, adding only enough additional flour to keep dough from sticking to board and hands. Sprinkle fruit-nut mixture, about ½ cup at a time, on the dough and knead in. Continue to add and knead until the fruit-nut mixture is all used. Place dough in a large, buttered bowl. Brush top of the dough with a little melted butter. Cover with a towel and let rise in a warm place about 2 hours, or until double in bulk. Punch down dough.

Turn onto the board again and work it for a minute or two. Let stand for 10 minutes. Divide dough into 2 parts and roll each into an oval shape. With the rolling pin, make a deep indentation a little to the right of center on each oval. Brush the indentations with melted butter and fold each oval over along the indentation. Press the edges together lightly.

Place the loaves on a buttered baking sheet. Brush them with melted butter and let stand in a warm place about 45 minutes or until double in bulk. Preheat oven to 350°F. Bake loaves 35 to 40 minutes, or until golden brown. Cool on cake racks. Sift confectioners' sugar generously over tops.

Swiss Pear Loaves

1 cup chopped dried pears
½ cup golden raisins
½ cup chopped blanched
   almonds
¼ cup chopped citron
1 teaspoon grated lemon rind
½ teaspoon cinnamon
½ teaspoon cloves
½ teaspoon nutmeg
¼ cup pear brandy

¼ cup butter
¾ cup milk
½ cup sugar
2 teaspoons salt
1 egg, well beaten
½ cup warm water (105°
   to 115°F.)
2 packages active dry yeast
5½ cups flour (approx.)
Confectioners' sugar

Combine dried pears, raisins, almonds, citron, lemon rind, spices, and pear brandy. Let stand overnight.

Warm butter and milk. Stir until butter melts. Add sugar, salt, and egg. Cool. Pour warm water into a warmed bowl, add yeast, and dissolve. Stir into milk mixture. Add enough flour to make a dough that is soft but not sticky. Knead on lightly floured board. Cover and let rise in a warm place until doubled in bulk. Punch it down and knead for about 3 minutes. Sprinkle fruit-nut mixture, about ½ cup at a time, on the dough and knead in. Continue to add and knead until the fruit-nut mixture is all used. Mold the dough into 2 loaves and put in greased 9- x 5-inch loaf pans. Let loaves rise until doubled in bulk.

Preheat oven to 350°F. Bake 50 minutes, or until golden brown. Turn breads out on a rack to cool. Sift confectioners' sugar over before serving.

Pies

Plain Pastry

2 cups sifted flour
1 teaspoon salt
⅔ cup shortening

5 tablespoons cold water (approx.)

Sift flour and salt together into a bowl. Cut shortening into flour with a pastry blender or 2 knives, scissors fashion, until size of small peas. Sprinkle water, a tablespoon at a time, over different parts of mixture, while tossing quickly with a fork, until all particles cling together when pressed gently. Form pastry into a ball and chill for 10 minutes before rolling out. For a baked pie shell, make half the recipe; line an 8- or 9-inch pie pan with the pastry. Prick all over with a fork and bake in oven preheated to 450°F. for about 12 minutes or until golden.

YIELD: Pastry for one 8- or 9-inch double-crust pie or two 8- or 9-inch pie shells.

Baked Crumb Shell

1½ cups crumbs—any of following: graham crackers, chocolate wafers, gingersnaps, zwieback, corn flakes, vanilla wafers

2 to 4 tablespoons sugar
¼ cup butter

Combine crumbs and sugar. (The amount of sugar used depends on the sweetness of the crumbs.) Mix with butter until mixture is crumbly. Press onto bottom and sides of a 9-inch pie pan, forming a small rim. Bake for 8 minutes in oven preheated to 375°F. Cool before filling.

YIELD: 9-inch pie shell.

Brandied Butter Pastry

2 cups sifted flour
½ teaspoon salt

¾ cup firm butter
3 to 5 tablespoons cold brandy

Sift together flour and salt. Cut in butter with pastry blender or two knives, scissors fashion, until mixture is crumbly. Gradually add brandy, sprinkling over different parts of mixture, until all particles cling together when pressed gently. Form pastry into a ball and chill for 10 minutes before rolling out. For a baked pie shell, make half the recipe. Line an 8- or 9-inch pan with pastry and prick all over with a fork. Bake in oven preheated to 425°F. for about 12 minutes or until golden.

YIELD: Pastry for one 8- or 9-inch double-crust pie or two 8- or 9-inch pie shells.

Rum and Butter Crust

1 package (5½ ounces)
   tea biscuits
¼ cup butter

½ cup sifted confectioners'
   sugar
4 teaspoons light rum

Crush tea biscuits to crumbs. One package yields 2 scant cups. Melt butter in a large skillet over low heat. Add biscuit crumbs and stir around for about 5 minutes, until lightly toasted. Remove from heat and let cool. Add confectioners' sugar and mix well. Stir in rum. Press the mixture on the bottom and sides of a 9-inch pie pan. Do not make a rim! Chill.

YIELD: 9-inch pie shell.

Bourbon Cookie-Dough Crust

1¼ cups sifted flour
1 tablespoon sugar
½ teaspoon salt

½ cup butter
1 egg yolk
2 tablespoons bourbon

Sift together flour, sugar, and salt. Blend in the butter. Stir in egg yolk and bourbon. Do not overmix. Press dough on bottom and sides of a 9-inch pie pan. For a baked pie shell, prick pastry all over and bake in oven preheated to 425°F. for about 12 minutes or until golden.
YIELD: 9-inch pie shell.

Glazed Apple Tart

9-inch Bourbon Cookie-
  Dough Crust (above)
9 large cooking apples
1 teaspoon lemon juice
⅔ cup sugar

¼ cup water
⅔ cup apricot preserves
⅓ cup Calvados
2 tablespoons butter

Bake pastry in oven preheated to 425°F. for 6 minutes, or until very lightly browned. Cool.

Peel, core, and slice 3 apples thinly. Mix with lemon juice and 2 tablespoons of the sugar. Set aside. Peel, core, and slice remaining apples. Turn into saucepan with water and cook, covered, over low heat until tender, about 20 minutes. Stir occasionally. Add remaining sugar, ⅓ cup apricot preserves, ¼ cup Calvados, and butter. Bring to a boil and cook, stirring constantly, until very thick. Let cool slightly.

Spoon apple mixture into partially baked pastry shell. Cover with an overlapping layer of the sugared apple slices. Bake in oven pre-heated to 375°F. for about a half hour, or until the sliced apples are tender and lightly browned. While pie is baking, bring remaining apricot preserves to a boil. Stir in remaining Calvados and simmer for about 3 minutes. Press through a sieve. When tart is removed from oven, spoon or brush apricot glaze over.
SERVES: 8.

Brandied Deep-Dish Apple Pie

8 large, tart apples
¼ cup butter
1 cup sugar

½ cup orange juice
Grated rind of 1 orange
Brandied Butter Pastry,
   half recipe (page 194)
¼ cup brandy

Peel and slice apples into a baking dish, about 2 inches deep. Melt butter and combine with sugar, orange juice, and orange rind. Pour over apples and stir in. Roll pastry to fit *over* top of dish. Cut 2 or 3 holes in the dough, then lay over the apples, pressing crust down at edges. Bake 10 minutes in oven preheated to 450°F. Reduce heat to 325°F. and bake until apples are tender, about 35 to 40 minutes. Remove from oven and insert a small funnel in one of the holes in the crust. Pour in brandy. Tilt pie back and forth to distribute brandy all through. Serve warm.
SERVES: 8.

Apricot Tart

1 package (11 ounces)
   dried apricots
2 cups water
1 teaspoon lemon juice
¾ cup sugar

2 tablespoons bourbon
Bourbon Cookie-Dough Crust,
   double recipe (page 195)
1 large can apricot halves,
   drained

Combine apricots, water, and lemon juice. Bring to a boil. Reduce heat and simmer 20 minutes or until almost tender. Add sugar and simmer 5 minutes longer. Add bourbon. Purée in a blender or press through a sieve. Let cool. Roll out two-thirds of pastry and fit into a 9-inch pie pan. Flute the crust. Spoon in puréed apricots. Arrange the apricot halves, cut side down, over the purée. Roll out remaining

pastry and cut into half-inch strips. Arrange lattice fashion over the pie. Bake in oven preheated to 350°F. for 50 minutes.
SERVES: 8 to 10.

Banana Rum Cream Pie

½ cup sugar	1 tablespoon Jamaica rum
5 tablespoons flour	9-inch Rum and Butter
¼ teaspoon salt	Crust (page 194)
2 cups milk	2 large, ripe bananas
3 egg yolks, lightly beaten	½ cup heavy cream, whipped
1 tablespoon butter	and sweetened to taste

Combine sugar, flour, and salt in a heavy saucepan. Gradually add the milk, stirring with a wire whisk. When blended, cook over low heat until mixture thickens. Continue cooking, stirring often, 15 minutes. Remove from heat. Stir a little of the hot mixture into the beaten egg yolks, then pour into sauce, stirring constantly. Return just to a boil and remove from heat. Stir in butter and cool slightly. Add rum.

Pour custard mixture into Rum and Butter Crust and chill. Slice bananas and arrange over custard. Garnish with whipped cream.
SERVES: 8.

Almond and Prune Tart

2 cups blanched almonds	2 tablespoons cornstarch
1½ cups pitted prunes,	3 eggs
chopped	⅓ cup cream
½ cup butter	¼ teaspoon salt
⅔ cup sugar	½ teaspoon almond extract
1 teaspoon grated lemon rind	9-inch baked pie shell
2 tablespoons lemon juice	(page 193)
⅓ cup Armagnac	

Grind or grate almonds (may be whirled in a blender). Reserve. Combine prunes, 1 tablespoon of butter, 2 tablespoons sugar, lemon peel, lemon juice, and Armagnac in a small saucepan. Simmer, stirring, until liquid is absorbed. Let cool.

Cream remaining butter with remaining sugar until fluffy. Blend in cornstarch, eggs, one at a time, cream, salt, almond extract, grated almonds, and prune mixture. Pour mixture into prepared pie shell. Bake in oven preheated to 350°F. for 35 minutes. Cool at least 15 minutes before cutting.

SERVES: 8.

Mandarin-Orange Chiffon Pie

1 can (11 ounces) mandarin
   oranges
1 envelope unflavored gelatin
½ cup water
4 eggs, separated
½ cup sugar
2 tablespoons grated orange
   rind

¼ cup mandarino liqueur
¼ cup frozen orange-juice
   concentrate, thawed
⅛ teaspoon salt
9-inch Rum and Butter Crust
   (page 194)

Drain can of mandarin oranges and reserve ¼ cup syrup. Reserve 8 mandarin-orange sections for garnish. Cut rest of orange sections in half. Sprinkle gelatin over water. Let soften for 5 minutes. In the top of a double boiler, combine egg yolks, ¼ cup sugar, orange rind. Add gelatin. Cook, stirring, over hot water until thickened. Remove from heat and stir in reserved ¼ cup syrup, mandarino, and orange-juice concentrate. Refrigerate until mixture thickens a bit. Beat 4 egg whites with salt until foamy. Gradually add remaining ¼ cup sugar and beat until stiff. Stir about one-quarter of the beaten egg whites into gelatin mixture. Stir in halved mandarin-orange sections. Fold in remainder of egg whites. Pour into prepared Rum and Butter Crust. Garnish with whole mandarin-orange sections. Chill until set.

SERVES: 8.

Cherry Pie

2 cans (1 pound 4 ounces)
  pitted red sour cherries
1 cup sugar
⅛ teaspoon salt
2 tablespoons kirsch
1 tablespoon cornstarch

¼ teaspoon almond extract
Few drops red food coloring
  (optional)
Plain pastry (page 193)
1 tablespoon butter, in bits

Drain cherries and reserve the juice. Combine drained cherries with sugar, salt, and kirsch, and let stand for about an hour. Drain liquid from sugared cherries and add enough of the reserved juice from the cans to make ¾ cup. Combine this liquid with cornstarch and bring to a boil, stirring constantly. Simmer 2 or 3 minutes until thickened and clear. Remove from heat; add cherries, almond extract, and red food coloring. Stir gently.

Preheat oven to 425°F. Line a 9-inch pie pan with half of Plain Pastry. Pile cherry mixture into prepared pie pan. Dot with butter and cover with remaining pastry. Make several slits in top crust, near center. Bake 55 minutes.
SERVES: 8.

Peach Crumb Pie

1 package (11 ounces)
  dried peaches
4 cups water
Brandied Butter Pastry, half
  recipe (page 194)
½ cup brown sugar, firmly
  packed
¼ cup butter

⅓ cup sifted flour
½ teaspoon cinnamon
1 tablespoon cornstarch
½ cup sugar
Pinch salt
2 tablespoons Southern
  Comfort liqueur
1 tablespoon butter

Bring peaches and water to a boil. Reduce heat and simmer about 45 minutes or until peaches are tender. Remove from heat and drain, reserving ½ cup of the cooking liquid. Line 9-inch pie pan with Brandied Butter Pastry. With a fork, blend together brown sugar, butter, flour, and ½ teaspoon cinnamon until crumbly. Set aside.

Heat reserved ½ cup of peach liquid. Combine cornstarch, sugar, salt and ¼ teaspoon cinnamon. Stir into hot peach juice. Add liqueur. Boil, stirring, until thick and clear. Remove from heat and stir in 1 tablespoon of butter.

Preheat oven to 425°F. Arrange drained peaches in pastry-lined pan. Pour over cooked peach syrup. Top with prepared crumb mixture. Bake for 40 minutes.
SERVES: 8.

London Dock Pecan Pie

Brandied Butter Pastry,
  half recipe (page 194)
½ cup butter
½ cup sugar
¾ cup white corn syrup
¼ cup maple-flavored syrup

3 eggs, lightly beaten
2 tablespoons Jamaica rum
¾ cup coarsely chopped
  pecans
¾ cup pecan halves

Line a 9-inch pie pan with Brandied Butter Pastry. Heat oven to 350°F. Cream butter with sugar until light and fluffy. Slowly stir in corn syrup, maple-flavored syrup, eggs, rum, and coarsely chopped pecans. Pour into pie shell. Top with pecan halves. Bake 55 minutes.
SERVES: 8 to 10.

Pumpkin Pie

1½ cups canned pumpkin
1 cup brown sugar, firmly
  packed
2 tablespoons molasses
½ teaspoon cinnamon
½ teaspoon ginger
¼ teaspoon nutmeg
¼ teaspoon powdered cloves

½ teaspoon salt
3 eggs, lighly beaten
1½ cups half-and-half
  (milk and cream)
¼ cup rye whiskey
9-inch unbaked pastry shell
  (page 193)

Preheat oven to 425°F. Combine pumpkin, brown sugar, molasses, spices, and salt. Mix eggs, half-and-half, and whiskey. Stir into pumpkin mixture. Pour mixture into pastry shell. Bake 15 minutes. Reduce heat to 350°F. Bake 35 to 40 minutes longer or until set. SERVES: 8.

Brandied Mince Pie

Plain Pastry (page 193)
2 cups prepared mincemeat
½ cup chopped walnuts

½ cup peeled, diced apple
½ cup orange marmalade
¼ cup brandy

Preheat oven to 425°F. Line a 9-inch pie pan with half of pastry. Combine mincemeat, walnuts, apple, orange marmalade, and brandy. Turn into prepared pan. Cover pie with remaining pastry and cut slits in several places. Bake for 30 to 35 minutes, until crust is golden brown. Serve warm. SERVES: 8.

Plantation Pie

1½ cups mashed, cooked
  sweet potatoes
½ cup sugar
1 teaspoon cinnamon
¼ teaspoon ginger
¼ teaspoon nutmeg
½ teaspoon salt

2 eggs, lightly beaten
½ cup milk
2 tablespoons melted butter
¼ cup bourbon whiskey
8-inch unbaked pastry shell
  (page 193)

Preheat oven to 400°F. Combine sweet potatoes, sugar, spices, and salt. Combine eggs, milk, melted butter, and bourbon. Stir into potato mixture. Pour into pastry shell. Bake about 40 minutes or until set. SERVES: 6.

Black Bottom Pie

1 envelope unflavored gelatin
1 cup sugar
2 cups milk
3 eggs, separated
1 tablespoon cornstarch
⅛ teaspoon salt
1 teaspoon vanilla
½ cup heavy cream, whipped

2 squares unsweetened
  chocolate, melted
2 tablespoons Jamaica rum
2 tablespoons grated
  semisweet chocolate
9-inch Baked Crumb Shell
  (page 193)

Combine gelatin and ½ cup of sugar in the top of a double boiler. Gradually stir in the milk and set over boiling water until the milk is scalded. Beat egg yolks with cornstarch, salt, and vanilla until light. Slowly stir in about a half cup of scalded milk. Stir egg mixture into remainder of milk in the top of a double boiler. Cook, stirring until thickened. Chill until it starts to set.

Beat egg whites until foamy. Gradually beat in remaining half cup sugar until whites are stiff. Beat chilled custard until fluffy. Fold in egg whites and whipped cream. Divide mixture in half. Fold melted chocolate into one half. Stir rum into other half. Turn chocolate mixture into pie shell. Chill 5 minutes. Top with rum mixture. Sprinkle with grated chocolate. Chill until firm.
SERVES: 8.

Eggnog Pie

1 envelope unflavored gelatin
¾ cup cold milk
3 eggs, separated
½ cup sugar
½ cup heavy cream
⅛ teaspoon salt

¼ teaspoon nutmeg
⅓ cup bourbon
½ cup seedless raisins
1 9-inch Baked Crumb Shell
  (page 193)

Soften gelatin in ¼ cup cold milk. Beat egg yolks slightly in top of double boiler; stir in ¼ cup sugar, ½ cup cream, ½ cup milk, salt, and nutmeg, and cook over hot (not boiling) water, stirring constantly, until mixture thickens and coats spoon. Remove from heat. Add softened gelatin and stir until dissolved. Cool thoroughly. Stir in bourbon. Chill until slightly thickened. Beat egg whites until foamy. Gradually beat in remaining ¼ cup sugar, until whites are stiff. Fold egg whites and raisins into bourbon mixture. Turn into pie shell. Sprinkle with additional nutmeg if desired. Chill until firm. SERVES: 8.

Angel Pie

4 eggs, separated
1½ cups sugar
¼ teaspoon cream of tartar
1 envelope gelatin
¼ cup water

¼ cup cognac
1½ cups heavy cream
2 tablespoons shaved bitter
 chocolate

Preheat oven to 275°F. Butter a 9-inch pie pan. Sift 1 cup of sugar with cream of tartar. Beat egg whites until stiff but not dry. Gradually beat in sugar–cream of tartar mixture until whites are very stiff and glossy. Spread over bottom and sides of pie pan, just to rim. Bake for 1 hour, until crisp and very lightly brown. Cool.

 Beat egg yolks until thick and lemon-colored. Gradually beat in ½ cup of sugar. Soften gelatin in the water and add 2 tablespoons of cognac. Heat over boiling water until gelatin dissolves. Pour gelatin mixture into the yolks, stirring well. Stir in remaining cognac. Whip 1 cup of the cream and fold in. Pour the filling into the meringue crust and chill. Whip remaining cream and spread over pie. Decorate with chocolate curls.
SERVES: 8.

Nesselrode Pie

1 envelope unflavored gelatin
1½ cups milk
3 eggs, separated
2 tablespoons Gold Label rum
1 teaspoon vanilla
Dash salt
1 cup macaroon crumbs

2 tablespoons finely chopped
 candied chestnuts
½ cup chopped raisins
½ cup chopped candied
 mixed fruit
⅓ cup sugar
9-inch pastry shell (page 193)
Shaved semisweet chocolate

Soften gelatin in the milk in the top of a double boiler. Beat in egg yolks and heat over hot water, stirring, until mixture coats a metal spoon, about 10 minutes. Stir in rum, vanilla, and salt. Chill until partially thickened. Stir in macaroon crumbs, chestnuts, raisins, and candied fruit. Beat egg whites until foamy. Gradually beat in sugar until whites are stiff. Fold into custard mixture and pour into pastry shell. Chill until set. Decorate with chocolate curls.
SERVES: 8.

Daiquiri Pie

2 eggs, separated
½ cup lime juice
1 teaspoon grated lime rind
2 tablespoons light rum

1 can (15 ounces) sweetened
  condensed milk
¼ cup sugar
9-inch Rum and Butter Crust
  (page 194)

Beat egg yolks until thick and lemon-colored. Add lime juice, lime rind, and rum. Beat in sweetened condensed milk. Beat egg whites until foamy. Gradually beat in sugar until whites are stiff. Fold into lime mixture and pour into prepared pie shell. Bake in oven pre-heated to 325°F. for 10 minutes. Cool and then chill.
SERVES: 8.

Cookies

Pecan-Bourbon Balls

2½ cups vanilla wafer crumbs
  (about 5 dozen)
1½ cups sifted confectioners'
  sugar

2 tablespoons cocoa
1 cup finely chopped pecans
3 tablespoons dark corn syrup
⅓ cup bourbon

Combine crumbs, 1 cup confectioners' sugar, cocoa, pecans, corn syrup, and bourbon. Mix thoroughly. Form into small balls and roll

in remaining ½ cup of confectioners' sugar. Store in a tightly covered container for several days to ripen before using.
YIELD: About 3½ dozen.

Irish Snap

¼ pound salt butter, at room temperature
½ cup sugar

¼ cup Irish whiskey
1 cup sifted flour
¼ teaspoon ground nutmeg

Cream butter with sugar until light and fluffy. Add whiskey alternately with flour. Sprinkle nutmeg over. Mix thoroughly. Chill for at least 1 hour. Preheat oven to 375°F. Drop very small amounts off the tip of a teaspoon, about 2 inches apart, on an ungreased cookie sheet. Bake for 5 minutes, or until edges are golden. Cool slightly on cookie sheet. Lift cookies off carefully with a spatula, and place on cake rack to cool.
YIELD: About 4 dozen.

Scotch Scrolls

1¼ cups sifted cake flour
¼ teaspoon salt
⅔ cup sugar
1 teaspoon cinnamon

1 teaspoon ginger
½ cup molasses
½ cup butter
3 tablespoons Scotch whisky

Preheat oven to 300°F. Sift flour with salt, sugar, cinnamon, and ginger. Heat molasses to boiling. Remove from heat and add butter. Stir until butter is melted. Add sifted dry ingredients gradually, stirring constantly. Stir in Scotch. Drop by half-measuring teaspoonfuls, 3 inches apart, on greased cookie sheets. Bake, 6 cookies at a time, for 8 to 10 minutes. Cool for about 1 minute. Remove with spatula and roll at once around the handle of a wooden spoon. If cookies should become too hard to remove easily or to roll, return to oven for half a minute.
YIELD: About 6 dozen.

Whiskey Chews

3 squares unsweetened chocolate	1 tablespoon slivered candied ginger
4 tablespoons butter	1 cup sugar
1½ cups sifted flour	1 egg
1½ teaspoons baking powder	½ cup bourbon whiskey
½ teaspoon salt	¼ cup sesame seeds

Melt chocolate and butter over hot water and then cool to lukewarm. Grease cookie sheets. Cover with waxed paper and grease again. Preheat oven to 375°F. Sift flour, salt, and baking powder into a mixing bowl and stir in the slivered ginger. Stir sugar into cooled chocolate-butter mixture, beat in egg, and then stir in whiskey. Stir this mixture into the dry ingredients. Blend well.

Take a teaspoonful of cookie dough. Hold over a dish and sprinkle with sesame seeds. (Excess seeds will fall into the dish and can be used again.) Slip cookie gently off the spoon onto prepared baking sheet. Repeat, placing cookies about 2 inches apart on the baking sheet. Bake ten minutes. Cookies should be slightly moist in the center and chewy.

YIELD: About 5 dozen.

Rum Dums

3 cups seedless raisins	½ cup brown sugar, firmly packed
½ cup Gold Label rum	2 eggs
1½ cups sifted flour	2 cups coarsely chopped walnuts
1½ teaspoons baking soda	
1½ teaspoons cinnamon	½ pound chopped candied mixed fruit
½ teaspoon nutmeg	1 pound whole candied cherries
½ teaspoon ginger	
¼ cup butter	

Put raisins in a bowl and pour rum over. Mix well and let stand at least 1 hour. Preheat oven to 325°F. Sift together flour, baking soda, and spices. Cream butter until soft. Add sugar and beat until light and fluffy. Beat in eggs, one at a time. Add flour mixture and blend. Stir in raisins, nuts, candied fruit, and cherries. Drop from teaspoon onto greased cookie sheets. Bake for about 15 minutes or until firm. Cool on wire racks.
YIELD: About 8 dozen.

Cognac Nut Balls

1 cup sifted flour	2 tablespoons cognac
3 tablespoons sugar	1 cup very finely chopped
¼ teaspoon salt	walnuts
½ cup sweet butter	Confectioners' sugar

Sift flour, sugar, and salt into a bowl. Blend in butter with spoon (or fingers) until all ingredients are combined. Add cognac and walnuts, and mix well. Chill dough for a half-hour.

Preheat oven to 325°F. Shape dough into ½-inch balls and place on *ungreased* cookie sheets. Bake for 20 to 25 minutes, or until pale brown. While cookies are baking, sift confectioners' sugar onto a sheet of waxed paper. Remove baked cookies very carefully with spatula and place on the confectioners' sugar. Sift additional sugar over. Cool cookies on wire rack. Work carefully as cookies are very fragile at this point. After cookies have cooled, roll in additional confectioners' sugar. An easy way to do this is to shake gently 4 or 5 cookies at a time in a plastic bag containing confectioners' sugar.

Mellow for 24 hours before eating! You'll find that these cookies continue to mellow and improve on standing.
YIELD: About 3 dozen.

Kourabiedes

1 pound sweet butter	3 tablespoons Metaxa
1¾ cups sifted confectioners' sugar	4½ cups sifted flour
1 egg yolk	Whole cloves

Cream butter until light. Gradually add ¾ cup confectioners' sugar and continue beating until well combined. Add egg yolk and Metaxa, and beat well. Add flour gradually and beat until well blended. Chill for about 1 hour.

Preheat oven to 350°F. With floured hands, shape pieces of the dough into balls about 1½ inches in diameter. Put them on un-greased baking sheets and stick a whole clove in the top of each. Bake for 15 minutes. Let them cool on the baking sheet for several minutes and then carefully transfer to a wire rack. While cookies are still warm, very gently shake 4 or 5 cookies at a time in a plastic bag containing remaining confectioners' sugar.
YIELD: 5 dozen.

Sugar Snaps

2 cups sifted flour	½ cup soft butter
1 cup sugar	1 egg
¼ teaspoon salt	2 tablespoons Jamaica rum
½ teaspoon baking powder	½ teaspoon vanilla

Sift flour, sugar, salt, and baking powder. Add butter and mix in with a pastry blender or 2 knives, scissors fashion, as for pie crust, until mixture forms coarse crumbs. Blend in egg and rum. Add vanilla and knead until dough holds together. Form into a ball and refrigerate, covered, for about 2 hours.

Preheat oven to 400°F. Divide dough into thirds. Roll out each third between two sheets of waxed paper until ⅛ inch thick. Cut and place about 2 inches apart on lightly buttered cookie sheets.

Use several cookie cutters to get a variety of shapes. Bake 5 to 7 minutes.
YIELD: About 6 dozen.

Mocha Crisps

1 cup butter	¼ teaspoon cinnamon
1 cup sugar	2 tablespoons coffee liqueur
1 egg yolk	2½ cups flour
1 tablespoon grated semisweet chocolate	½ teaspoon baking powder
¼ teaspoon salt	Finely chopped almonds

Cream butter until soft and gradually beat in sugar until light and fluffy. Beat in egg yolk, grated chocolate, salt, and cinnamon. Add coffee liqueur, flour, and baking powder. Mix until dough holds together. Refrigerate, covered, for several hours.

Preheat oven to 350°F. Roll a small amount of dough at a time very thin. Cut with small cutters and transfer to ungreased cookie sheets, allowing about ½ inch between cookies. Sprinkle with chopped almonds. Bake 10 minutes until lightly brown. Loosen at once with a spatula and let stand until cool. Store in airtight containers.
YIELD: About 12 dozen.

Orange Cordial Bars

⅓ cup butter	1 cup (6-ounce package) semisweet chocolate bits
⅔ cup brown sugar, firmly packed	1¼ cups finely chopped walnuts
1 egg	¼ cup sugar
½ cup milk	2 tablespoons orange liqueur
1 cup sifted flour	1 tablespoon orange juice
¼ teaspoon soda	1 teaspoon grated orange rind
½ teaspoon salt	

Preheat oven to 375°F. Grease a 9-inch square pan. Cream butter and brown sugar until well mixed. Beat in egg and stir in milk. Sift flour with soda and salt and stir into batter. Add chocolate bits and walnuts. Blend well. Spread in pan and bake 25 to 30 minutes. Meanwhile, combine sugar, orange liqueur, orange juice, and orange rind. Bring to a boil. Pour evenly over cake as soon as it comes out of the oven. Cool and cut into small bars.

YIELD: About 30.

Milosti
Middle European Fried Cookies

2 cups sifted flour	2 tablespoons milk
3 tablespoons sugar	3 tablespoons brandy
¼ teaspoon salt	1 teaspoon grated lemon rind
2 tablespoons butter	Oil for deep-frying
1 egg	Confectioners' sugar
1 egg yolk	

Sift flour with sugar and salt. Cut in butter, as for pie crust. Beat egg and egg yolk, and stir into flour-butter mixture. Add milk, brandy, and grated lemon rind. Mix well. Turn dough out on a lightly floured board and knead 20 turns. If dough is too soft, work in a little more flour. Chill dough for a half-hour.

Divide dough into three parts and roll out, one part at a time, on a lightly floured board to ⅛ inch thick. Cut into strips 1½ inches by 3 inches. Make a slit in the center of each strip and pull one end of the dough through.

Heat oil to 375°F. Fry cookies, a few at a time, until golden brown. Drain on absorbent paper and sprinkle generously with confectioners' sugar.

YIELD: About 3 dozen.

Anise Toast

You might call this Italian zweiback.

2¾ cups sifted flour
1½ teaspoons baking powder
½ teaspoon salt
1 cup sugar
½ cup butter, melted
2 tablespoons anise seed

2 tablespoons anisette liqueur
1½ tablespoons blended
  whiskey
1 cup coarsely chopped
  filberts
3 eggs

Sift flour with baking powder and salt. Combine sugar, melted butter, anise seed, anisette, whiskey, and filberts. Beat in eggs, one at a time. Mix in dry ingredients and blend well. Cover dough and chill for about 3 hours.

Preheat oven to 375°F. Butter cookie sheets. On a lightly floured board, shape dough with your hands to form flat loaves about ½ inch thick and 2 inches wide, the length of your cookie sheet. Place no more than 2 loaves on a cookie sheet, parallel to each other but well apart. Bake for 20 minutes.

Remove from oven and let loaves cool on pans until they can be touched. Cut into diagonal slices about ½ inch thick. Lay slices on cut sides, close together, on cookie sheet and return to oven for 15 minutes more, or until lightly toasted. Cool on wire racks and store in airtight containers.

YIELD: About 5 dozen.

Candies

Brandied Almond Truffles

2 cups finely chopped
  blanched almonds
2 cups sifted confectioners'
  sugar
1 egg white
2 tablespoons brandy

1½ cups semisweet chocolate
  bits
¾ cup sweetened condensed
  milk
1 tablespoon butter

Combine almonds, confectioners' sugar, egg white, and brandy. Press mixture evenly into a buttered 8-inch square pan. Melt chocolate in the top part of a double boiler over boiling water. Stir in condensed milk and butter, and cook until thickened (about 5 minutes). Pour chocolate mixture over almond layer. Let stand in a cool place until firm. Cut into small squares.
YIELD: About 5 dozen.

Mansion House Pralines

2½ cups sugar
¼ cup white corn syrup
1 small pinch baking soda
1 tablespoon butter

1 cup evaporated milk
2 tablespoons bourbon
3 cups pecan halves

Combine sugar, corn syrup, baking soda, butter, and evaporated milk in a heavy saucepan. Cook over medium-low heat to firm-ball stage (242°F. on a candy thermometer). Remove from heat and stir in bourbon and pecan halves. Beat until candy thickens and looks creamy. Drop by spoonfuls onto waxed paper and let cool.
YIELD: About 3 dozen pralines.

Jamaica Nuggets

1 cup (6-ounce package)
  chocolate bits
1 cup (8-ounce can) almond
  paste
1 cup sifted confectioners'
  sugar

2 tablespoons Jamaica rum
1 tablespoon soft butter
1½ tablespoons cinnamon
½ cup cocoa

Grate chocolate. (This is most easily done in a blender.) Put almond paste into a large bowl and break up with a wooden spoon. Add grated chocolate, confectioners' sugar, rum, and butter. Blend very well. Form into small balls, about the size of a marble. Mix cinnamon and cocoa in a plastic bag. Shake balls gently, 4 or 5 at a time, in this mixture. Place on a cake rack to dry. Store in an airtight container.

YIELD: About 3 dozen.

Spiced Rye Nuts

2 cups unsalted mixed nuts
2 cups sifted confectioners'
  sugar
½ teaspoon cinnamon

½ teaspoon nutmeg
½ teaspoon ginger
¼ cup butter
¼ cup rye whiskey

Preheat oven to 350°F. Spread nuts on a cookie sheet and heat in oven for about 15 minutes, until lightly toasted. Meanwhile, combine confectioners' sugar, cinnamon, nutmeg, and ginger. Cream butter and add sugar-spice mixture gradually, alternating with whiskey. Beat until smooth and well blended. Add warm nuts and stir around until all are well coated. Spread on a cool cookie sheet to dry. Separate nuts and store in an airtight container.

DESSERTS
I
CHAPTER
18

Dessert Sauces

The sauces in this group are fairly simple and allow the cook a lot of latitude in application. They go over all manner of fruit, ice cream, puddings, custards, and cakes—or wherever the imagination leads. The Chocolate Sauce classically goes over *profiteroles*—miniature cream puffs stuffed with ice cream or whipped cream. But it enhances plain cake or chocolate roll, too.

Cherries Jubilee is merely a brandy-laced cherry sauce, ladled over vanilla ice cream. Try it over pudding or custard for a treat. You get the idea now.

Use these sauces freely, following your own taste preferences. Perhaps you'll invent another "Cherries Jubilee."

Cordial Sundae

One of the easiest, pleasantest desserts is ice cream or sherbet with liqueur poured over. A tablespoon (½ ounce) per portion is about right. Just to start, here are some suggestions—but the combinations are virtually unlimited:

Orange liqueur: orange, raspberry, or strawberry sherbet; chocolate, vanilla, or cherry ice cream.

Cherry liqueur: orange or lemon sherbet; vanilla, chocolate, peach, or cherry ice cream.

White crème de menthe: strawberry, raspberry, lemon sherbet; chocolate or coffee ice cream.

Green crème de menthe: lemon sherbet, vanilla or pistachio ice cream.

Crème de cacao: vanilla, chocolate, pistachio, or coffee ice cream.

Crème de bananes: vanilla, chocolate, or strawberry ice cream.

Crème de cassis: raspberry sherbet; vanilla or strawberry ice cream.

Coffee liqueur: coffee, banana, or butter-pecan ice cream.

Anisette: coffee or butter-pecan ice cream.

Ginger: lemon sherbet; vanilla ice cream.

Blackberry liqueur: any fruit flavor.

216

Bourbon-Apricot Sauce

½ cup dried apricots
1½ cups water

¼ cup sugar
2 tablespoons bourbon

Combine apricots, water, and sugar, and bring to a boil. Reduce heat, cover pan, and simmer for 20 minutes, or until apricots are tender.

Rub the fruit and liquid through a sieve, or purée in a blender. Stir in bourbon and refrigerate.

YIELD: About 2 cups.

Cherry Cardinale

1 package (10 ounces)
  frozen raspberries
¼ cup sugar

2 teaspoons lemon juice
2 tablespoons cherry liqueur

Thaw raspberries. Purée in a blender or rub through a fine sieve. Put in a saucepan; add sugar and lemon juice. Bring to a boil and simmer for 5 minutes. Remove from heat. Stir in cherry liqueur. Chill. Serve with ice cream or custard.

YIELD: About 1 cup.

Cherries Jubilee

1 large can pitted Bing
  cherries (1 pound 14
  ounces)
¼ cup currant jelly

1 tablespoon lemon juice
1 tablespoon cornstarch
1 tablespoon cold water
⅓ cup cognac, warmed

Drain cherries, reserving 1 cup of liquid. Combine this liquid with jelly and lemon juice. Bring to a boil, stirring. Remove from heat. Blend cornstarch and water and stir into hot liquid. Add cherries. Return to heat and bring to a boil, stirring. Pour into a heatproof

bowl and bring to the table. Ignite cognac and pour over sauce. Ladle flaming sauce over ice cream.
SERVES: 8.

Cherry Sauce

½ cup sugar
¾ cup water
2 cups pitted sour cherries
1 teaspoon cornstarch

1 tablespoon cold water
1 teaspoon lemon juice
¼ cup kirsch

Combine sugar and ¾ cup water. Bring to a boil and boil for 5 minutes. Add cherries and cook for 5 minutes. Combine cornstarch and remaining tablespoon of water. Stir into fruit. Cook until the sauce is clear and slightly thickened. Remove from heat, cool, and then stir in lemon juice and kirsch. Serve with cake or ice cream.
YIELD: About 3 cups.

Flaming Nesselrode Sauce

1 jar prepared Nesselrode
   (10 ounces)

1 can crushed pineapple,
   drained (8½ ounces)
¼ cup light rum, warmed

Heat Nesselrode and pineapple just until boiling. Turn into a heat-proof bowl and bring to the table. Ignite rum and pour over fruit. Ladle flaming sauce over ice cream.
SERVES: 6 to 8.

Triple Orange Caramel

2 cups sugar
½ cup orange juice, heated
½ cup boiling water

3 tablespoons triple sec
   (orange liqueur)

Put sugar in a deep, heavy skillet and cook over moderate heat until it becomes a caramelized syrup. Watch carefully to see that it doesn't burn. Stir in orange juice and water. Cook over low heat for about 20 minutes. Remove from heat and stir in triple sec. Cool and then refrigerate.

YIELD: About 2½ cups.

Sauce Tropicana

1 cup orange marmalade
½ cup Gold Label Puerto
  Rican rum
2 teaspoons lemon juice

2 ripe peaches, peeled, pitted
  and sliced
1 banana, sliced
1 cup crushed pineapple
½ cup flaked coconut

Combine orange marmalade and rum in a small saucepan and heat just to the boiling point. Sprinkle lemon juice over peaches and banana to prevent darkening. Combine with marmalade, pineapple, and coconut.

Serve over vanilla, strawberry, or peach ice cream.

YIELD: About 1 quart.

Butterscotch Rum Sauce

½ cup sugar
½ cup dark corn syrup
Pinch of salt
¼ teaspoon instant-coffee
  powder

2 tablespoons butter
2 tablespoons Jamaica rum
1 cup light cream

Stir the sugar and syrup together in the top of a double boiler. Heat over boiling water, stirring occasionally, until sugar melts. Add all remaining ingredients and continue cooking over hot water until *slightly* thickened, about 20 minutes. Cool.

NOTE: This sauce thickens as it cools.

YIELD: About 1½ cups.

Bourbon Chocolate Sauce

6 ounces semisweet
  chocolate chips
½ cup black coffee

1 tablespoon bourbon
3–4 tablespoons cream

Combine chocolate chips and coffee in a heavy saucepan. Place over low heat and stir until melted and smooth. Add bourbon and cream. Serve warm or at room temperature.
YIELD: About 1½ cups.

Mocha Sauce Flambé

1 cup semisweet chocolate
  bits
1 tablespoon butter
½ teaspoon instant-coffee
  powder

¼ cup light corn syrup
¼ cup milk
¼ cup blended whiskey,
  warmed

Melt chocolate bits and butter in the top of a double boiler over hot, not boiling, water. Gradually stir in instant-coffee powder, corn syrup, and milk, beating until smooth. Pour into heatproof serving bowl.

At the table, ignite whiskey and pour into chocolate sauce. When flames subside, stir sauce and spoon over coffee ice cream.
YIELD: About 1½ cups.

Sauce Sabayon

4 egg yolks
½ cup sugar

¾ cup Marsala
1 tablespoon kirsch

Beat egg yolks and sugar in the top of a double boiler. Stir in the Marsala. Place over hot water and cook, stirring constantly, until thick and creamy. Stir in kirsch. May be served warm or chilled with fruit, over chocolate desserts and cake.
SERVES: 6 to 8.

Irish Velvet Sauce

4 egg yolks
¼ cup sugar
1 teaspoon cornstarch

⅛ teaspoon salt
1¾ cups milk, scalded
2 tablespoons Irish whiskey

Beat egg yolks with sugar until thick and pale. Beat in cornstarch and salt. Gradually stir in milk.

Pour into a heavy pan and cook over low heat, stirring constantly, until mixture thickens and lightly coats back of spoon.

Remove from heat and stir in Irish whiskey. Serve warm or cold with steamed puddings.

YIELD: About 2 cups.

Hard Sauce

½ cup sweet butter
1½ cups superfine granulated
  sugar

2–3 tablespoons cognac

Cream the butter well and gradually beat in the sugar. Beat the sauce until it is very light and fluffy. Gradually stir in the cognac. Chill well.

Served with steamed puddings like plum pudding. Hard Sauce can be molded with butter paddles or forced through a pastry tube into stars or rosettes.

Minty Dip

¾ cup sour cream
1 tablespoon crème de menthe

1 tablespoon light-brown
  sugar

Combine all ingredients and chill. A very nice dip for fresh fruit, especially strawberries.

Sauce Café

1½ cups strong coffee
¾ cup sugar
1 tablespoon arrowroot or
  cornstarch

2 tablespoons cold water
2 tablespoons coffee liqueur

Heat the coffee with the sugar. Combine the arrowroot and water and stir into the coffee. Cook over low heat, stirring until thickened. Add coffee liqueur and chill before serving.
YIELD: About 2 cups.

Fruit

Make-Your-Own Compote

Lemon juice
Sliced fresh peaches, peeled
Sliced bananas
Sliced cantaloupe, peeled
Hulled, washed strawberries
Orange sections
Fresh pineapple wedges

Halved plums, pitted
Confectioners' sugar
Triple sec
Crème de menthe
Maraschino
Kirsch

Squeeze lemon juice over peaches and bananas, coating fruit well to prevent darkening. Arrange fruits on individual plates or trays. Sprinkle generously with confectioners' sugar and refrigerate. At serving time, place trays and liqueurs on table—half-bottle liqueurs are fine. Guests can "make their own" fruit combinations and then sprinkle with the spirit of their choice.

Fruits Afire

1 can (1 pound) pears
1 can (1 pound) Bing cherries
1 can (1 pound) peeled whole
  apricots

2 tablespoons lemon juice
1 cinnamon stick
½ cup apricot preserves
6 tablespoons Gold Label rum

Drain pears, apricots, and cherries, reserving syrup. Combine syrups in a saucepan with lemon juice, cinnamon stick, apricot preserves, and 2 tablespoons rum. Bring to a boil and cook until reduced by half. Remove cinnamon stick and pour over fruits. Refrigerate until about a half-hour before serving.

Preheat oven to 350°F. Turn fruit and syrup into an ovenproof casserole. (Use one attractive enough to be brought to the table.) Cover casserole and heat in oven just until fruit is hot. Warm remaining ¼ cup rum. At the table, ignite the rum and pour flaming over the fruit. Serve when flames have died out.
SERVES: 8 to 10.

Apples Normandy

5 large apples
¼ cup butter
4 tablespoons sugar, or more

½ teaspoon vanilla
¼ cup Calvados, warmed
1 cup sour cream

Peel, core, and thinly slice apples. Melt butter in a large skillet. Add apple slices and sprinkle with sugar (amount depends on tartness of the apples). Cook over medium-low heat, turning the apple slices occasionally. When they are tender and transparent, transfer to a heatproof serving dish. Pour Calvados over and ignite. When flames die down, serve with sour cream.
SERVES: 6.

Apricots Framboise

8 large firm apricots
1¼ cups sugar
2 cups water
1 package frozen raspberries

3 tablespoons framboise
⅓ cup blanched almonds,
   slivered and toasted

Cover apricots with boiling water and let stand 5 minutes. Drain and peel, reserving the peelings. Halve apricots and remove pits.

Combine sugar and water, bring to a boil, and boil for 5 minutes. Add apricots to the boiling water and remove from heat immediately. Cool apricots in syrup and then chill.

Remove apricots from syrup and arrange in a serving dish. Add the frozen raspberries and reserved apricot peel to the syrup and bring to a boil, gently separating the block of frozen berries. Simmer for 10 minutes. Strain through a fine sieve and return to heat. Cook syrup for 10 minutes longer, or until the syrup has thickened and reduced slightly. Cool the syrup to room temperature, stir in framboise, and pour over the apricots. Sprinkle with toasted almonds.

SERVES: 8.

Banana High

4 firm, ripe bananas	½ cup dark corn syrup
2 tablespoons orange juice	1 teaspoon grated orange rind
¼ cup butter	⅓ cup bourbon, warmed

Cut bananas in half lengthwise, and brush with orange juice. Melt butter in a large skillet. Add corn syrup and orange rind to butter. Heat to boiling point over low flame, stirring occasionally. Add bananas and sauté over low heat 3 minutes, frequently basting with syrup.

Arrange bananas on warmed, flameproof serving dish. Pour bourbon over bananas. Ignite and serve.

SERVES: 4.

Cherry Compote Flambé

1 can (1 pound 13 ounces) Bing cherries	6 almond macaroons
1 tablespoon lemon juice	3 tablespoons Jamaica rum, warmed
1 teaspoon grated orange rind	

Drain cherries, reserving syrup. Pour syrup into a chafing dish, add lemon juice and orange rind, and bring to a boil. Simmer for 5 minutes. Add cherries and simmer 5 minutes more. Break up macaroons and add to pan. Ignite rum and pour over. Serve when flames have died out.
SERVES: 6.

Cranberry Confections

4 cups (1 pound) cranberries   4 to 6 tablespoons gin
2½ cups sugar

Preheat oven to 350°F. Pick over cranberries and place in a shallow baking pan in which they can lie in a single layer. (A 15- by 10-inch jelly-roll pan is a good size.) Sprinkle with 2 cups of sugar and cover tightly with a double thickness of aluminum foil.

Bake 45 minutes. Lift up one end of foil and check to see if cranberries are tender. If they don't seem quite done, cover and bake 5 to 10 minutes longer.

Remove pan from oven and loosen cranberries gently with a spatula. After about 15 minutes, sprinkle with gin and remaining sugar. Let cool completely and then store in a covered jar.
YIELD: About 3 cups.

Dates-on-the-Side

Serve with roast pork or poultry or as a garnish for fruit salad.

2 cups pitted fresh dates   3 tablespoons brandy
¼ cup lemon juice   1 tablespoon slivered lemon
¼ cup sugar   peel (zest)

Place dates in a bowl. Combine remaining ingredients and stir until sugar has dissolved. Pour over dates. Cover and refrigerate for several days before using. Stir occasionally.
YIELD: About 2 cups.

Fig Fancy

1 can figs
1 pint vanilla ice cream

2 tablespoons bourbon or
   blended whiskey
2 tablespoons fig syrup

Chill 4 dessert dishes. Drain figs and reserve syrup. Place 2 or 3 figs in each dish and top with ice cream. Mix bourbon with 3 tablespoons of fig syrup and divide equally over the four portions.
SERVES: 4.

Broiled Grapefruit

2 grapefruit
4 tablespoons Gold Label rum

4 tablespoons brown sugar,
   packed

Cut grapefruit in halves. Remove seeds and loosen sections. Combine rum and brown sugar. Spread on grapefruit halves. Broil under flame until hot and bubbly, about 3 minutes.
SERVES: 4.

Melon Richelieu

1 ripe honeydew melon
½ pound Bing cherries
   (approx.)

¼ cup orange juice
2 tablespoons grenadine
3 tablespoons kirsch

Cut slice off stem end of melon, about 1 inch down, and set aside. Remove seeds from center and scoop out inside, using a melon-ball cutter. Pit the cherries and combine with melon balls. Pack the fruit into the melon shell, filling to the top. Combine orange juice, grenadine, and kirsch and pour into melon. Replace the top and set the melon in a container where it can stand upright. Refrigerate at least 6 hours.
SERVES: 6 to 8.

Watermelon Souse

1 medium-size watermelon   1 pint bourbon

Cut several parallel, diagonal gashes, through the rind down to the meat, on either side of the watermelon. With a sharp knife, cut a circle about 2 inches in diameter on the top center of the watermelon. Cut down about 5 inches deep, remove "plug," and reserve.

Place melon in a deep pan and refrigerate for about an hour. Pour off juice in cavity. Pour bourbon into cavity, replace plug. Chill melon for at least 6 hours before serving.
SERVES: 12.

Orange Orientale

6 large navel oranges   1 cup light corn syrup
3 cups water   3 tablespoons lemon juice
1 cup sugar   ⅓ cup orange liqueur

Remove orange outer peel from oranges (no white) with a vegetable peeler. Cut this "zest" into small julienne strips. Combine peel with 2 cups of water in a saucepan. Bring to a boil and simmer, covered, for about 10 minutes. Drain, reserving peel. Remove all of the white underskin from the whole oranges. Cut in halves crosswise and store in a large bowl.

Combine remaining cup of water, sugar, and corn syrup in a large saucepan. Bring to boil over high heat, stirring until sugar is dissolved. Lower heat and cook for 10 minutes. Add reserved peel. Continue cooking about a half-hour longer until syrup is slightly thickened. Add lemon juice and orange liqueur, and remove syrup from heat. Pour over oranges. Refrigerate, covered, for at least 8 hours, turning oranges in syrup from time to time.
SERVES: 6.

Baked Stuffed Oranges

½ cup finely cut pitted dates
¼ cup miniature
  marshmallows
¼ cup finely chopped walnuts

⅓ cup cognac
8 medium navel oranges
½ cup light-brown sugar

Combine dates, marshmallows, walnuts, and cognac. Refrigerate, covered, overnight. Next day, cut a ½-inch horizontal slice off the top of each orange. Also, remove a thin slice from the bottom of each orange, so that the orange will stand upright. Carefully scoop out pulp from the oranges, cut up, and combine with date mixture. Stuff oranges with date-orange mixture. Preheat oven to 350°F. Place oranges in a shallow baking pan, and sprinkle them with brown sugar. Bake for 30 minutes. Serve at room temperature. SERVES: 8.

Orange-Pineapple Snow

1 package orange gelatin
  dessert
1 cup pineapple juice, heated
½ cup hot water
¼ cup light rum
¼ cup orange juice

1 cup crushed pineapple,
  drained
1 tablespoon orange liqueur
2 egg whites
2 tablespoons sugar

Dissolve orange gelatin in hot pineapple juice and hot water. Stir in rum and orange juice. Chill until syrupy. Stir in crushed pineapple and orange liqueur. Beat egg whites with 2 tablespoons sugar until stiff. Gently fold into gelatin mixture. Spoon into individual dessert dishes. Chill until firm. SERVES: 6.

Baked Peaches Amandine

½ cup ground almonds
½ cup confectioners' sugar
2 tablespoons butter
½ teaspoon grated lemon peel

⅓ cup orange liqueur
6 ripe freestone peaches
¼ cup granulated sugar

Combine ground almonds, confectioners' sugar, butter, and lemon peel, and mix well. Stir in about 1 tablespoon orange liqueur, or enough to get a good consistency for forming into balls.

Dip peaches into boiling water, then plunge immediately into cold water. Remove skins, halve, and pit. Put a small ball of almond mixture in each peach half, and then put halves together. Carefully place peaches in a buttered baking pan. Pour remaining orange liqueur over peaches and sprinkle with granulated sugar.

Bake in oven preheated to 375°F. for about 25 minutes, or until peaches are tender, basting several times with juices in the pan. Serve warm or chilled.
SERVES: 6.

McPeach

1 large can freestone peaches, drained	1 tablespoon confectioners' sugar
3 tablespoons Irish whiskey	⅛ teaspoon cinnamon
1 cup heavy cream, cold	

Place well-chilled peaches in serving bowl and sprinkle with 2 tablespoons of whiskey. Whip cream; add sugar, cinnamon, and remaining tablespoon of whiskey, gradually. Pipe whipped cream around peaches in bowl, or serve individually, and top each portion with cream.
SERVES: 6.

Poached Virgin Pears

1½ cups brown sugar, firmly packed	½ cup Virgin Islands rum
1 cup water	4 tablespoons candied fruit, finely chopped
¼ cup butter	½ cup heavy cream, whipped
4 firm, ripe Bartlett pears	

Combine brown sugar, water, and butter in a large skillet. Bring to a boil and simmer 10 minutes. Peel, halve, and core pears. Add pears and ¼ cup rum to syrup. Cover skillet and simmer until pears are tender, 10 to 15 minutes. Remove pears from syrup. Cook syrup until slightly reduced and thickened. Pour over pears and chill.

Soak candied fruit in remaining ¼ cup rum. At serving time, put ½ tablespoon candied fruit in the center of each pear. Spoon a little syrup over each serving and garnish with whipped cream.
SERVES: 4.

Fresh Pineapple Wedges Kirsch

1 medium-size ripe pineapple   ¼ cup kirsch
½ cup superfine granulated
   sugar (or to taste)

Cut pineapple in quarters lengthwise and peel each quarter, removing the eyes. Cut away hard core and then slice each quarter crosswise into ¼-inch slices. Sprinkle with sugar and kirsch, and chill.
SERVES: 4 to 6.

Prunes Armagnac

1 pound pitted prunes   1 cup Armagnac (approx.)

Put prunes into a 2-quart jar. Pour in enough Armagnac to cover. Let stand 10 days before using. As prunes are consumed, they can be replaced with more. Just add a little Armagnac from time to time.

Use in fruit compote, with ice cream, duck or game. Purée for use in cake filling, etc.

Strawberries Romanoff

1 quart strawberries
½ cup superfine granulated
   sugar (or to taste)
1 pint vanilla ice cream

1 cup heavy cream
3 tablespoons orange liqueur
3 tablespoons cognac

Wash and hull strawberries, and set aside 6 large ones for garnish. Slice remaining berries into a bowl, sprinkle with sugar, and refrigerate. Chill 6 sherbet glasses. Just before serving time, let ice cream soften slightly. Whip cream until stiff, and beat in half the liqueur and rum. Mix remaining liqueur and cognac into ice cream, and then quickly fold in the whipped cream. Spoon sliced berries into chilled glasses, top with cream mixture and a whole strawberry. Serve at once.
SERVES: 6.

Strawberries Alexandra

1 ripe pineapple
¼ cup Gold Label rum
1 cup sugar (approx.)
1 quart strawberries

1 cup apricot preserves
1 cup heavy cream, whipped
   and sweetened to taste

Cut pineapple into ½-inch slices and peel. Cut the 4 center slices in half and remove cores. Sprinkle with 2 tablespoons rum and sugar to taste. Chill.

Dice remaining pineapple. Wash and hull strawberries, and reserve a dozen of the nicest for garnish. Quarter remaining berries, mix with diced pineapple, sweeten to taste, and chill.

Heat apricot preserves until melted, push through a strainer, and add remaining 2 tablespoons rum. Chill.

To serve, mound diced fruit in the center of a serving dish. Surround with half slices of pineapple and whole berries. Drizzle apricot preserves over all. Serve with bowl of whipped cream.
SERVES: 8.

Frozen Desserts

INTRODUCTORY NOTE: Unless otherwise specified, freezer should be turned up to coldest point when making any of the following frozen desserts. Freezing times given are approximate, since freezer temperatures vary according to type.

Simple Raspberry Sorbet

1 package frozen raspberries, unthawed	¼ cup framboise (dry raspberry brandy)

Cut unthawed block of frozen raspberries into 3 parts. Blend one part at a time in an electric blender with ⅓ of the framboise. Blend until well mixed. When all the raspberries have been puréed, pour into a freezing tray. Freeze to a soft, firm consistency.
SERVES: 4.

Peach Sip

4 ripe peaches	¼ cup bourbon
4 teaspoons sugar (or to taste)	4 cups finely crushed ice

Dip peaches in boiling water and then in cold water. Skin and slice fruit into a bowl. Add sugar and bourbon. Refrigerate for several hours. At serving time, divide crushed ice among four dessert dishes. Spoon peaches and liquid over the ice. Plant a short straw in each dish. After eating the fruit, sip the liquid through the straw.
SERVES: 4.

Crème de Menthe Sherbet

1 teaspoon unflavored gelatin	3 tablespoons crème de menthe
¼ cup lemon juice	1 egg white, stiffly beaten
1 cup sugar	
1½ cups water	

Sprinkle the gelatin over the lemon juice and let stand for 5 minutes. Combine sugar and water, and cook over medium heat, stirring, until sugar dissolves. Bring to a boil and cook for 5 minutes without stirring. Pour hot syrup over softened gelatin, stirring until completely dissolved. Pour into an ice tray and freeze until mushy, about 1½ hours.

Turn into a small chilled bowl. Add crème de menthe and beat until smooth. Fold in beaten egg white. Pour back into ice tray. Freeze until partially set (about 1 hour) and then stir with a fork. Freeze until firm, about 2 hours more.
SERVES: 4.

Café Granité

¾ cup sugar	½ cup crème de cacao
1 cup water	1 cup heavy cream
3 cups strong coffee (preferably espresso)	

Combine sugar and water, and cook over medium heat, stirring, until sugar dissolves. Bring to a boil and cook for 5 minutes without stirring. Add the coffee and cool. Pour into ice trays and freeze, stirring frequently, until mushy (about 1½ hours).

At serving time, pour crème de cacao and cream into pitcher. Spoon granité into chilled dessert dishes. Serve immediately, pouring some of crème de cacao-cream mixture over each portion. Those who wish may add more.
SERVES: 4.

Orange Freeze

1 cup sugar	2 tablespoons lemon juice
1¼ cups water	1 cup orange juice
¼ cup orange liqueur	Grated rind of 2 oranges

Combine sugar, water, and liqueur. Cook over medium heat, stirring, until sugar dissolves. Bring to a boil and cook for 5 minutes without stirring. Cool. Add remaining ingredients. Pour into 2 freezer trays. Freeze for about 1 hour, or until it is frozen around the sides but still mushy in the middle. Turn the mixture into a chilled bowl and beat until frothy. Return to the freezer trays and freeze for about 4 hours, or until firm, stirring the ice every hour. SERVES: 6.

Frozen Grasshopper

Chocolate Crust:
1 cup chocolate cookie
   crumbs, finely crushed
2 tablespoons melted butter

Filling:
1¼ cups half-and-half
   (milk and cream)

36 marshmallows
½ cup green crème de menthe
⅓ cup white crème de cacao
6 drops green food coloring
2 egg whites
3 tablespoons sugar
1½ cups heavy cream

Crust: Combine chocolate cookie crumbs and melted butter. Pat mixture evenly over the bottom of an 8-inch or 9-inch spring-form pan that is at least 2 inches deep. Set aside in refrigerator.
Filling: Pour half-and-half into a small saucepan, add marshmallows, and cook, stirring, until marshmallows are melted. Set pan in cold water and stir until mixture is cooled. Blend in crème de menthe, crème de cacao, and green food coloring. Chill mixture until it begins to thicken. Beat egg whites until stiff, gradually add the sugar, and continue to beat until whites hold short, distinct peaks. In a large bowl, whip cream until stiff. Fold marshmallow mixture and egg whites into the whipped cream. Pour into pan lined with chocolate crust. Cover with plastic film and freeze until firm (at least 8 hours).

About 15 minutes before serving, remove pan from freezer. Dip a towel in hot water, wring dry, and wrap around pan. Let stand 30 seconds. Remove towel, run a knife blade around the edge of the

crust, and remove the pan sides. Set "Grasshopper" on a serving dish and hold in refrigerator until ready to serve.
SERVES: 12.

Rum-Raisin Cream

⅓ cup Gold Label rum
1 cup raisins
1 can (15 ounces) sweetened
   condensed milk
1 cup water

½ teaspoon salt
2 teaspoons vanilla
1 tablespoon lemon juice
2 cups heavy cream, whipped
1 cup chopped walnuts

Pour rum over raisins and let stand several hours. Combine condensed milk, water, salt, vanilla, and lemon juice. Chill. Fold in whipped cream. Turn into refrigerator trays and freeze until partially frozen (about 1 inch in from edge of tray). Turn into a chilled bowl and beat until fluffy. Fold in raisins and walnuts. Return to trays and freeze until firm.
YIELD: About 1½ quarts.

Bourbon Fruit Cream

1 teaspoon unflavored gelatin
¼ cup cold water
1 cup milk
½ cup sugar
¼ cup bourbon

1 cup heavy cream, whipped
½ cup chopped candied fruits
¼ cup macaroon cookie
   crumbs

Soften gelatin in cold water. Heat milk to boiling point; remove from heat. Add gelatin and sugar to milk, and stir until dissolved. Add bourbon; mix well. Turn into refrigerator tray and freeze until partially frozen. Turn into chilled bowl and beat until smooth. Fold whipped cream and fruits into gelatin mixture. Return to refrigerator tray. Sprinkle with cookie crumbs. Freeze until firm (about 2–3 hours).
SERVES: 6 to 8.

Biscuit Tortoni

2 eggs, separated
½ cup confectioners' sugar
2 tablespoons clear white
   Jamaica rum

½ teaspoon vanilla
1 cup heavy cream, whipped
⅔ cup crushed almond
   macaroons

Beat egg yolks with sugar until fluffy. Stir in rum and vanilla. Beat egg whites until stiff. Fold yolk mixture into whites. Fold in whipped cream and ½ cup macaroon crumbs. Spoon into 4-ounce paper dessert dishes. Sprinkle each portion with a little of the remaining macaroon crumbs. Freeze until firm.
SERVES: 6 to 8.

Apricot Parfait

1 cup dried apricots
2 tablespoons Armagnac
1½ teaspoons lemon juice
3 egg yolks
⅛ teaspoon salt

⅓ cup granulated sugar
⅓ cup brown sugar, firmly
   packed
⅓ cup water
2 cups heavy cream, whipped

Cook apricots until very tender; drain. Purée by whirling in a blender or pressing through a sieve. Add Armagnac and lemon juice to purée. Beat egg yolks with salt until thick and light. Combine sugars and water and cook over medium heat, stirring until sugar dissolves. Bring to a boil and cook for 3 minutes without stirring. Immediately, pour this hot syrup in a fine stream into the beaten egg yolks, beating constantly at high speed. Continue beating until mixture has cooled. Add the apricot purée and stir until smooth. Fold in the whipped cream and pour into refrigerator trays. Freeze, without stirring, until firm. At serving time, let stand at room temperature for several minutes before spooning into serving dishes.
YIELD: About 1½ quarts.

San Juan Banana Mousse

2 cups mashed ripe bananas
¼ cup Gold Label rum
⅛ teaspoon salt
⅓ cup light corn syrup

½ cup sugar
1 cup milk
1 cup heavy cream, whipped
1 egg white, stiffly beaten

Combine bananas, rum, salt, corn syrup, sugar, and milk. Fold in whipped cream and beaten egg white. Pour into ice trays and freeze, stirring occasionally, until firm.
SERVES: 6.

Bourbon Chocolate Parfait

½ cup cocoa powder
⅔ cup hot water
1 tablespoon butter
½ cup honey
⅓ cup light corn syrup

½ teaspoon vanilla
¼ cup bourbon
1 quart vanilla ice cream
½ cup heavy cream, whipped

Blend cocoa, water, butter, honey, and corn syrup in a saucepan, and cook, stirring occasionally, until boiling. Remove from heat; stir in vanilla and bourbon. Cool. Place alternate layers of ice cream and chocolate sauce in parfait glasses. Place in freezer until ready to serve. Top with whipped cream.
SERVES: 6 to 8.

Cherry Bombe

¼ cup kirsch
½ cup drained maraschino
    cherries, chopped

1 quart cherry ices or sherbet
3 pints vanilla ice cream

Pour kirsch over drained, chopped cherries and let stand for several hours. Chill a 2-quart mold in the refrigerator. Let cherry ices soften slightly and then spread over the inside of the mold to form a layer about ½ inch thick. Put mold in freezer until cherry ices firm up again.

Meanwhile, let vanilla ice cream soften slightly. Drain chopped cherries and quickly stir into vanilla ice cream. Pack the ice cream into the center of the mold. Cover the mold with foil, return to the freezer, and freeze for about 8 hours.

To serve, remove the foil and place the mold on a chilled serving plate. Wipe the outside of the mold several times with a cloth wrung out in hot water, and then lift bombe off. The unmolding can be done ahead of time and the bombe returned to the freezer until serving time.

SERVES: 8 to 10.

Dubliner

1 pint vanilla ice cream
4 cups hot, double-strength
   coffee

4 ounces Irish whiskey
Whipped cream

Place one scoop vanilla ice cream in each of 4 tall glasses. Pour hot coffee over ice cream until glass is two-thirds full. Add second scoop ice cream and fill glass almost to the top with coffee. Put an ounce of whiskey into each glass. Stir. Garnish with whipped cream. Serve with long-handled spoons.

SERVES: 4.

Norwegian Omelet

1 pint strawberry ice cream
1 9-inch sponge-cake layer
¼ cup kirsch
8 egg whites
1 cup sugar

4 egg yolks
1 teaspoon vanilla
1 tablespoon confectioners'
   sugar

Let ice cream soften slightly at room temperature. Sprinkle cake with kirsch, then spread evenly with ice cream. Place on a baking sheet and freeze, unwrapped, until ice cream is firm.

Beat egg whites until foamy; gradually beat in sugar until whites have stiff, glossy peaks. Beat egg yolks with vanilla until thick and lemon-colored. Fold yolks gently into whites. Preheat oven to 500°F. Place ice cream-covered cake (cake side down) on a heatproof serving plate. Working quickly, smooth egg mixture over. Dust with confectioners' sugar. Place on a board and put in oven for 3 minutes, or until lightly browned. Serve at once.

SERVES: 8 to 10.

Baked Alaska

4 egg whites
⅛ teaspoon cream of tartar
⅔ cup sugar
1 thin layer of sponge cake
1 quart ice cream, frozen hard

1 tablespoon confectioners' sugar
3 tablespoons blended whiskey, warmed

Beat egg whites with cream of tartar until foamy. Gradually beat in sugar until whites are very stiff. Reserve 3 half eggshells. Preheat oven to 450°F. Cover a small board with several thicknesses of brown paper. Place the cake layer on the board.

Cake layer should be of a size to allow for a half-inch rim when ice cream is placed on the cake. Place the hard-frozen ice cream on the cake and quickly cover with meringue. Dust with confectioners' sugar. Now, carefully set half eggshells into top of meringue like little cups. Place in oven for about 5 minutes, or until lightly browned.

Slide Baked Alaska onto a chilled platter. Pour whiskey into eggshell halves and ignite. Serve blazing.

SERVES: 6 to 8.

DESSERTS
II
CHAPTER
19

Creams and Custards

Mocha Bavarian

1 cup milk
¾ cup sugar
1 tablespoon instant-coffee
  powder
1 envelope unflavored gelatin

2 eggs, separated
1 cup semisweet chocolate bits
  (6-ounce bag)
2 tablespoons coffee liqueur
½ cup heavy cream

Combine ½ cup milk, ¼ cup sugar, instant-coffee powder, and gelatin in a saucepan. Cook over moderate heat, stirring constantly, until gelatin dissolves and mixture just comes to a boil. Remove from heat. Beat the egg yolks slightly. Add some of the hot coffee mixture to eggs and then pour back into pan, stirring rapidly. Cook over moderate heat 2 minutes, stirring constantly. Remove from heat and stir in chocolate bits until melted. Blend in remaining ½ cup milk and coffee liqueur. Chill until thickened but not set. Beat egg whites until stiff but not dry. Gradually beat in remaining ½ cup sugar until egg whites are stiff and glossy. Whip cream. Fold chocolate mixture into egg whites, then fold in whipped cream. Pour into 1½-quart mold. Chill until set.
SERVES: 8 to 10.

Mincemeat Bavarian

¼ cup sugar
2 tablespoons cornstarch
1 envelope unflavored gelatin
1 cup milk

4 egg yolks, slightly beaten
1½ cups heavy cream
2 cups prepared mincemeat
2 tablespoons brandy

In a medium saucepan, mix together sugar, cornstarch, and gelatin. Gradually stir in milk until smooth. Cook over medium heat, stirring constantly, until gelatin dissolves and mixture comes to a boil. Reduce heat and simmer, stirring, about 2 minutes. Add some of hot milk mixture to egg yolks. Pour back into saucepan. Stir over low heat about 3 minutes. Cool completely.

Whip ½ cup of cream and fold into mixture. Combine mincemeat and brandy in a large bowl. Fold in custard mixture. Whip remaining cream and fold in. Turn into 6-cup mold. Chill overnight. SERVES: 6.

Nesselrode Bavarian

2 envelopes unflavored gelatin
¾ cup sugar
¼ teaspoon salt
1½ cups milk
4 eggs, separated
1 teaspoon vanilla
¼ cup Jamaica rum
¼ cup chopped blanched
   almonds

2 tablespoons raisins
2 tablespoons chopped
   candied citron
¼ cup chopped dates
½ cup halved candied
   cherries
½ cup heavy cream, whipped

Mix gelatin, ¼ cup sugar and salt in the top of a double boiler. Add milk and egg yolks, and beat until blended. Set over simmering water and cook, stirring constantly, until mixture thickens slightly and coats a metal spoon. Remove from heat and add vanilla, rum, almonds, and fruits. Chill until thickened but not firm. Beat egg whites until frothy. Gradually add ½ cup sugar and beat until stiff. Fold into fruit-nut mixture along with whipped cream. Pour into 1½-quart mold and chill until firm. SERVES: 8 to 10.

Arctic Soufflé au Grand Marnier

½ cup cold water
1 envelope unflavored gelatin
3 eggs, separated
¼ teaspoon salt

1 can frozen orange-juice
   concentrate (6 ounces)
¼ cup Grand Marnier
½ cup sugar
½ cup heavy cream, whipped

Pour water into the top of a double boiler and sprinkle with gelatin. Beat egg yolks lightly with salt. Add to water-gelatin mixture and place over boiling water. Beat with a whisk until the gelatin dissolves and the mixture thickens. Remove from hot water. Add undiluted orange-juice concentrate and Grand Marnier. Chill until mixture is thickened but not firm.

Meanwhile, prepare soufflé dish. Tear off a strip of waxed paper long enough to circle a 1-quart soufflé dish. Fold in thirds and tie around the dish so that a 2-inch collar extends above the top.

Beat egg whites until frothy. Gradually add sugar and beat until stiff. Fold the whites into the orange mixture and then fold in whipped cream. Pour into prepared dish and chill until firm. Carefully remove paper collar before serving.
SERVES: 8 to 10.

Danish Rum Pudding

1 envelope unflavored gelatin
¼ cup cold water
5 egg yolks
¾ cup sugar
2 cups milk, scalded
½ cup light rum

1 cup heavy cream, whipped
1 package frozen raspberries, thawed
2 tablespoons sugar
1 teaspoon cornstarch

Soften gelatin in cold water. Beat the egg yolks with sugar until thick and lemon-colored. Slowly stir in scalded milk. Pour into the top of a double boiler and cook over boiling water, stirring constantly, until thick and smooth. Stir in gelatin until dissolved; cool. Stir in rum and fold in whipped cream. Turn into a 1½-quart mold and chill for at least 4 hours.

Crush thawed raspberries and heat with sugar and cornstarch, stirring, until slightly thickened. Cool. Spoon over rum cream at serving time.
SERVES: 6 to 8.

Sour Cream Mousse au Kirsch

1 cup heavy cream
½ cup milk
½ cup sugar
⅛ teaspoon salt
1 envelope unflavored
gelatin

¼ cup cold water
1 cup sour cream
1½ tablespoons kirsch
1 pint strawberries, crushed
and sweetened

Combine heavy cream, milk, sugar, and salt, and cook over low heat until sugar is dissolved. Remove from heat. Soften gelatin in cold water and stir into cream mixture. When gelatin is dissolved, beat in the sour cream until mixture is smooth and blended. Stir in kirsch. Pour into individual serving dishes. Chill until firm. Serve with strawberries.
SERVES: 4 to 6.

Paddy's Parfait

Coffee jelly and whipped cream.

¼ cup Irish whiskey
2 envelopes unflavored gelatin
4 cups hot strong coffee
¾ cup superfine sugar

1 cup heavy cream, whipped
and sweetened
¼ cup chopped pecans

Soften gelatin in whiskey. Add hot coffee and sugar, and stir until gelatin is dissolved. Pour into a shallow pan to a depth of a half inch. Chill until firm, then cut into half-inch cubes. Alternate layers of coffee jelly cubes and whipped cream in parfait glasses. Top with whipped cream and sprinkle with chopped pecans.
SERVES: 6 to 8.

Mousse au Chocolat

1 cup semisweet chocolate
  bits (6-ounce package)
5 tablespoons boiling water

4 egg yolks
2 tablespoons bourbon
4 egg whites, stiffly beaten

Put chocolate bits in a blender container and blend at high speed for 6 seconds. Turn motor off and scrape chocolate down from sides of container. Add boiling water and blend at high speed for 10 seconds. Add egg yolks and bourbon, and blend for 5 seconds more, or until smooth. Very carefully fold chocolate mixture into beaten egg whites (a whisk is recommended). Spoon into small serving dishes and chill for at least one hour before serving.
NOTE: To make without a blender, put chocolate and water in a heavy pan and stir over low heat until chocolate has melted. Beat in egg yolks, one at a time, and then stir in bourbon. Remainder of recipe is the same.
SERVES: 6 to 8.

Chocolate Whipped-Cream Mousse

4 squares semisweet chocolate
  (4 ounces)
3 tablespoons orange liqueur
4 eggs, separated

⅛ teaspoon salt
⅛ teaspoon cream of tartar
2 tablespoons sugar
½ cup heavy cream, whipped

Melt chocolate over hot water. Remove from heat and stir in orange liqueur. Beat egg whites until foamy. Add salt and cream of tartar, and beat until soft peaks form. Add sugar and beat until stiff but not dry. Beat egg yolks until thick and lemon-colored, and stir into the chocolate mixture until well blended. Add about one-quarter of the beaten egg whites and mix in. Fold in whipped cream and remainder of egg whites. Spoon into dessert dishes and chill. Garnish with extra whipped cream just before serving (optional).
SERVES: 4 to 6.

Sabayon

6 egg yolks
6 tablespoons sugar

Pinch salt
¼ cup cognac

Put the egg yolks into the top of a double boiler and beat lightly. Gradually beat in sugar. Add salt. Set pan over hot (not boiling) water. Continue beating while adding cognac slowly. Remove from heat as soon as thickened. Pour into small sherbet glasses and serve warm.
SERVES: 4 to 6.

Crème Brûlée

2 cups cream
6 egg yolks
¼ cup sugar
⅛ teaspoon salt

2 tablespoons cognac
1 teaspoon vanilla
1 cup granulated brown sugar

Heat cream until scalded, in the top of a double boiler. Beat egg yolks with sugar and salt until well blended. Gradually stir in a little hot cream. Pour back into the top of the double boiler and place over hot (not boiling) water. Cook, stirring constantly, until the mixture coats a metal spoon. Remove from heat and place in a pan of cold water to cool quickly. Stir in cognac and vanilla. Pour into an ovenproof (not metal) 9-inch pie pan or baking dish. Chill.

Sprinkle the granulated brown sugar evenly over the surface of the chilled custard. Set the pan of custard in an ovenproof dish of cracked ice. Place about 6 inches below a preheated broiler, just until sugar caramelizes. Watch to make sure it doesn't burn. This can be done immediately before serving or any time within 3 hours of serving.
SERVES: 6.

Flan

5 eggs	⅛ teaspoon salt
⅔ cup sugar	2 tablespoons Spanish brandy
1 tall can evaporated milk	⅓ cup light brown sugar,
(or 1¾ cups half-and-half)	firmly packed

Beat eggs with sugar and salt until well blended. Scald milk and gradually beat into the egg mixture. Stir in brandy.

Sift the brown sugar into the bottom of a 3-cup baking dish. Pour the egg-milk mixture gently over. Place in a shallow pan of hot water and bake in an oven preheated to 350°F. for about 30 minutes or until a knife blade inserted in the center comes out clean.

Refrigerate. Before serving, run a knife around the edge of the pan and turn out onto a serving platter.

SERVES: 6.

Flaming Cream Squares

3 egg yolks, lightly beaten	2 cups cream, scalded
¼ cup sugar	½ cup graham-cracker
⅛ teaspoon salt	crumbs
⅓ cup Canadian whisky	1 beaten egg
4 tablespoons cornstarch	⅓ cup ground almonds
3 tablespoons milk	Oil for frying

In the top of a double boiler, combine egg yolks, sugar, salt, and 1 tablespoon whisky. (Reserve rest of whisky for flaming.) Mix cornstarch and milk to a smooth paste and stir into egg yolks. Very slowly stir in heated cream. Place over hot water and cook, stirring constantly, until thick and smooth. Pour into a buttered 8-inch square pan. Chill until firm.

Several hours before serving, cut the cream into small squares. Dip in graham-cracker crumbs, then in beaten egg, and finally in ground almonds. Chill.

Heat oil, to the depth of 1½ inches, in a deep skillet or electric fryer to 375°F. Fry the squares, a few at a time, until golden on top and bottom. Drain on paper towels and keep warm. Arrange the fried cream squares on a heatproof platter. Warm the remaining whisky. Ignite and pour over.

SERVES: 6.

Tight Little Island

2 cups milk
6 tablespoons sugar
½ teaspoon vanilla
3 eggs, separated

¼ teaspoon cornstarch
Dash salt
1½ tablespoons kirsch

Bring milk to a boil in a large skillet. Add 3 tablespoons sugar and the vanilla. Stir to dissolve sugar. Beat egg whites until foamy. Gradually add 3 tablespoons sugar, cornstarch, and salt, and beat until stiff. Using two large spoons, shape beaten egg whites into ovals. Gently drop, a few at a time, into the heated milk, which should be barely simmering. Cook for about 30 seconds and then carefully turn over. Cook on other side for 30 seconds. Lift meringues out of milk with a slotted spoon and drain on paper towels.

Strain the milk in which the egg whites were cooked. Beat egg yolks until light and lemon-colored. Add some of warm milk to yolks, then gradually stir mixture into milk. Stir over low heat until mixture coats the spoon. Stir in kirsch.

Pour custard into a wide, shallow serving dish. Place meringues on top. Chill.

SERVES: 4 to 6.

Zuppa Inglese

2 cups milk
2 tablespoons butter
¾ cup sugar
3 tablespoons cornstarch
½ teaspoon salt
2 eggs, beaten
1 teaspoon vanilla

1 9-inch sponge cake
6 tablespoons Jamaica rum
3 tablespoons water
¾ cup raspberry jam
2 cups heavy cream
⅓ cup chopped candied fruit

Heat milk and butter in a heavy saucepan to scalding. Combine ½ cup sugar, cornstarch, and salt, and gradually add to milk. Blend smoothly. Cook, stirring, until mixture thickens. Stir a little of the hot mixture into the beaten eggs, and then pour all back into saucepan, slowly. Cook, stirring, until thick and smooth. Remove from heat and add vanilla.

Carefully cut cake into 3 layers. Mix rum with water. Lay bottom layer on a large serving plate. Sprinkle with 3 tablespoons rum mixture. Spread half of the raspberry jam over. Spread half of the custard over that. Top with second layer. Repeat procedure as for first layer. Top with third layer. Sprinkle with 3 tablespoons of rum mixture. Whip cream with remaining ¼ cup sugar until stiff. Spread over top and sides of cake. Decorate with candied fruit. Chill. SERVES: 10 to 12.

Scotch Whisky Trifle

2 cups milk	12 ladyfingers
2 eggs	4 tablespoons Scotch whisky
2 egg yolks	½ cup currant jelly
½ cup vanilla	½ cup heavy cream, whipped
¼ teaspoon salt	3 tablespoons blanched,
1 teaspoon vanilla	slivered almonds

Scald milk in top of double boiler. Beat together eggs and egg yolks. Stir sugar and salt into eggs. Gradually add a little of the heated milk to the eggs, stirring constantly. Pour back into milk in double boiler and cook over hot, not boiling, water until mixture thickens enough to coat a spoon. Remove from heat, cool; add vanilla.

While custard is cooling, split ladyfingers and place in serving bowl. Sprinkle with Scotch, then dot with currant jelly. Cover with custard, chill 1 hour, then top with whipped cream. Garnish with slivered almonds.
SERVES: 6.

Dessert Omelets and Soufflés

Brandy Mocha Omelet

Filling:
¼ cup semisweet chocolate
   bits
2 tablespoons heavy cream
1 tablespoon brandy
1½ teaspoons sugar

Omelet:
3 eggs, separated
2 teaspoons instant-coffee
   powder
2 tablespoons butter
1½ teaspoons sugar

Filling: Melt chocolate in top of double boiler over hot water. Remove from heat. Stir in cream, brandy, and sugar. Cover and keep warm.

Omelet: Beat egg yolks with coffee powder until well blended. Beat egg whites until stiff peaks form. Gently fold yolk mixture into egg whites until just blended. Heat butter in an omelet pan. Turn egg mixture into pan and quickly spread over bottom. Cook over medium heat until omelet is golden underneath. Place under broiler, 6 inches from heat, until top is lightly browned—about 2 minutes.

Turn out on serving plate, broiled side down. Place 3 tablespoons filling in center and fold omelet in half. Sprinkle with sugar. Spoon rest of filling over top.

SERVES: 3.

Omelette aux Pommes

2 cooking apples
3 tablespoons butter
2½ tablespoons sugar

1 tablespoon apple brandy
   (applejack)
3 eggs, separated
2 tablespoons heavy cream

Peel, core, and chop the apples. Cook with 1 tablespoon butter and 1 tablespoon sugar until soft. Stir in apple brandy.

Beat egg yolks with cream and 1 tablespoon sugar. Beat egg

whites until stiff and gently fold in yolks. Heat remaining butter in an omelet pan. Turn egg mixture into pan and quickly spread over bottom. Cook over medium heat until omelet is golden brown underneath. Spoon apple mixture over the cooked omelet, and fold. Sprinkle with remaining sugar and glaze under a hot broiler.
SERVES: 2.

Raspberry Omelet Soufflé

6 eggs, separated
½ cup seedless raspberry jam
3 tablespoons framboise

¼ cup sugar
3 tablespoons butter
Confectioners' sugar

Beat the egg yolks with ¼ cup jam and framboise (raspberry brandy) until thick and light in color. Beat egg whites until stiff, then gradually beat in sugar until they form stiff peaks. Fold yolks thoroughly into the whites.

Preheat oven to 350°F. Melt the butter in a shallow pan (at least 10 inches in diameter) in the oven. Stir remaining jam into butter and top with the egg mixture. Bake 15 to 20 minutes, or until omelet soufflé is set around the edge but still slightly creamy and moist in the center. Serve at once, spooning some butter-jam sauce over each portion. Dust with confectioners' sugar.
SERVES: 6 to 8.

Salzburger Nockerln

4 egg whites
3 tablespoons sugar
2 egg yolks
2 tablespoons sifted cake
 flour
½ teaspoon butter

2 tablespoons confectioners'
 sugar
1 tablespoon Jamaica rum
2 large cooked prunes
Confectioners' sugar for
 sprinkling

Preheat oven to 400°F. Beat egg whites with 3 tablespoons sugar until stiff. Using a whisk, fold in 1 egg yolk (unbeaten) at a time. Do this carefully so that air is retained in beaten whites. Gently fold in flour.

Butter a 9- or 10-inch ovenproof platter. Sprinkle with 1 tablespoon confectioners' sugar. Pour batter onto platter. Sprinkle top with 1 tablespoon confectioners' sugar. Bake for 5 minutes, or until top is just golden. Remove from oven; sprinkle with additional confectioners' sugar and rum. Garnish with prunes and serve at once. SERVES: 2.

Grand Marnier Soufflé

⅓ cup butter	3 egg whites
¾ cup flour	1 cup sugar
½ teaspoon salt	2 tablespoons lemon juice
1½ cups milk	1 teaspoon grated lemon rind
5 eggs, separated	½ cup Grand Marnier

Lightly butter a 2-quart soufflé dish, then sprinkle with sugar. Cut a strip of waxed paper or foil about 30 inches long and 6 inches wide, and fold in half lengthwise. Grease one side with butter and sprinkle with sugar. Tie the paper around the soufflé dish, sugared side in, so that it extends at least 2 inches above the dish.

Melt butter over low heat in a heavy saucepan. Remove from heat, add flour and salt, and mix until smooth. Add the milk, a little at a time, stirring constantly. Return to heat and cook, stirring constantly, until thickened and smooth. Remove from heat. Beat egg yolks until thick and lemon-colored. Add hot sauce, a little at a time, beating constantly until all the sauce has been added and the mixture is creamy. Cool to room temperature.

Preheat oven to 350°F. Beat all 8 egg whites until soft peaks form. Add sugar gradually, beating constantly until whites are stiff. Beat in the lemon juice, a few drops at a time. Stir the lemon rind and Grand Marnier into the egg-yolk mixture, mixing well. Add all at

once to the egg whites, and fold in thoroughly, using quick, light strokes. Pour into the prepared soufflé dish and set dish in a pan containing 1 inch of hot water. Bake for 1 hour. Remove from oven and carefully remove paper collar. Serve at once.
SERVES: 6 to 8.

Double Chocolate Soufflé

3 tablespoons butter
3 tablespoons flour
1 cup milk
½ cup sugar
¼ teaspoon salt

2 squares unsweetened
   chocolate, melted
1 teaspoon vanilla
½ cup crème de cacao
4 egg yolks
5 egg whites

Butter a 1½-quart soufflé dish and sprinkle with sugar. Refrigerate while preparing the soufflé. Melt butter in a saucepan. Blend in flour. Gradually add milk, stirring constantly. Mix in sugar, chocolate, and vanilla, and cook over low heat until thick and smooth. Remove from heat; add crème de cacao. Beat yolks lightly, and add a little of the hot chocolate mixture. Stir both into the rest of the chocolate mixture in the saucepan.

Preheat oven to 400°F. Beat egg whites until stiff and fold into yolk mixture. Pour into prepared soufflé dish. Set dish in a pan containing 1 inch of hot water. Bake soufflé for 15 minutes. Reduce heat to 350°F. and bake 20 to 25 minutes longer. Serve immediately.
SERVES: 6.

Mocha Soufflé

Use the recipe above and make the following substitutions:

1. ½ cup strong coffee and ½ cup milk instead of 1 cup milk.
2. ½ cup crème de café instead of crème de cacao.

Soufflé Rothschild

3 tablespoons butter
4 tablespoons flour
1 cup milk
½ cup cream
½ cup sugar
⅛ teaspoon salt

4 egg yolks
⅓ cup candied fruit, finely
   chopped
2 tablespoons kirsch
5 egg whites

Butter a 1½-quart soufflé dish and sprinkle with sugar. Refrigerate while preparing the soufflé. Melt butter in a saucepan. Blend in flour. Gradually add milk and cream, stirring constantly. Mix in sugar and salt, and cook over low heat until thick and smooth. Cool for a few minutes, then beat in yolks, one at a time. Return to heat and cook another mintue or two, until thick and smooth. Cool slightly and stir in candied fruit and kirsch.

Preheat oven to 375°F. Beat egg whites until stiff and fold into mixture. Pour into prepared soufflé dish and bake for 25 to 30 minutes.
SERVES: 6 to 8.

Puddings

Steamed Pudding De-Light

2 cups fine dry bread crumbs
¾ cup bourbon
2 eggs, beaten
½ cup orange juice
¼ cup molasses
¼ cup melted butter
½ teaspoon baking soda
½ cup currants

1 jar (4 ounces) diced candied
   pineapple
2 tablespoons flour
1 teaspoon cinnamon
⅛ teaspoon nutmeg
⅛ teaspoon cloves
Hard Sauce

Combine crumbs and ½ cup bourbon. Let crumb mixture stand 15 minutes; mix well. Add eggs, orange juice, molasses, melted butter, and baking soda; beat well. Combine currants, pineapple, flour, and spices. Add fruit mixture to molasses mixture; mix well. Turn into greased 1-quart mold. Cover tightly. Place mold in a pot with enough boiling water to come halfway up the side. Cover pot. Steam 1½ hours.

Turn pudding out onto flameproof serving dish. Warm remaining ¼ cup bourbon; ignite and pour over pudding. Serve pudding with Hard Sauce.

SERVES: 6.

Really Brandied Plum Pudding

¾ cup currants
¾ cup seedless raisins
¾ cup seeded raisins
½ cup finely chopped dates
½ cup chopped candied fruit
¼ cup slivered candied orange peel
½ cup sliced blanched almonds
½ teaspoon grated lemon rind

1 cup brandy (approx.)
2 cups soft bread crumbs
⅔ cup sifted flour
½ cup finely chopped suet
½ teaspoon nutmeg
½ teaspoon cinnamon
¼ teaspoon ginger
⅛ teaspoon cloves
3 eggs
¾ cup sugar

Marinate fruits and almonds overnight in ½ cup brandy. Next day, add crumbs, flour, suet, and spices to the marinated fruits. Mix together lightly. In another bowl, beat eggs with sugar until light. Pour over fruit mixture. Mix lightly, using your hands.

Butter and flour a 1½-quart mold. Fill with mixture almost to the top. Cover mold tightly with buttered lid (or use buttered aluminum foil). Place mold in a pot with enough boiling water to come halfway up the side. Cover pot. Simmer for 5 hours, adding more boiling water as needed. Remove mold from water and cool. When cool, uncover and pour about ¼ cup brandy over. Cover pudding and keep in a cool place for at least 2 weeks before serving. Additional brandy can be added from time to time.

To serve, heat covered pudding in hot water for 1 hour. Unmold

on a serving platter. Warm ¼ cup brandy, ignite, and pour flaming over pudding at table.
SERVES: 6.

Paleface Indian Pudding

3¾ cups milk	1 teaspoon salt
¼ cup yellow cornmeal	¼ cup sugar
¼ cup Scotch whisky	1 teaspoon cinnamon
½ cup dark molasses	4 tablespoons butter

In a double boiler, scald 2 cups of milk. Mix cornmeal smoothly with Scotch and stir into the hot milk. Cook over hot water 20 minutes, stirring frequently. Add molasses, salt, sugar, cinnamon, and butter. Stir well and pour into a buttered pudding dish. Pour 1¾ cups cold milk over the top. Bake for 3 hours in oven preheated to 250°F. Serve warm with heavy cream or vanilla ice cream.
SERVES: 4 to 6.

Riz à l'Impératrice

1 cup candied fruit, chopped	1 envelope unflavored gelatin
¼ cup blended whiskey	4 egg yolks, lightly beaten
1 cup raw rice	1 cup sugar
2 cups boiling water	1 teaspoon vanilla
2 cups milk	1 cup heavy cream, whipped
¼ teaspoon salt	

Soak fruit overnight in whiskey. Cook rice in boiling water about 10 minutes. Pour off water and add 1⅓ cups milk and the salt. Cook in milk until very tender. Set aside to cool. Sprinkle gelatin on remaining ⅔ cup milk, in top part of double boiler. Set over boiling water and cook until milk has scalded. Add eggs, sugar, and vanilla, and cook, stirring constantly, until smooth and thickened. Mix into rice and cool until mixture begins to set. Stir in undrained candied fruit. Fold in whipped cream. Chill.
SERVES: 6.

Meringue Rice Pudding

1 cup raw rice	2 tablespoons lemon juice
2 cups boiling water	½ cup orange juice
½ teaspoon salt	2 tablespoons hot water
3 cups milk	2 tablespoons bourbon
1¼ cups sugar	2 egg whites
¼ cup butter	2 tablespoons apricot jam

Cook the rice in boiling water and salt for 5 minutes. Drain thoroughly. Add milk and simmer until the rice is very tender and all the milk is absorbed. Melt butter and ¾ cup sugar over very low heat until sugar is golden. Add lemon juice, orange juice, and hot water. Bring to a boil. Add to the cooked rice and simmer together for 3 minutes. Cool the rice.

Preheat oven to 325°F. Butter a 1½-quart baking dish. Stir bourbon into cooled rice. Beat egg whites with ⅓ cup sugar until stiff. Put half the rice into prepared baking dish. Dot with apricot jam. Spread with remaining rice and carefully cover with meringue. Sprinkle with remaining sugar. Bake for 20 minutes, or until meringue is golden brown. May be served warm or chilled.
SERVES: 8 to 10.

Bread and Fruit Pudding

2 cups small bread cubes	¼ teaspoon nutmeg
3 cups milk, scalded	⅛ teaspoon salt
½ cup chopped pitted dates	3 eggs, well beaten
½ cup sugar	3 tablespoons melted butter
¼ teaspoon cinnamon	2 tablespoons full-bodied rum

Butter a 2-quart baking dish. Put in bread cubes and pour scalded milk over. Soak for 10 minutes. Add dates. Combine sugar, cinnamon, nutmeg, and salt in a small bowl. Stir in eggs, melted butter, and rum. Pour over bread-cube mixture. Stir well. Bake in oven preheated to 350°F. for about 1¼ hours, or until knife inserted in center of pudding comes out clean. Serve warm or cold.
SERVES: 8.

Marlborough Pudding

1 cup thick unsweetened
    applesauce
2 tablespoons Calvados
¾ cup sugar

3 eggs, lightly beaten
2 tablespoons melted butter
¼ teaspoon salt

Preheat oven to 325°F. and butter a 1-quart casserole. Combine all ingredients and blend well. Pour into casserole. Bake 50 to 60 minutes, or until knife inserted in center comes out clean. Serve warm or cold. Good with heavy cream, plain or whipped.
SERVES: 4 to 6.

Rum-Raisin Ricotta

3 tablespoons seeded raisins
¼ cup Gold Label Puerto
    Rican rum
1 pound ricotta cheese

¼ cup sugar
1 teaspoon grated lemon rind
Instant espresso-coffee powder

Steep raisins in rum for about 1 hour. Whip cheese until smooth and soft. Add raisins and rum, sugar, and lemon rind, and beat until completely mixed. Spoon into sherbets and chill. Dust lightly with instant-espresso powder.
SERVES: 6.

Fritters, Pancakes and Crêpes

Beignets

1 cup water
½ cup butter
½ teaspoon salt
2 tablespoons sugar
1 cup sifted flour

5 eggs
2 tablespoons cognac
Salad oil for frying
Confectioners' sugar

Combine water, butter, salt, and sugar in a saucepan. Bring to a boil. Add flour all at once, stirring constantly over low heat until mixture forms a ball and leaves the sides of the pan. Remove from heat. Add eggs one at a time, beating hard after each addition. Beat in cognac. Refrigerate batter while heating oil in an electric skillet or deep-fryer to 385°F.

Drop batter by rounded tablespoons into hot oil. Fry only a few at a time. Cook until golden brown, about 5 minutes on each side. Drain and sprinkle with confectioners' sugar. Serve warm.
SERVES: 8.

Apple Fritters

3 large apples
¼ cup sugar plus 1 tablespoon
4 tablespoons Calvados
¾ cup sifted flour
¼ teaspoon salt

¼ cup beer
1 tablespoon melted butter
1 egg, separated
Salad oil for deep frying
Confectioners' sugar

Peel and core apples and cut in ¼-inch slices. Sprinkle ¼ cup sugar and 2 tablespoons Calvados on apple slices. Cover and let stand for 1 hour.

Mix flour, salt, 1 tablespoon sugar, beer, butter, and 2 tablespoons Calvados until smooth. Beat egg yolk and add to flour mixture. Cover and refrigerate for 2 or 3 hours. When ready to fry, whip egg white until stiff and fold in. Heat oil in an electric skillet or deep-fryer to 375°F. Drain apple slices and dip into the batter to coat well. Fry, a few at a time, until well browned. Drain and sprinkle with confectioners' sugar.
SERVES: 6.

Variation:

Pineapple Fritters

Prepare as above with following changes:
1. Substitute drained canned pineapple slices for the apple.
2. Eliminate ¼ cup sugar.
3. Substitute light rum for Calvados.

Banana Fritters

4 firm, ripe bananas	½ teaspoon salt
⅓ cup bourbon	½ teaspoon cinnamon
2 teaspoons lemon juice	2 eggs
3 tablespoons sugar	½ cup milk
1 cup sifted flour	1 teaspoon melted butter
1 teaspoon baking powder	Salad oil for frying

Peel bananas and cut in half lengthwise and then crosswise. Marinate for 1 hour in mixture of bourbon, lemon juice, and 2 tablespoons sugar.

Sift flour with baking powder, salt, cinnamon, and remaining tablespoon of sugar. Beat eggs with milk, melted butter, and 1 tablespoon of banana marinade. Gradually beat in flour mixture and beat until smooth.

Heat oil in electric skillet or deep-fryer to 375°F. Drain banana pieces and dust with flour. Dip in batter to coat well. Fry, a few at a time, turning once, until golden brown on all sides. Drain and keep warm. Serve at once.
SERVES: 6 to 8.

Applejack Pancakes

1 cup sifted flour	2 tablespoons melted butter
½ teaspoon salt	1 tablespoon applejack
⅛ teaspoon baking soda	¾ cup shredded raw apples
¼ cup sugar	Butter for frying and serving
2 eggs	with pancakes
1 cup milk	Cinnamon-sugar

Sift together flour, salt, baking soda, and sugar. Combine eggs with milk and beat very well. Add to flour mixture. Stir in melted butter and mix batter with a rotary beater until completely smooth. Pour applejack over apples and add to batter.

Heat a little butter in a 6-inch skillet. For each pancake, pour in 2 tablespoons of batter all at once and quickly tilt and rotate pan so that the bottom of the pan is completely covered. When lightly brown on the bottom, turn pancake and lightly brown the other side. Repeat until all batter is used. Keep pancakes hot. To serve, put about a half-teaspoon of softened butter in the center of each pancake, fold over, and sprinkle generously with cinnamon-sugar. SERVES: 6.

Cakes and Rum

½ cup seedless raisins
¼ cup Jamaica rum
2 cups sifted flour
2 cups milk
4 eggs, separated

5 tablespoons sugar
½ teaspoon salt
4 tablespoons melted butter
¼ pound butter (for frying)
Confectioners' sugar

Pour rum over raisins, stir, and let stand for several hours.

Combine flour and milk, and mix well. Add egg yolks, sugar, salt, and melted butter, and beat until smooth. Drain raisins and stir in. Beat egg whites until stiff and fold in.

Heat ¼ pound of butter in a heavy 10-inch skillet. Add batter (about 1 inch deep) and cook, covered, until a golden-brown crust forms on the bottom. Turn, using 2 pancake turners, and let brown, uncovered, on other side.

Remove from pan, break into pieces with a fork, and sprinkle generously with confectioners' sugar. SERVES: 4.

Walnut-Brandy Palacsinta

Filling:
¾ cup walnuts, finely
  chopped
1 cup sugar
2 tablespoons milk
2 tablespoons brandy
1 teaspoon grated orange rind

Pancakes:
3 eggs

6 tablespoons flour
1 tablespoon sugar
½ teaspoon salt
1 cup milk
Butter for frying

Topping:
1 cup heavy cream
1 teaspoon sugar
1 tablespoon orange liqueur

Filling: Combine ingredients and mix well. Reserve.

Pancakes: Beat eggs lightly. Add flour, sugar, and salt, and continue beating until batter is smooth. Add milk gradually, beating until completely smooth. Heat about a teaspoon of butter until bubbly in an 8-inch frying pan. Pour in 3 tablespoons of batter all at once and quickly rotate and tilt pan so that the bottom of the pan is completely covered. When lightly brown on the bottom, turn pancake and lightly brown the other side. Add ½ teaspoon of butter to the pan for each additional pancake and repeat above until all the batter is used. This makes about 12 pancakes. Keep pancakes warm.

Topping: Whip cream with sugar and orange liqueur. Spread pancakes with filling and roll up. Fold in the sides to hold filling inside. Heat a little butter in a frying pan or chafing dish and quickly reheat filled pancakes. Garnish each portion with whipped-cream topping. SERVES: 6.

Dessert Crêpes

2 eggs, well beaten
¼ cup milk
¼ cup water
1 tablespoon melted butter
1 tablespoon cognac
½ cup sifted flour

¼ teaspoon salt
2 teaspoons sugar
½ teaspoon vanilla extract
Clarified butter for frying (see below)

Add all ingredients, except clarified butter, to beaten eggs. Beat with a rotary beater until smooth. Let batter stand at room temperature for at least an hour.

To clarify butter: Melt 4 to 6 tablespoons butter in a heavy pan. Let stand a few minutes and then carefully pour off clear, golden liquid, clarified butter, discarding milky residue which is left.

Heat an 8-inch skillet or omelet pan until a couple of drops of water sprinkled in the pan bounce across and then evaporate. Brush pan with clarified butter. Pour in 2 tablespoons of batter and quickly rotate and tilt pan so that the bottom is covered. It will set and brown

in about 20 seconds. Turn and brown other side. Slide onto a warmed plate. Repeat above until all batter has been used.
YIELD: 12 to 15 crêpes.

Crêpes Suzette

12 Dessert Crêpes (page 263)	Juice of one orange (½ cup)
¼ cup sweet butter	6 tablespoons orange liqueur
¼ cup confectioners' sugar	2 teaspoons sugar
Grated zest of one orange	¼ cup cognac, warmed

Prepare Dessert Crêpes. Cream butter and confectioners' sugar. Stir in orange zest, orange juice, and 3 tablespoons orange liqueur.

Put mixture in a heated chafing dish and heat until it bubbles. Add crêpes, one at a time, bathing in the sauce. Fold each crêpe in quarters and push to one side of the pan.

When all the crêpes are folded in the pan, sprinkle with sugar and add remaining 3 tablespoons of orange liqueur and ¼ cup cognac. Ignite, using a long (fireplace) match. Spoon flaming sauce over crêpes and serve as soon as the flames die out.
SERVES: 4.

Crêpes Soufflé Bourbon

12 Dessert Crêpes (page 263)	2 egg yolks
½ cup milk	½ teaspoon vanilla
2 tablespoons flour	2 tablespoons bourbon
¼ cup sugar	4 egg whites, stiffly beaten
Pinch salt	Superfine granulated sugar

Prepare Dessert Crêpes as directed and keep warm. Blend milk, flour, sugar, and salt until smooth. Cook, stirring, until thick. Combine egg yolks, vanilla, and bourbon, and beat lightly. Gradually beat flour mixture into eggs and blend well. Cool, then fold in the beaten egg whites.

Preheat oven to 450°F. Butter a large heatproof serving dish and sprinkle with superfine sugar. Place about 2 or 3 tablespoons of soufflé mixture in the center of each crêpe. Fold crêpes in half and place in a single layer in the prepared dish. Sprinkle with superfine sugar and bake until lightly browned and puffed, about 3 minutes. Serve at once.

SERVES: 6.

Crêpes Blueberry

1 pint fresh blueberries	½ teaspoon grated lemon rind
¼ cup sugar	1½ tablespoons kirsch
1 tablespoon lemon juice	12 Dessert Crêpes (page 263)
1 tablespoon water	

Wash and drain berries. Combine sugar, lemon juice, and water in a saucepan. Add the berries and bring to a boil, stirring constantly. Remove from heat and stir in lemon rind. Add kirsch.

Prepare Dessert Crêpes and keep warm. Meanwhile, heat blueberry sauce over a low flame. Roll crêpes and place on dessert plates. Ladle warmed blueberry sauce over. Serve at once.

SERVES: 4 to 6.

WHISKEY
IN THE
GLASS
CHAPTER
20

How To Be a Good Mixer

The knack of mixing tasty, satisfying drinks is easily acquired. A drink is simply a group of ingredients, a formula if you will, combined in a precise manner. The formulas are neither sacrosanct nor immutable. We've seen changes in the classic martini and Manhattan, as an instance, in the last dozen years. So by all means experiment, until you find the recipe that pleases you most. Then, do as the professionals do—measure all ingredients carefully, follow the prescribed mixing method and use good materials. A working bartender may seem to toss ingredients together with raffish ease. He has the measurements in his eyes and in his fingers, from long practice. Don't allow yourself similar liberties. Here are further professional mixing tips—everything you need to know to make superb drinks:

1. *Stir* clear drinks like the Manhattan or the martini; otherwise they turn cloudy.
2. *Shake* drinks that contain sugar, cream, juices or egg whites.
3. Use ice cubes when stirring. Stir until drink is well chilled, and no longer. Too much stirring dilutes a drink.
4. Use chipped or cracked ice when shaking. Shake vigorously, to mix all ingredients thoroughly and get a creamy consistency.
5. Use fresh fruit and good-quality mixers for tastier drinks. Squeeze fruit just before you use it. However, frozen juices are practical and satisfactory for punches and quantity preparation.
6. When stripping peel from fruit, pare thinly to avoid the bitter, white under part. Take only the colored "zest." To use, twist peel over the drink to spray surface with the flavorful oils. Drop peel into drink or not, as specified.
7. Rub the rim of the liquor bottle with waxed paper before pouring, to prevent dripping. An occasional rub will do.
8. Stir drinks containing carbonated beverages briefly, to retain all the bubbles you can. Tilt the glass and pour soda down the side, to hold the sparkle in a highball.

9. Soak lemons in warm water for ten minutes, then roll on a hard surface before squeezing. You'll get more juice.

10. Never use confectioners' sugar—it contains cornstarch and will cloud your drink.

11. Sweeten with superfine or granulated sugar dissolved in a little liquid. Even better, make up a simple syrup: Heat 2 cups sugar and a pint of water just to the boil. Store covered in a cool place and use as needed. It keeps well.

12. To frost the rim of a glass, moisten edge with juice or some other liquid, invert, and swirl in sugar or salt. Chill until the moist area hardens to form a crust.

13. Don't drown a drink. Serve a pitcher of ice water or cold soda with highballs so guests can add more as desired. When serving drinks made with juices or tonic, follow same principle.

14. A twist of lemon or orange rind adds interest to "on-the-rocks" drinks.

15. Try a few dashes of orange liqueur to smooth out cocktails made with lemon.

16. To give a Daiquiri a frothy top, add a drop of milk to your mix before shaking.

17. Ice should go into the glass first, to avoid splashing and to facilitate chilling. Add alcohol before juice or soda—the alcohol, being lighter, rises and starts the mixing process.

18. Keep everything cold for best results. Prechill the pitcher or shaker, mixers, glassware, and utensils. To chill glass quickly, fill with crushed ice while you're mixing the drinks. Spill ice out just prior to pouring.

19. Don't stint on ice when preparing drinks. A good rule of thumb is to be generous in the shaker or pitcher, and cut down on ice in the glass.

20. Water freezes at 32°F., but can vary in temperature as much as 10 degrees. Use hard-frozen ice directly from the refrigerator, if possible.

21. Use fresh ice and glassware every time you mix a new round of drinks. Mix only the required quantity. The "dividend" left in the shaker waters down and tastes flat.

22. Ice will pick up food odors if it has been in the freezer any length of time. Discard "stale" ice periodically.

23. For purposes of calculating or measuring, figure that one ice cube displaces one ounce of liquid. Remember, it will also add an ounce of water to the drink when melted.

24. A canvas bag and a mallet are all you need to make cracked ice from ice cubes.

Bar Equipment

Good tools are a pleasure to work with, and an economy in the long run. Shun elaborate gadgets. The only people who use them successfully are the pitchmen paid to demonstrate them. Here's a list of what you should have. Quite a few are familiar kitchen tools—no need to duplicate for the bar.

Shaker: The best type of shaker consists of two containers, a bottom, made of heavy glass, and a tight-fitting metal top. Glass retains cold better than metal and will give less dilution to your drink.

Pitcher: A martini pitcher with a lip to hold back ice can be used for stirring all drinks.

Strainer: A flat wire strainer with coiled-spring edge is ideal for home use.

Corkscrew: A plain wing-type corkscrew works very well and costs about a dollar. Don't be tempted by the decorative bone or silver-plated fancies featured before the holidays.

Measuring cup: Get the double-enders. One side measures a full jigger—1½ ounces—the other side a pony—1 ounce.

Other essentials are:

Lime squeezer
Juicer: A hand juicer is adequate.
Bottle opener
Long-handled bar spoon
Ice bucket: Make sure the cover fits tightly.

Stoppers: To recork opened soda bottles.
Canvas bag and mallet: For crushing ice.

Other items which are helpful but *not necessary:*

Muddlers, wooden cutting board, stainless-steel paring knife, long plastic or metal stirring rod, ice scoop, funnel, set of measuring spoons, fine wire strainer, lemon zester or **potato peeler.**

Glassware

You don't really need special glasses for serving liquor, but it adds to the pleasure. The following sizes are recommended:

A stemmed **cocktail glass** of 4-ounce capacity. This will hold a generous drink and you won't have to fill it to the brim.

A 7-ounce **old-fashioned glass** for "on-the-rocks" drinks and frappes, as well as old-fashioneds.

A 12-ounce **Collins glass** that will double for highballs and coolers. This size holds a good-sized drink, and enough ice to keep the drink cold.

Several 2-ounce **shot glasses** with heavy base are handy to have.

Sours and some medium-size drinks are quite attractive served in **wine goblets.**

Standard Measures

A quart, whether it's milk, water or whiskey, holds 32 ounces.
A fifth is ⅕ of a gallon, ⅘ of a quart or 25.6 ounces.
A half-gallon is 64 ounces.
A gallon is 128 ounces.
A jigger is 1½ ounces.
A pony is 1 ounce.
2 tablespoons equal 1 ounce.
6 teaspoons equal 1 ounce.
A dash is ⅙ teaspoon or about 8 drops.

Practical Party Guide

The caterer's rule of thumb in estimating the number of bottles needed for a party is one fifth for every four people. This is fairly generous, allowing four 1½-ounce drinks per person, plus spillage. Obviously there will be variations, depending on the crowd, the occasion, season of year, drink preferences and the bartender. You wouldn't want guests to take more than two cocktails before dinner, if that. On the other hand, people will imbibe more at a party that runs into the small hours. You certainly don't want to run out, so keep a reserve supply. It's reassuring to have more liquor on hand than you expect to use. Savings may be effected by purchasing the half-gallon or gallon size, where available.

One last reminder—have plenty of ice. You can overcome almost any shortage but ice. Arrange for a supply from a dealer or vending machine, allowing the equivalent of 3 ice cubes per drink. That should take care of the shaker or pitcher and the glass.

Cheers!

DRINKS
CHAPTER
21

Cocktails

Gin with a Wedge

Since gin is already flavored with juniper berries, fruit peels and other bontanicals, it's a kind of ready-made cocktail just as it comes from the bottle.

Pour 2 ounces good-quality gin over plenty of ice. Drop a wedge of orange, both fruit and peel, into the glass. Stir very well to chill and dilute.

Martini

Not so long ago the martini was considered an urban tipple, fashionable with that exotic species known as "communications" men. It is today the nation's most popular cocktail. Controversy and martinis go together. Bernard De Voto, in his now legendary *Harper's* magazine article, prescribed a ratio of 3.7 gin to 1 vermouth for "the true martini." Hemingway's Col. Cantwell drank his martinis 15 to 1 and Winston Churchill "glanced at the vermouth bottle" as he poured the gin. Some bartenders shake a few drops of Scotch whisky into the glass before mixing. The single point of agreement among martiniphiles is that a martini should be frigid. Prechill everything, including the gin and vermouth. Following is a more or less conventional martini and a few stirring variations.

2 ounces gin   Lemon peel or olive
½ ounce dry vermouth

Stir gin and vermouth with ice until well chilled. Pour into chilled cocktail glass over ice cubes. Add twist of lemon peel or olive.

Variations:

Vodka Martini

Just substitute vodka for gin.

274

Garlic Martini

5 ounces gin
1 ounce dry vermouth
Garlic powder, a few grains

1 drop salad oil
4–5 grains salt (optional)

Mull garlic powder, oil, and salt in a mixing glass. Add chilled gin
and vermouth, and stir well with cracked ice until cold. Strain into
cocktail glasses.
SERVES: 2.

Gibson

Regular martini but substitute a cocktail onion for the lemon peel.

Pernod Martini

Swirl a few drops of Pernod around cocktail glass, then drain. Pour
in regular martini. Omit garnish.

Ginger Martini

Add ¾ inch of dried ginger root to gin and vermouth, and let stand
for 5 minutes. Stir with ice and strain into chilled glass. Omit garnish.

Manhattan

1½ ounces blended whiskey
    or bourbon
½ ounce sweet vermouth

Dash of bitters
Maraschino cherry

Stir well with cracked ice and strain into a cocktail glass. Garnish
with cherry.

Variation: As a change, substitute cherry liqueur for the vermouth
and leave out bitters.

Rob Roy

1½ ounces Scotch whisky   ½ ounce sweet vermouth

Stir with ice until well chilled. Strain into a cocktail glass.

Variation:

Dry Rob Roy

Substitute dry vermouth for sweet vermouth.

Bourbon Old-Fashioned

½ teaspoon sugar   Twist of lemon peel
2 dashes Angostura bitters   Fresh pineapple stick or
1 teaspoon water   half orange slice
2 ounces bourbon

In a medium old-fashioned glass, muddle sugar with Angostura and water. When thoroughly mixed, add cracked ice or cubes. Pour in bourbon. Stir. Add lemon peel. Garnish with pineapple or orange slice.

Bourbon Sour

1½ ounces bourbon   Half slice orange
1 ounce lemon juice   Maraschino cherry
1 teaspoon sugar or simple
    syrup

Shake bourbon, lemon juice, and sugar with cracked ice. Strain into a sour glass. Garnish with orange slice and cherry.

Variation:

Boston Sour

1½ ounces blended whiskey
1 ounce cranberry-juice
  cocktail

½ ounce lemon juice
½ teaspoon sugar or simple
  syrup

Shake with ice and strain into a sour glass. Garnish with orange slice.

Daiquiri

1½ ounces rum
1 ounce lime juice

1 teaspoon sugar or
  simple syrup

Shake well with cracked ice and strain into a cocktail glass.

Variations:

Frozen Daiquiri

Same as above, but shake or blend with ⅓ cup shaved ice. Pour unstrained into cocktail glass and serve with short straws.

Bacardi Cocktail

1½ ounces Bacardi rum
1 ounce lime juice

½ teaspoon grenadine
½ teaspoon sugar

Shake well with cracked ice and strain into a cocktail glass.

Daiquiris by the Pitcher

12 ounces rum
1 6-ounce can frozen
  Daiquiri mix, thawed

6 ounces ice water

Half-fill a 2-quart pitcher with cracked ice. Pour in rum, Daiquiri mix, and water. Stir until completely blended. Strain into cocktail glasses, or over ice in old-fashioneds.
SERVES: 8.

Kipinski

1 ounce white Puerto Rican
  rum
1 ounce triple sec

1 ounce unsweetened
  grapefruit juice

Shake with ice until chilled. Strain into cocktail glass.

Gimlet

1½ ounces vodka
1 tablespoon lime juice

½ teaspoon sugar or
simple syrup

Shake with ice and strain into cocktail glass. Garnish with slice of fresh lime. A teaspoon of Cointreau is a pleasant addition.

Cape Codder

1½ ounces vodka
1 teaspoon lime juice

Cranberry-juice cocktail

Pour vodka and lime juice over ice cubes in an old-fashioned glass. Add cranberry juice to fill. Stir.

Dubonnet Cocktail

1½ ounces gin
1 ounce Dubonnet

Twist of orange peel

Stir with ice. Strain into old-fashioned glass over ice cubes. Garnish with orange peel.

Waverly Cocktail

1½ ounces gin
1 teaspoon crème de cassis

1 teaspoon orange juice

Shake with cracked ice and strain into a chilled cocktail glass.

White Lady

1 ounce gin
½ ounce Cointreau

½ ounce lemon juice

Shake with cracked ice and strain into a chilled cocktail glass.

Sidecar

1 ounce brandy
1 ounce triple sec

1 ounce lemon juice

Shake well with ice. Moisten rim of cocktail glass with lemon juice and swirl in superfine sugar. Strain drink into glass.

Negroni

1 ounce gin
1 ounce Campari

1 ounce Italian (sweet) vermouth

Shake with ice and strain into a cocktail glass. For a dryer drink, use half dry vermouth and half sweet vermouth.

Jack Rose

1½ ounces applejack
Juice of ½ lime

1 teaspoon grenadine

Shake well with cracked ice and strain into cocktail glass.

Margarita

Salt
1½ ounces white tequila

½ ounce triple sec
½ ounce lime juice

Moisten rim of cocktail glass with lime juice. Invert glass and swirl in salt to frost rim. Tap glass to knock off excess salt. Shake all ingredients with cracked ice until chilled. Strain into prepared glass. Be careful of rim.

Brawny Broth

1 ounce vodka
Thin slice of lemon
4 ounces hot bouillon

Grind of pepper
Salt, if necessary

Put vodka and lemon slice in a cup or mug. Add bouillon and season to taste.

Whisky-Mac

1 ounce Scotch whisky

1 ounce ginger wine

Stir with ice until well chilled. Strain into cocktail glass.

Scotch Mist

Mound chipped ice in a small old-fashioned glass or small-footed glass. Pour 2 ounces Scotch whisky over. Serve with short straws.

Sazerac

2 ounces bourbon
1 dash Peychaud bitters
2 dashes Pernod

1 scant teaspoon sugar or
    simple syrup
Strip of lemon peel

Stir all ingredients except lemon peel with ice and strain into cocktail glass. Twist lemon peel over glass but do not drop in.

NOTE: You can substitute 2 teaspoons of anisette for the Pernod and sugar in recipe above.

Tall Drinks

Tom Collins

1½ ounces gin
1 ounce lemon juice

1 teaspoon sugar or
    simple syrup
Club soda

Shake gin, lemon juice, and sugar with cracked ice. Strain into a tall glass. Add ice cubes and club soda to fill. Stir lightly.

Ramos Fizz

2 ounces gin
2 ounces cream
½ ounce lemon juice
1 teaspoon sugar

1 teaspoon grenadine
1 egg white
Several dashes Orange
    Flower Water

This drink requires long, vigorous shaking with lots of cracked ice. Use a drink mixer (not a blender) if you have one. Strain into a tall glass.

Le Screwdriver

1½ ounces vodka
½ ounce triple sec or
   curaçao

Chilled orange juice

Place two or three ice cubes in an 8-ounce glass. Add vodka, triple sec, and orange juice to fill. Stir.

Salt Lick

2 ounces vodka

2 ounces chilled grapefruit
  juice

2 ounces chilled tonic

Moisten rim of 8-ounce glass with lemon juice; then swirl in fine salt
to form a frosted ring around edge. Put ice cube into glass. Add
vodka, grapefruit juice, and tonic. Stir lightly.

Dill Mary

1½ ounces vodka

½ teaspoon dried dill weed

3 ounces tomato juice

1 drop Tabasco

⅛ teaspoon salt, or to taste

Light grind of black pepper

Rub dill between fingers to powder, and drop into bar glass or cup.
Pour in vodka and tomato juice. Let steep for 10 minutes. Add salt
and Tabasco. Stir. Strain through fine mesh strainer over ice cubes
into an 8-ounce glass. Stir briskly until chilled. Grind a light sprinkle
of black pepper on top.

NOTE: Surprisingly, the dried dill is much preferable to fresh in
this recipe.

Moscow Mule

1½ ounces vodka

Juice of ½ lime

Ginger beer

Pour vodka and lime juice over ice cubes in a copper mug. Stir.
Drop in lime hull. Add ginger beer to fill. Stir quickly.

Ginger Highball

Ginger snap minus the sweetness of ginger ale.

1½ ounces blended whiskey   Club soda
Slice fresh ginger root, the size
   of a nickel

Pour whiskey over ice cubes in a highball glass. Place ginger root in a thoroughly clean garlic press. Squeeze ginger into whiskey, add soda, stir gently.

Mint Julep

6 sprigs fresh mint   2 ounces Kentucky bourbon
1 teaspoon sugar   Crushed ice

In a large, chilled, dry highball glass, place 3 sprigs of fresh mint. Cover with 1 teaspoon sugar and a little water. Muddle lightly, just bruising the mint. Fill the glass with finely crushed ice and slowly add bourbon. Stir slowly to frost the glass. Add more crushed ice to fill glass, and stir again. Plant 3 or 4 sprigs of mint in ice at top of glass. Dust lightly with sugar and serve with straw.

Primavera

12 sprigs watercress   3 ounces White Label rum
8 ounces pineapple juice

Trim off stem ends of cress. Whirl leaves with pineapple juice in blender for 30 seconds. Pour over ice cubes, into two 8-ounce glasses. Add 1½ ounces of rum to each glass. Stir until chilled.
SERVES: 2.

Planter's Punch #1

3 ounces Jamaica rum
Juice of ½ lime, plus shell
½ ounce orange juice

1 teaspoon grenadine
Dash aromatic bitters
Club soda

Pour all ingredients, except club soda, into a tall glass, half-filled with ice. Stir. Add more cracked ice to within 1 inch of rim. Fill with club soda to just above level of ice. Garnish with sprig of mint or orange slice.

Planter's Punch #2

1½ ounces Puerto Rican rum
1 ounce Jamaica rum
1 tablespoon each lemon,
    lime and orange juice

1 teaspoon sugar
Club soda
Half slice of orange
Pineapple stick

Shake rums, juices, and sugar with ice until very cold. Strain into tall glass two-thirds filled with cracked ice. Add club soda. Garnish with orange and pineapple.

Variation: In Jamaica, honey is sometimes used in place of sugar. It's very pleasant in this variation of a famous drink.

Zombie

2 ounces Puerto Rican rum
1 ounce Jamaica rum
½ ounce 151-proof rum
1 ounce curaçao

1 ounce lemon juice
1 ounce orange juice
½ ounce grenadine
1 dash Pernod

Stir vigorously with cracked ice. For one, strain into tall glass over ice. For two, pour over ice in old-fashioned glasses. For three, pour over ice in cocktail glasses.

Mai-Tai

1 ounce White Label Puerto
   Rican rum
½ ounce Gold Label Puerto
   Rican rum

½ ounce curaçao
½ ounce lime juice
½ teaspoon Falernum

Pour into a tall glass filled with shaved ice. Stir briskly with a long-handled spoon.

Brandy Milk Punch

2 ounces brandy or cognac
6 ounces cold milk

1 scant teaspoon sugar or
   simple syrup

Shake well with ice. Strain into a 10-ounce glass. Dust with a little freshly grated nutmeg.

Pimm's Cup

2 ounces Pimm's No. 1
1 slice lemon

7-Up (or other lemon-flavored
   soda)
Sprig of borage

Pour Pimm's over several ice cubes in a 10-ounce glass. Add lemon slice. Fill with 7-Up and garnish with sprig of borage—leaves and flowers.

Refreshments or After-Dinner Drinks

Alexander

1 ounce crème de cacao
1 ounce gin or brandy

1 ounce cream

Shake well with cracked ice. Strain into cocktail glass. Sprinkle with nutmeg for a pleasant change.

Black Russian

1 ounce coffee liqueur   1 ounce vodka

Pour over ice cubes in old-fashioned glass. Stir.

Rusty Nail

1 ounce Scotch whisky   ¾ ounce Drambuie

Pour over ice cubes in an old-fashioned glass. Stir.

Stinger

1½ ounces brandy   ¾ ounce white crème de
                                        menthe

Stir well with cracked ice. Strain into cocktail glass.

Variation:

White Spider

Substitute vodka for brandy.

Fire and Ice

1 ounce Cherristock or   1 ounce kirsch (cherry
   Cherry Heering   brandy)

Stir with ice until very cold. Strain into chilled cocktail glass.

Scarlett O'Hara

1½ ounces Southern Comfort   Juice of ¼ lime
1½ ounces cranberry juice

Stir well with ice and strain into cocktail glass.

Angel's Tip

Pour crème de cacao into a liqueur glass until two-thirds full. Carefully pour heavy cream over back of teaspoon so that it floats over the liqueur.

Grasshopper

½ ounce white crème de   ½ ounce green crème de
   cacao   menthe
                                 ½ ounce cream

Shake briskly with cracked ice. Strain into small cocktail glass.

Pousse Café

⅙ grenadine   ⅙ crème de violette
⅙ Maraschino   ⅙ chartreuse
⅙ green crème de menthe   ⅙ brandy

Slowly pour, *one by one,* into a cordial glass, *in order given.* Each cordial should form a layer, floating on top of others, without mixing.

Hot Drinks

Auld Man's Milk

1 egg, beaten
1 teaspoon sugar

1 cup hot milk
2 ounces Scotch whisky
½ ounce Drambuie

Shake briskly in a preheated cocktail shaker. Strain into 2 warmed mugs.
SERVES: 2.

Big Apple

3 ounces apple juice, warmed
Pinch of powdered ginger

½ baked apple
1 ounce applejack

Heat apple juice and ginger to simmer in a small pan. Scald a thick-sided, heat-resistant old-fashioned glass by filling with boiling water, then emptying. Now put in the baked apple half, with just a little of its syrup. Apple should be at room temperature. Ignite liquor and pour into glass. Add warmed apple juice. Stir. Sip slowly, and spoon up the liquor-drenched apple.

Hot Buttered Rum

1 scant teaspoon butter
1 teaspoon maple syrup
Dash each of cinnamon,
   allspice, and bitters

Slice of lemon
2 ounces Jamaica rum
4 ounces boiling water

Place butter in preheated ceramic mug or heavy glass. Leave spoon in mug. Add syrup, spices, lemon, and rum. Mix. Pour in boiling water. Stir. Dust with extra cinnamon or nutmeg, if you like.

Tom and Jerry

1 egg

1 teaspoon brown sugar

¼ teaspoon allspice

1 ounce Puerto Rican rum

½ ounce cognac

Hot milk or water

Separate egg. Beat yolk with sugar and allspice. Gradually beat in liquors. Beat egg white. Fold into egg-yolk mixture and pour into cup or mug. Add hot water or milk to fill.

Punches and Bowls

Flaming Glögg

This is a holiday favorite in all Scandinavian countries. The "floating torch" is our own bright idea. Gin, vodka, and light rum may be used instead of aquavit.

1 fifth aquavit

1 bottle red table wine

10 cardamom pods (split)

5 cloves

Juice of 3 oranges

Grated rind of 1 orange

1 cup blanched almonds

1 cup raisins

2-inch piece of stick cinnamon

Sugar to taste—about ½ cup
   to 1 cup

4 dried figs (traditional but
   optional)

Save out 6 ounces of aquavit. Place all other ingredients, except sugar, in a kettle. Heat slowly to simmer. Don't boil! Stir in as much sugar as you require. Remove from fire; pour into punch bowl. YIELD: About 25 small portions.

Variation:

Floating Torch

Grapefruit half

6 ounces aquavit

Granulated sugar

Remove pulp cleanly from grapefruit half, being careful not to tear the rind. Serrate rim by cutting hatch marks with a paring knife. Moisten cut edges with a little aquavit, then sprinkle with granulated sugar. Warm remaining aquavit and pour as much of it into grapefruit shell as it will reasonably hold. Carefully set filled grapefruit cup into punch. Set aflame with long fireplace match. Turn out lights and enjoy the dramatic effect as "torch" flames. When ready to serve, tip contents of torch into punch. Stir. Ladle into cups. Dip a few raisins and almonds into each cup.

Eggnog

12 eggs
1½ cups sugar
1 fifth bourbon
3 ounces rum

1½ quarts heavy cream, whipped
Bittersweet chocolate for garnish

Separate eggs. Beat yolks with 1 cup sugar until thick and light. Very slowly add bourbon and rum. Fold in whipped cream. Beat egg whites with ½ cup sugar until stiff. Fold in. Top with thin curls of bittersweet chocolate.

NOTE: This nog is not for calorie counters. It is so rich and thick that it can be spooned as well as sipped.
SERVES: 25 to 30.

Garden Punch

2 cans frozen lemonade
   concentrate, thawed
1 quart gin

1 cucumber, unpeeled
1½ quarts chilled club soda

Combine lemonade concentrate and gin, and pour over ice in a 4-quart punch bowl. Slice cucumber very thin and add to bowl. Pour in club soda just before serving. Stir just enough to mix. Garnish each serving with a slice of cucumber.
SERVES: 25 to 30.

Coffee Drinks

Coffee and liquor have a natural affection for each other. Almost any spirit goes. In these days of the trim silhouette and the low-cholesterol diet, a coffee-liquor concoction can serve as beverage *and* dessert. Following are several you're bound to enjoy.

Irish Coffee

1½ ounces Irish whiskey
Hot black coffee

Sugar to taste
Slightly whipped cream

Prewarm a 7-ounce goblet. Pour in Irish whiskey and add coffee to within a half inch of the top. Add sugar and stir. Carefully float whipped cream on top. Sip drink through the cream.

Variations:

Iced Irish Coffee

4 ounces double-strength
   black coffee
1½ ounces Irish whiskey

1–2 teaspoons superfine
   granulated sugar
Slightly whipped cream

Chill double-strength hot black coffee. Pour into cocktail shaker with whiskey, sugar, and cracked ice. Shake well until thoroughly chilled. Strain and pour into 7-ounce goblet. Top with slightly whipped cream. *Do not stir.*

Irish Mist Coffee

Substitute Irish Mist Liqueur for the whiskey, and cut down or eliminate sugar.

Café Brûlot Diabolique

8 whole cloves	6 ounces cognac, warmed
1 small cinnamon stick	4 cups hot double-strength
6 lumps sugar	coffee
Peel of 1 lemon, finely cut up	

Place spices, sugar, and peel in chafing dish or heatproof bowl. Add cognac. Ignite cognac and stir until well blended. After a minute or two, slowly pour the hot black coffee and continue to stir. Strain into Brûlot or demitasse cups.
SERVES: 8.

Variation:

Brûlot in Orange Cups

This is an interesting variation of the Brûlot Diabolique. Prepare beverage as in recipe above, substituting Metaxa, the Greek specialty, for cognac. Use 5-Star or 7-Star for easy flaming. Serve as follows:
   Scrub 4 large thin-skinned oranges. Cut in half and scoop out pulp. Carefully turn rind inside out, taking care not to split. Fit each half into a sherbet glass. Pour in hot Brûlot. Allow to stand for one minute while the orange flavor subtly perfumes the beverage.

Triple C

1 or 2 whole cardamom pods	1 ounce cognac per cup
per cup	Sugar—½ teaspoon per cup,
Hot coffee	or to taste

Place a dish of whole cardamom pods on the table. Each person skins his cardamom and drops the seeds into the coffee cup. Bruise seeds, then pour steaming-hot coffee over. Add cognac and sugar. Stir and sip.

Café Royale

Place a cube of sugar in a teaspoon or dessert spoon. Fill spoon with liquor—cognac, bourbon, rum or kirsch—dousing sugar as well, and hold directly over a cup or demitasse of hot coffee. Set spirits aflame. As flames subside, dip spoon in coffee and stir. For a "surefire" success, make it with 151-proof rum, but don't use too much.

Coffee Blazer

Granulated sugar
Lemon wedge
¾ ounce coffee liqueur,
    warmed

¾ ounce cognac, warmed
Hot coffee, about 6 ounces
Sweetened whipped cream,
    for garnish

Moisten rim of a heavy old-fashioned glass or cup by rubbing with lemon. Invert glass in sugar and swirl to coat rim. Hold glass under flame, turning slowly as sugar softens. Pour warmed spirits into large spoon or ladle and ignite. Add flaming to glass, and tilt so flames lick sugar on rim. Fill with hot coffee, and top with heaping tablespoonful of whipped cream.

INDEX
BY
SPIRIT

295

GIN AND VODKA

ALPHABETICAL
INDEX